THE INTERNATIONAL POLITICAL ECONOMY
OF INVESTMENT BUBBLES

good business is the best art...
Andy Warhol

The International Political Economy of Investment Bubbles

PAUL SHEERAN
King Alfred's University College, Winchester

AMBER SPAIN
Goldenberg Hehmeyer and Company

ASHGATE

Published by
Ashgate Publishing Limited
Gower House
Croft Road
Aldershot
Hants GU11 3HR
England

Ashgate Publishing Company
Suite 420
101 Cherry Street
Burlington, VT 05401-4405
USA

Ashgate website: http://www.ashgate.com

British Library Cataloguing in Publication Data
Sheeran, Paul
  The international political economy of investment bubbles
  1. Financial crises - Political aspects 2. Financial crises -
  History 3. Business cycles 4. Speculation 5. Power (Social
  sciences) 6. Investments - Government policy
  I. Title II. Spain, Amber
  338.5'42

Library of Congress Cataloging-in-Publication Data
Sheeran, Paul.
  The international political economy of investment bubbles / Paul Sheeran, Amber Spain.
    p. cm.
  Includes bibliographical references and index.
  ISBN 0-7546-1997-4
  1. Speculation. 2. Stocks--Prices. 3. Investment analysis. 4. Financial crises--
  History. 5. International economic relations. I. Spain, Amber. II. Title.

  HG6015.S336 2004
  332.63'228--dc22

2003025120

ISBN 0 7546 1997 4

Printed and bound by Athenaeum Press, Ltd.,
Gateshead, Tyne & Wear.

Contents

Introduction

The pages that follow are concerned with fear and greed and the everyday struggle associated with the rapid acquisition of money. Faith, hope, trust, deception and stupidity are referred to, not in judgement, but as factors that influence the possibilities of speculation. Opportunism and chance are part of the investment process, but they do not form the exclusive pillars that determine success or failure. The phenomenon of speculation and its profitable outcome is influenced by a variety of factors, which multiply with animated activity.

The overriding need in this book is to understand the development and collapse of bubbles within the context of international political economy. The knowledge related to recognising why bubbles intensify nearing the peak (why do they pick up force and collapse suddenly?) is important to financial, economic and political policy through the nature of the damage it causes. The need to have forecasts to assess the potential instability of a bubble is therefore relevant to politicians, economists, investors and regulators.

The International Political Economy of Investment Bubbles includes an historical analysis to assess the growth and collapse of financial bubbles. The wider political, economic and social consequences arising from the emergence and collapse of bubble investments is introduced to explore the international ramifications of speculative financial acts.

A complementary but no less substantial concern is to analyse the formulation and application of legislation that may follow huge losses and gains. The connections between investment, politics and economics, both within and between states, will be linked and examined.

The content of the book fulfils several related aims. It assesses the growth, maturity and demise of investment bubbles. The analysis makes clear the collapse of investment bubbles, which invariably results in political and economic instability of some kind. It is suggested at the outset that the positive and negative direction of investment bubbles is influenced by the presence and intervention of power and authority. The point of reference is shaped around the debate on market volatility. Are spectacular booms and busts related to crowd behaviour or are bubbles driven, manipulated and deflated by cunning (the power exercised by key investors and institutions)?

The book seeks to identify the patterns and trends in speculation vis-à-vis the operation of power. The nature of power, its relevance to investment bubbles and its limitations in manipulating the markets, will be, in the pages that follow, considered in-depth.

Speculative Investment

Spectacular booms and busts have been studied elsewhere. Charles Kindleberger's well-known text, *Manias, Panics and Crashes*, written in the late 1970s looks incisively back on a range of investment adventures and events. This book differs significantly from Kindleberger. As well as presenting a study of the role of power in investment bubbles, it adds original value through an analysis of:

1. the fundamentals that underpin financial decisions and activity in relation to investment bubbles
2. the rationale of domestic and international regulation introduced as a measure to limit financial turbulence throughout the markets
3. the relationship between the dotcom bubble and the telecoms industry
4. the models that contribute to the understanding of financial movements and theoretical approaches that unravel bubble activity
5. the response to financial irregularities such as fraud and malfeasance
6. the political, economic, social, technological, legal and cultural factors that impact on the markets and shape possibilities
7. the degree of transparency in corporate balance sheets
8. the risks that prevail in speculative advantage
9. the role of experts and related financial advice
10. the relevance of ethics in business

Investment bubbles are notoriously difficult to define, but a surge in or fatigue of speculative activity is observable in a range of historical markets. In this context, finance is incorporated in economics via investment. It should be kept in mind that the basic fundamentals of all asset prices are expectations about the discounted value of future cash flow from investment. Bubbles could be interpreted through the examination of poor decision forecasting, but other factors need to be considered. An historical approach to previous 'bubbles' will be introduced to compare and contrast, and refute the appearance of speculative bubbles. It is intended that the subsequent analysis will provide a platform from which to assess the vagaries of speculative advantage. The actions that underpin a rapid escalation in investment or a flight from it need to be made clear because they severely affect both institutions and private investors and often lead to financial regulation in some form. Pettinger provides a useful definition of investment:

> Investment is anything on which a return of any sort is anticipated. Thus people invest time, energy, resources, and also personal interest and commitment in ventures, as well as money.[1]

The bubble phenomenon may indicate animation in speculative activity as it accelerates and reaches widely through an economy, a wave that creates a vacuum motored by speculation and enthusiasm. For example, the Dutch tulip mania in 1634 and the French Mississippi Bubble in 1717 demonstrate the infectious nature of speculation and the destructiveness associated with the fever. In seeking to understand the role and operation of power within speculative acceleration, the activity of social identity – *a person's sense of who he or she is*[2] – in relation to groups and crowds, is an important component in the study of investment bubbles. In light of the spectacular gains and losses of the dotcom bubble, it would appear that few lessons have been learned from the bubbles of the seventeenth and eighteenth centuries.

The financial disasters of Enron and WorldCom, and other high profile debacles such as Long Term Capital Management and its rescue by the Federal Reserve Bank of New York support the view that 'small firms in difficulties perish quickly: large firms, however, bring losses to many around them, not only to short term creditors but to financial institutions which have supported capital expenditure programmes and granted credits'.[3] The need to introduce regulation and compliance to various market exchanges should be complemented by an inherent improvement in the degree of accountability and responsibility exercised by senior management, without which abuse will not be curtailed in any meaningful way. This perhaps raises a series of questions relating to business education and the general absence of ethics in higher business programmes.

The speculative adventure associated with the dotcom bubble generated huge gains initially followed by spectacular losses and crashes. Following the arrival of dotcom start-ups, the late 1990s recorded an exponential rise in the IPOs (Initial Public Offerings) of technology shares. It was initially expected that the market could be sustained. Although the prices initially soared, by spring 2000, they fell rapidly. The subsequent losses incurred by the telecommunications industry and the increasing debt burden following the costs associated with the purchase of third generation phone licences impacted on other areas, the dotcom sector in particular. The bursting of the media bubble in the wake of the financial difficulties associated with ITV digital and the German media giant Kirch Gruppe, illustrates the difficulties associated with the study of bubbles.[4] They do not take on a neat form.

The question that particularly interests the authors of the book is: have 'bubbles' throughout history followed a pattern? The most recent model of a bubble is that of Cohen, written in the late 1990s, before the dotcom fallout, the telecommunications debacle and the media cull had been assessed. It therefore appears appropriate to reconsider existing models that have been established and contribute additional material to understand the vagaries of intensive speculation in its varied forms.

The model set out by Cohen in the book *The Edge of Chaos* (1997) provides a starting point to assess early bubbles. Clearly, the model is influenced by other studies in the wider literature on bubbles. The material in this book directs the reader to the role of the state and its influence on bubble activity.

The attacks on Washington and the World Trade Centre in New York on 11 September 2001 accelerated the fall in stocks around the world, which were suffering in the light of technology, media and telecommunications losses. Subsequently, the gradual recovery from the shock to the financial system included a new wave of regulatory measures aimed at the freezing of the assets of terrorism. The response highlighted, although ambiguously, the volume of 'dirty money' in the financial system. The difficulties in identifying and separating legal deposits from illegal transactions are compounded by the degree of confidentiality expected by depositors.

The period of de-regulation in the financial sector, initiated from the 1970s, needs to be reviewed carefully to limit continued and widespread abuse. For example the exponential rise in financial products, hedge funds in particular, will need some form of regulation to address the development and ever increasing sophistication of new financial products and the speed of execution.

The conflict of interests that abound in the overlap between politics and business needs to be recognised and the worst abuses checked. The working group set up by the George W. Bush administration, including the Treasury, the Federal Reserve, the Commodity Futures Trading Commission and the Securities and Exchange Commission, the main financial regulator, in response to the high profile collapses of the corporate giants Enron and WorldCom, highlights the difficulties of impartiality. The close links between the Bush administration and corporate America are not only fuel for the pen of Michael Moore, who exposes the problem succinctly.

The subsequent furore around WorldCom, through which expenses were booked as investment in order to make the company look much healthier than it actually was, provides further evidence for the view that financial irregularities are not necessarily isolated to particular sectors or corporations.[5] This is a fundamental problem that needs to be tackled to rebuild investor confidence (for example the wide condemnation by investors in response to the problems at Andersen is a clear warning to the industry). The cases of Enron and WorldCom and LTCM will be returned to throughout the book. It must be reiterated that the questions relating to the links between big business and governments, particularly in the context of donations by businesses and political parties,[6] is a key issue that will shape the development of global markets throughout the twenty-first century. States have messy relations with a range of actors.

The turbulence associated with financial speculation has concerned governments throughout history. In maintaining relative stability in international financial affairs, states have co-operated through various international institutions to limit the unstable nature of international markets. This is by no means achieved without error, suspicion and hostility in some form. The apparent need to harmonise and co-ordinate economic policy within and between states is increasingly accelerated by the global web of financial transactions, a project not without dissent.

International Political Economy

For the starting point of the book, international political economy will be defined as the 'complex interplay in the international context between politics and economics, between states and markets'.[7] The need to reflect on the changing nature of markets is widely recognised; the narrow recourse to the 'dismal science' is not sufficient in unpacking the content of phenomena associated with speculative investment. In response to the rapid interdependence prevalent in the international financial system, the suitability of an approach, attained through the study of the nexus of relations between economics and politics, is considered a viable approach in seeking to understand the contagion generated by bubble activity.[8] The integration of the financial and investment sector is one the most identifiable trends of globalisation.

Britain is leading the world in screen-based trading, having only one remaining floor-based exchange. Interestingly, the London Stock Market does not have a direct physical need to be located in the country to trade in markets, which in turn further globalises markets. Traders in the UK and Europe monitor the US markets as indicators in the immediate term – thus furthering the international economy. London is far more internationally orientated than either New York or Tokyo and has the largest slice of most international markets. Therefore, all exchanges need to be considered in the global setting.

In an international business context, numerous authors have commented on the 'implicit assumption that companies operate in an international arena, either because the firms have ventured abroad themselves or by virtue of their companies, suppliers, buyers or other stakeholders becoming more international'.[9] Clearly, the nexus of relations between states, firms and markets, mapped at an earlier juncture by Strange and Stopford, have become increasingly dense, prevalent and multifaceted.[10] The wrong doing associated with Enron generated far more damage than the financial position of its immediate shareholders. The global nature of products and services and the range of financial and investment tools linked to them need to be considered alongside the wider consequences they generate. For example, the exponential rise in financial products is generating a need for regulation in an international context,[11] which is repeatedly disabled through national uncoordinated action and penalties. In practice, the markets transgress regulation or innovate around it.

Political economy has had a long history in the academic departments of the United Kingdom, not necessarily as a stand-alone discipline, but as a body of thought that recognises the overlapping themes embedded in politics and economics.[12] Its evolvement has reflected, interpreted and analysed the shift to international and global political economy.

The standard text, *The Politics of International Economic Relations*, by Joan Spero (1977), filled a vast gap in the analysis of international politics and international economics, and the institutions that structure the response to politics and economics. The book is more weighted to a study of institutions than process but demonstrates the influence and power of hierarchies and bureaucracies active in the international system.

Richard Higgott's informative chapter 'International Political Economy' in Groom and Light's *Contemporary International Relations: A Guide to Theory* (1999) maps eloquently the development of the discipline and captures its fluidity through its on-going metamorphosis in 'constantly undergoing redefinition and reconceptualization'.[13]

The renewed interest in international political economy from the 1970s led also to an awareness of its limitations in a world increasingly dominated by corporate brands and consumer markets. The animation of integrated capital markets, the explosion in the service sectors, and the changing nature of change, notwithstanding its sophistication and ambiguities, generated the need for political and economic flexibility.

The eclecticism in academia that has accompanied complex interdependence and globalisation has in part attempted to move beyond the confines of neat prescriptions, and recognise – not ignore – the problems of separating economics, politics and socio-cultural phenomena in an integrated world increasingly premised on the uneven but conscious totalising experience.

In the early 1990s Murphy and Tooze led the analysis of non-institutional concerns in the cavalier but extremely informative *The New International Political Economy*, and a body of work interested in the marginalised issues of gender, poverty and development operational in the global political economy. This key text opened the discipline to a variety of theoretical approaches which were unconstrained from the masculine influence of mainstream international relations.

Journals such as the US journal *International Organization* and the *British Review of International Political Economy* have provided sites where studies that link politics and economics can be debated. This book will not delve into the intense theoretical debates that pitch author against author in the academic war zone. The aim will be to draw on theory to add clarity to areas of complexity that abound in the overlap between economics and politics in the study of bubbles. The links between governments, firms and consumers and investors will be unravelled to reveal the tangible connections that limit or accelerate damage to the national economy and international system. The canvas of the topic may be global, but intense financial activity seemingly takes place in specific geographical areas or electronic sites in the Western world (thus a geographical bias is noted).[14]

The International Political Economy of Investment Bubbles returns to the management of international economic and financial exchanges. In focusing on the fluctuations in and consequences of investment, the book (re)connects states and markets and maps the evolving and uneven terrain between them.

The Value of Wealth

The adventure of financial gain is conditioned by the spectre of failure, although reason can momentarily be suspended. The selection of indicators that inform investors will be assessed to infer the degree of irrationality that accompanies speculation. The vast collation of data needs to be reviewed with a strong awareness of the method of collection and analysis. The mistakes, flukes, recklessness and sheer absurdity embedded in the markets will not be driven into a neat taxonomy, but studied to present a full impression of flaws and anomalies.

Aristophanes, writing fifteen centuries ago in the classic play *Wealth* comments on the intoxication of wealth and its accumulation. An elderly, hard-up Athenian farmer speaks:

CHREMYLOS. But no one's ever had too much of *you.*
If someone's wealth should rise to thirteen talents,
He sets his sights the more on sixteen talents.
And if he gets to that, he aims at forty:
He swears that life's intolerable with less![15]

The above passage cautions against the abandonment of predetermined targets. Greed undermines the return of an investment and jeopardises the initial gain. The decision to pull out of a rising stock that may continue to perform well is a move fraught with tension. The decision should be informed by the return on the original investment and the need to secure a position before additional risk is initiated.

The Victorian classic *The Way We Live Now* (1875) by Anthony Trollope illustrates the above point. The book follows the fortunes of the city financier, Augustus Melmotte, and an investment bubble generated by the development of a railway in Mexico,[16] a project that is, in fact, not being built. Initially, the stock produces incredible returns and investors are encouraged to commit more to the project or lose out on an investment of a lifetime. The investment is flawed not by the initial idea that generated the interest, but the decision by Melmotte not to execute the intentions of the project through sound business principles. Melmotte uses his charisma and relies on his previous business wizardry to lure investors.

The piece demonstrates the dangers of not paying close attention to the underlying value of the project. In the case of the railway, the implementation of the business plan and the ability of the management team to get it built within forecasted budgets is crucial to the sustained performance of the stock. The character, Melmotte, is destroyed when the scam is realised. He ends in ruin and takes his life. The investor who had not gambled on ever increasing stock prices in relation to the investment, but consolidated on the initial success of the return, would not be in the position of considering a similar fate.

The bubble scenario and its consequences are not confined to fiction. The bubble leading up to the 1929 Stock Market Crash (an event accelerated by an earlier cut in US interest rates by the Federal Reserve to alleviate the high prices in Europe, particularly Britain, which resulted in the wider availability of money to invest in stock market speculation) illustrates the intoxication that can drive speculation in short term selling and buying. The song *I'm in the market for you* captured the excitement that accompanied the rush to stocks:

> *I'll have to see my broker*
> *Find out what he can do*
> *'Cause I'm in the market for you.*
>
> *There won't be any joker,*
> *With margin I'm all through*
> *'Cause I want you outright it's true.*
>
> *You're going up, up, up in my estimation*
> *I want a thousand shares of your caresses too.*
>
> *We'll count the hugs and kisses,*
> *When dividends are due,*
> *'Cause I'm in the market for you.*[17]

John Kenneth Galbraith, writing in *The Great Crash,* considered the parallel boom that saw the creation of new companies issuing stock, without management expediency and order books that could indicate solid growth. There are some similarities with the revenue negative companies of the late 1980s and 1990s. The passage below gives one example from the stock market of 1987 where investment descends into blind speculation:

> I was in New York on the morning of 19 October 1987, and felt the foundations of that religion tremble. That morning, I concluded that the failure of money in two of its instrumental aspects – measure of value and means of payment – was not so much impossible as quite likely; and even more so as money increased in abstraction, lost even its gossamer physicality of banknotes and became mere impulses in electronic ledgers, girdling the city at the speed of light, a million million dollars in motion every day. In London and New York, I met people who invested fortunes in financial enterprises they simply could not describe or explain. No doubt soon, a bank would discover it had lost its capital in those obscure speculations; other banks would fail in sympathy; there would be a depression in trade; trade wars; killing wars.[18]

In the rush to be part of the bull market of the dotcom era, investors ignored the fundamentals that allow businesses to stay in business. This is not a unique pattern: wealth and short-term gain attracts crowds. The failure of an investment and the general fall in the markets generates opportunities that will eventually be acted upon; all parts of the cycle will be inspected.[19]

Fear and Greed

The damage done to the market from the financial malfeasance that occurred not exclusively in the United States, led to the loss of confidence amongst investors. Private investors particularly, who provide extensive liquidity to the markets, have taken flight; sensitive to the loss of trust, however tenuous its previous foundations.

Greed in the corporate sector is exposed in the collapse of companies such as Enron. 'Enron was once the seventh biggest company in the US, but was forced into bankruptcy on 2 December 2001 after rescue take-over bids failed.'[20] It would appear that senior managers recognised the extensive flaws in the balance sheet and took action to secure personal positions. Employees throughout the company were not so fortunate:

> The problem centred on Enron's 401(k)-employee retirement programme. 401(k) accounts are employee directed investment accounts that companies help fund and administer. Enron's programme, worth about $2.1 bn a year ago [from December 2001], was 60 per cent invested in the company's own stock, and employees were prevented from selling even as shares plummeted.[21]

The blame lies with the cunning of influential figures in senior management and the prevalence of greed in the boardroom and beyond. The culture of greed and materialism is often viewed as a measure of success, which promotes an international business class vying for advantage in an intensely competitive environment.

> But the biggest danger of all comes down to simple human ambition. Throughout corporate history, the finance director was regarded as the managing director or chief executive in waiting, someone serving time in a worthy but dull job until the top seat fell vacant. But as the CFO's role has expanded, and especially in the very biggest of companies, a new range of pretenders have emerged. The top of the corporate tree is now populated with presidents, chief operating officers, chief information officers and others, all of whom see themselves at the head of the queue. Increasingly, multinationals want their CFOs to be pointy-headed financial specialists – accountants or bankers with PhDs in statistics. And they want their chief executives to be natural leaders, whose job is to look good on TV and keep the markets happy. That shift has meant that the CFO has lost the natural right of succession,

leaving many seething in their well-paid – but not well-paid enough – subordinate roles. The combination of thwarted ambition, near-unlimited power and the right to sign billion-dollar cheques is a potent one.[22]

The value of company reports and annual accounts has been severely damaged by loose practices. 'Ratios, on their own, will not be sufficient providers of information about a company. Information of a non-financial nature will generally be required before meaningful analysis is possible.'[23] The debate on corporate America reiterates the wider discussion of the need to balance regulation and flexibility.

Investors, like companies succumb to greed. Human behaviour appears conditioned by greed and lust. Otherwise religion would be redundant. Genomics and brain imaging may offer intricate variations on human nature, history offers a convincing perspective. The history of avarice as the deadliest vice in Western Europe has been said to begin in earnest only with the rise of capitalism or, earlier, the rise of a money economy. Richard Newhausrer's book *The Early History of Greed* (2000) traces vices back further, elucidating the nuances of gain and its destructive capacity.

Whilst greed is an important factor in the rise and decline in financial products of any kind, it is suggested in this book that the condition of greed and financial speculation needs to be viewed through the lens of power. Power is the vehicle through which actions and practice are shaped. The relevance of the actualisation of power to bubbles will be considered in the next chapter.

Methodology and Content

To gain insight into the complex world of financial speculation, the authors intend to use widely available secondary data. Qualitative research will, where possible, seek to limit ambiguities and make clear the points pertinent to understanding bubbles. The views of professional investors will be carefully cross-referenced to maintain objectivity, whilst recognising and respecting anonymity where requested.

Chapter One introduces a general theory of bubble activity. A wider assessment of business and market cycles relating to bubbles will be applied to highlight the economic and political consequences of distorted speculation.

The material in Chapter Two considers the management of risk and the prevalence of fear amongst investors. The former limits exposure to potential danger and the latter undermines even the most solid position.

Chapter Three considers the psychological relationship between trends and the emergence of bubbles. In particular, crowd mentalities and collective decision making in market environments will be analysed to make clear group speculation.

The material in Chapters Four to Seven is concerned with historical bubble activity. Chapter Four looks at the Tulipomania Bubble. Chapter Five presents an analysis of the South Sea Bubble. The Florida Real Estate and The Wireless Bubble are considered in Chapter Six. Chapter Seven analyses the Dotcom Bubble and its relationship to the telecoms sector.

Chapter Eight assesses the widely held view that the financial markets and 'the markets' in general can often appear to be chaotic and disorganised. The authors contend that this position ignores the increasing volume of regulation associated with international financial trading. The material in this section will explore the operation of international institutions in managing the balance between growth and inflation, promoting transparency and limiting fraud.[24]

A key theme of the book is an inspection of the role of investors close to the inception and the growth of the bubble. There is a distance between the quality of information available to actors who form the initial bubble and actors that arrive later. Chapter Nine includes an assessment of the various stages of the bubble. Theoretical approaches to understanding bubbles are studied to add insight into an evolving model, omitting the stages which are of less relevance and adding new features analysed in the book.

Chapter Ten concludes the study of investment bubbles and considers future movements in speculative activity.

Thanks are due to the following for lending their valuable time to the project: Dr Loykie Lomine, Professor Tom James, Gillian Sheeran, Gwen White, Dr Richard Brown, Jane Fairclough, Dr Paul Redford, Sue Odowd and Dr Richard Grover.

The views of Amber Spain are her personal considerations on the topic of investment bubbles.

Notes

[1] Pettinger (2000) p.1.

[2] The theoretical compass is taken from the book by Rupert Brown (2002) p.2, *Group Processes: Directions within and between groups...*

[3] See M.W.E Glautier and B. Underdown, *Accounting Theory and Practice*, (1991) p.253.

[4] BBC News Front Page reported on the succession of collapsed technology, telecommunications and media bubbles, which led to high losses amongst investors (27 March 2002), http://news.bbc.co.uk/default.stm, 'The Bursting of the Media.'

[5] See the US Chamber of Commerce for insight on how corporate accounting scandals have affected American businesses: http://www.uschamber.com.

[6] Susan Strange (1991) 'An Eclectic Approach', highlighted the need for the international political economy academic community to explore the relationship between big business, the state and markets.

[7] See Jackson and Sørensen in *Introduction to International Relations* for a general overview of international political economy. For an earlier snapshot of the field see Higgott (1994) 'International Political Economy'.

[8] Ferguson (2001) p.20. *The Cash Nexus*, Penguin.

[9] See Bob D Wit and Richard Meyer (1997), *Strategy – Process, Content, Context. An International Perspective*, for a series of classic papers and articles that debate the international fragmentation and international integration issue.

[10] For a detailed look at the increasing commercialisation of politics see, Susan Strange, John Stopford and John Henley (1991) *Rival States, Rival Firms: Competition for World Market Shares*.

[11] See Peter D Spencer (2000) *The Structure and Regulation of Financial Markets* and Dimitris N Chorafas (2000) *New Regulation of the Financial Industry*, for incisive comment in this area.

[12] See W.C.Olson and A.J.R. Groom (1991) pp .296-300, *International Relations Then and Now*.

[13] Higgott, R. (1994) p.156.

[14] See the notes on Zip's Law outlined in the chapter 'Geographical economies' in the book by Charles Marrewijk (2002) pp 265-289 *International Trade and the World Economy*. See also R..Johnson *et al* (2002) *Geographies of Global Change*. The book provides a series of critical insights into the economic, political, socio-cultural and ecological dimensions of change at every geographical scale from the local to the global.

[15] Aristophanes (388) 'Wealth', in *Birds and Other Plays*.

[16] The Trollope Society suggests, 'some find his original in George Hudson, the railway king, whose world collapsed in ruins in 1849. Some find him in Albert Gottheimer, a central European who was perhaps the first to discover how a gullible public could be exploited by the unscrupulous, which were in turn protected by the Limited Liability Company'.

[17] Olsen, G. (1930) *I'm In The Market For You*, Victor, Berliner Gram-O-Phone Co.

[18] James Buchan, (1997) *Frozen Desire*.

[19] In the 1960s, Edwin Coppock sought to devise an indicator that would avoid the 'madness of crowds'. He bewailed the short-terminism of market sentiment. He consulted members of the Episcopalian church, who told him it takes between 11 and 14 months for human beings to adjust to bereavement or to recover from a serious illness. Using this idea, he devised an indicator that would signal stock market lows. See 'The Trader: The Long View, The Coppock Indicator IS a Valuable Tool Because...' *Investment Chronicle*, 1 Feb, 2002.

[20] *Financial Times* (2002) p. 1, 11 January 2002.

[21] *ibid*, p. 8.

[22] BBC News, 'Greed, fear and loathing in the boardroom', 27 June 2000, http://news.bbc.co.uk/1/hi/business/2069255.stm.

[23] The techniques of interpreting and comparing financial reports are, however, crucial to success in investment. 'The collection of ratios on a systematic basis allows trends to emerge, and throws into relief the significance of changes indicated by the analysis of current events. Since the future is uncertain, the analyst has to rely on past behaviour for predicting future changes.' See M.W.E Glautier and B. Underdown, *Accounting Theory and Practice*, p.250.

[24] A survey was conducted during 2001 into the 'Top 100 Corporate Criminals of the Decade' (1990s). It lists the 100 under fourteen categories of crime ranging from pollution offences, through fraud and financial crime, illegal exports, bribery and worker death to tax evasion. The 100 recorded offences resulted in fines totalling nearly US$2½ billion. The scale of this criminality is horrendous, far exceeding those offences, which are thought of as 'normal criminality'. For example, the US Federal Bureau of Investigation estimates that street crime (burglary and robbery) costs the United States $3.8 billion a year. The estimated cost of corporate crime is $955 billion. See: http://www.corporatepredators.org/top100.html.

Chapter 1

Pascal and the Gambler: The Theory of Speculative Advantage

Introduction

This chapter will seek to reflect on the inflation and deflation of bubble activity – a model will be introduced to map its development in a basic form. The operation of business and market cycles will be considered to highlight the relationship between investment and the wider economy. The social, economic and political consequences of distorted speculation will be introduced, but this point will be expanded on in a later chapter.

It is argued that the progress of bubbles follows a particular pattern, although not necessarily linear or replicated exactly in every situation. Despite anomalies, stages can be identified and recorded. For example, a financial environment may be conducive to encouraging speculative activity. A caution relevant to the study of bubbles relates to the complex range of economic, social and political variables which are not necessarily transferable to similar investment bubbles at other times. 'History doesn't repeat itself', said Mark Twain, 'but it rhymes.' It is the rhymes and disobedient harmonies that this chapter seeks to unpack. It is argued that the search for similarities and differences in the recurring bursts of investment speculation is related to authority and power. The intention throughout the book is to assess to what degree the acceleration and flight from bubble activity is related to overt and covert forms of manipulation. How this transpires throughout society and initiates regulation is relevant to both investors and society in general.

The Nature of Bubbles

The term 'bubble' describes a particular phenomenon that appears spontaneously, although on close inspection it develops in stages and emits a degree of order. The object of desire: a particular stock, property, work of art, a tulip bulb or a commodity initially generates interest. The curiosity, through enthusiasm and wider participation in its circulation and exchange, accelerates the popularity of the item, whereby it becomes a cult, an obsession, a passion resulting in its perceived value no longer equating to its perceived and inflated price (a condition that invariably leads to opportunity, disappointment and loss).

Bubbles have a long history. The bubble in Middle English is associated with excitement. The word speculation (spek'yuh-LAY'shuhn) n. Definition – n. 1. a. The act of speculating. b. Contemplation of a profound nature. c. A conclusion, opinion, or theory reached by speculating; 2. a. Engagement in risky business transactions on the chance of quick or considerable profit. b. An instance of speculating. The word investment (in-VEST'muhnt) n. Definition – n. 1. The act of investing. 2. An amount invested. 3. Property or another possession acquired for future income or benefit. 4. Investiture. 5. Archaic. A garment; vestment. 6. An outer covering or layer. 7. A military siege.[1] The definition differs from the word gambler, which did not make its appearance in the language until the second half of the century, before which 'gambler' was a slang term for a fraudulent gamester, a sharper, or one who played for excessive stakes.[2]

Bubbles are formulated through the initial objective of seeking financial and material gain from a specific investment. From the definition of a bubble as a self-fulfilling reinforcing price change, the propensity of change operates through a range of indicators and social exchanges between agents and the markets. The degree of return is related to supply and demand, which correlates with the velocity of the bubble.

> The average investor hears just enough about the latest market trend to spark his interest. Growing pressure from friends, colleagues and the media make him feel afraid that perhaps he is 'missing out' on a major opportunity to profit. The trend remains in tact, causing the investor to regret his past caution and start to question his own judgement. By now the trend has hit the headlines, which is the final straw for his sense of caution. His resistance breaks down and he panics into the market.[3]

Despite the rush to market, it is easy to forget that a ceiling exists. For example, if you had considered buying x stock at 75 and have watched it climb to 100, you will convince yourself that you have already missed out on that 25 profit and thus had better buy quickly before missing the next climb. The important thing here is to calculate and re-calculate (based on sociological, political and economic factors) where 'fair value' is.

Driven by the spectacular, the unusual and the grandiose, the bubble generates and spreads its attraction, re-enforcing its longevity through its apparent momentum, which appears unstoppable. The bubble is inherently a statement about irrational behaviour, a phenomenon whereby participation is viewed as an end in itself.

> The essence of a speculative bubble is a sort of feedback, from price increases, to increased investor enthusiasm, to increased demand, and hence further price increase. The high demand for the asset is generated by the public memory of high past returns, and the optimism those high returns generate for the future. The feedback can amplify positive forces affecting the market, making the market reach higher levels than it would if it were responding only to these positive forces. Moreover, a bubble is not indefinitely sustainable. Prices cannot go on forever, and when price increases end, then the increased demand that the price increases generated ends too. Then, a downward feedback can replace the upward feedback.[4]

Despite previous bubbles and their implosion, it appears that a suspension of reason is adopted when a return on investment exceeds the market norm.[5] Investment is no longer a calculated risk, but a gamble that resembles a turn at the roulette wheel.

> In September, 1824, it was said 'Another thing in the shape of a Poyais loan,[6] has been brought into the market'. Great as the excitement was, there were not many disposed to risk their money; but those who did were persons who had saved a small amount, which, though insufficient to live upon, was sufficient to excite a desire for more. By this class a considerable sum was advanced; and the ruin that fell upon them was tremendous. The Poyais loan was an epoch from which many dated for the remainder of their lives; and the figure of one of these unhappy speculators must still be familiar to some readers, as she wandered daily through the offices of the Bank of England, and the purlieus of the Stock Exchange, exposed to all the annoyances which fall upon those who earn their bread in the public thoroughfares.[7]

The separation between a calculated investment and unexpurgated risk is determined by the degree of risk. Speculation and gambling share similarities, but are differentiated by probability, risk and the various social perceptions on methods that measure gain and loss.[8] Investing in stocks can also be driven by explicit fraud. The movement of traders abroad to work in the 'boiler room' scenario, basically selling completely dodgy stocks over the phone, is an increasing problem. The demand however is driven by customers who are willing to buy these stocks, which may not even exist, and certainly come with 'no questions asked' instructions. Notwithstanding outright fraud, gambling in stocks has a long history.

[The] problem of gambling in stocks was by no means new to the early Victorian period, although the debate about gambling focused attention on it. 'Stock jobbing' had been the cause of the infamous South Sea Bubble fiasco in 1720, entailing the excessive wholesaling of securities on the Stock Exchange. Here, remuneration – or profit – was determined by the difference between the price at which the jobber bought and sold stocks. This activity led to the excessive and unscrupulous buying up of stocks in order to secure maximum and often excessive income from the selling price. Yet over inflated prices led to the 'bubble' bursting, and hundreds of speculators were ruined. Hence 'An Act to prevent the infamous Practice of Stock Jobbing' was passed. This was designed to prevent a repetition of such events but, over a century later, the Act was 'habitually, and even daily, broken'.[9]

Gambling has historically been associated with the lower classes and the desperate. Financial speculation is not without frustration and economic casualties seeking to redress their loss. Without doubt, the early part of the new century is a most dangerous time for anyone to speculate – whether a day trader, fund manager or private investor. It is the point at which speculation becomes gambling as the psychological state of the investor is completely wrong to make unemotional decisions – which is the basis of good trading.

It would appear that despite previous warnings, speculators are willing to engage in a bubble, regardless of the failure of previous bubbles, which may have taken futures as well as fortunes. Whilst some may be aware of financial crashes, the operation of a bubble may have missed their attention.

Almost every generation sees some bubble or other floated to gull the punters with the shortest memories. Another bout of gambling mania in the 1840s saw a manic speculation on the London Stock Exchange in canal bonds and foreign securities, with spin-offs into other commodities, until the mania got out of control. By 1847, speculation in railway shares had reached insane heights. Then the frenzy shifted to gambling in corn because of the potato blight in Ireland. They went long on corn and sent the price rocketing. This merely compounded the misery of the Irish, of whom a million died, because their potato crop was ruined and they could not afford corn at the speculators' price.[10]

The vocabulary of money capitalism has features in common with gambling. Dostoyevsky's book, *The Gambler*, captures the thrill and despair of the gamble, with which those who fail to impose a stop loss on their investments are familiar. The desperation that can be evident at the table or with poker is similar to the final acceleration of the investment bubble and the flight from it. In Michael Lewis's, *Liar's Poker*, the need to succeed in extremely competitive environments is, regardless of success or failure, the language of the gambler. Despite the mentality of the gambler being relatively generic, success or failure seemingly relies mainly on the eloquent passage below:

> I know a trader who bought SCI shares on a tip around bubble proper build up/peak and as he was so confident, simply carried on buying the cheaper they got. I think the first lot were about 5 pounds, and by the bottom (about 30p) his average was 70p. – He then waited 2-3 years (!) whilst they crept back up and I think has a get out planned at 2 pounds. I can get all the proper figures if you want them, but the point is that an experienced trader/investor (with capital and balls!) can use these techniques to get out of a hole, or at least minimise losses, whilst the virgins are getting f***ed![11]

Until recently the private investor had limited direct access to the markets. Ironically, as investors can speculate virtually on any stock or trade through development in Internet trading and related software, the well publicised fall in stocks is limiting the take up of this on-line opportunity. It is however, likely, when a sustained rise is popularised, that investors will return, precisely when the real gains have been made, to generate a bubble.

The passage below is insightful in highlighting the participants in the growth bubble, but it ignores the key investors that shape the bubble and often take flight before it is fully expanded, a factor shaped by the operation of power within its trajectory. From the cases mentioned, the downside is ignored and compulsion heightened. The fluctuations in the markets are also affected by the increase in options and managed funds which tie markets together in a way the layman (or private/virgin investor) cannot appreciate. Sometimes someone will have to buy/sell when a particular price is reached, and often in volumes completely out of sync with what has been trading that day/month etc. This then moves the market sharply and throws the price out totally.

There are two types of speculators who participate in the growth of the bubble. The first is the type of person who believes that, for some reason, the price of this object of speculation will move tremendously higher, and remain there indefinitely. While this type of expectation clearly adds to the bubble, this alone will not:

> cause the market to rise tremendously. For example, consider a theoretical market consisting of 10 investors and speculators, and one stock. If the stock is currently at $100, and one of the speculators suddenly realizes for some reason that the stock is worth $1000, they will commit all of their capital, driving the

price of the stock temporarily higher until they have purchased all that their credit or margin will allow, after which the price will return to $100, or at least cease to climb. However, the situation changes when the second type of speculator enters the picture. This type of person subscribes to the 'greater fool theory' which says that an asset should be purchased as long as there exists at least one 'greater fool' to whom that same asset can be sold at a higher price. This theory is also known as the 'Castle-in-the-air' method of valuation. This strategy is what throws the market out of balance and fuels the second half of the bubble. These individuals will continue to purchase regardless of market levels, considering only the willingness of other individuals in the market to pay higher prices. At this point the bubble inflates itself, because a growing portion of the market is self-referencing, making decisions while looking inward.[12]

The early growth of bubbles is related to the success or failure of initial performance. A series of gains attracts interest. As the recommendation or prediction is seen to exhibit substance or opportunity, more investors become willing to take part. The interest can be estimated through different indicators: increase in the number of books published on the topic, increase in the subscriptions to specialised journals. Moreover, the well-known empirical rule according to which the volume of sales is growing during a bull market finds a natural interpretation in this framework: sales increases in fact reveal and pinpoint the progress of the bubble's diffusion throughout society. In opposition to the conception of a bubble and a crash at times of disorder, it would appear that it is the operations of countertrend before the peak, when the consensus is too strong,[13] that determines the outcome of the investment. This may not necessarily involve an initial dramatic shift, but it indicates a signal, which other astute investors' notice, whilst financial disaster can momentarily be avoided.

The History of Bubbles

The appearance of investment bubbles is recorded in a range of historical texts. Sakolski (1932), Erleigh (1933), Schabacker (1934), Carswell (1960), Cowles (1960) and Schama (1997) have each examined activity associated with bubbles. Earlier references include the book of Ecclesiastes, which informs of the need to engage in foreign trade and gives advice on taking and hedging risks:

> Send your grain across the seas, and in time you will get a return. Divide your merchandise among seven ventures, eight maybe, since you do not know what disasters may occur on earth.[14]

The first recorded case in England was that of a State Lottery in 1569. The tickets were on sale at the west door of St. Paul's Cathedral in London. The name of the winner is not recorded. In the early eighteenth century, the term bubble was widely associated with the South Sea Bubble.[15] The inflated share price and its subsequent collapse affected the entire country and led to regulation.

> Robert Walpole, who had always been against the South Sea Company from the beginning, took charge and sorted out this terrible financial mess. He was made Chancellor of the Exchequer and he divided the National Debt that had been the South Sea Company into three, between the Bank of England, the Treasury and the Sinking Fund. The Sinking Fund was made up of a portion of the country's income that was put aside every year, and eventually stability returned to the country.[16]

Despite widespread loss and the need for intervention and regulation the prevalence of bubbles was not eradicated. Financial gain continued to be an enticing activity, attracting novices and professional speculators.

> Throughout history, speculative bubbles have had some common features. There are certain financial preconditions, which invariably include leverage coupled with some other financial '(re)discovery' such as the power of the joint-stock company, the option, or risky debt (junk bonds). In some cases this financial innovation is replaced by changes in government policy that either favour easy credit or lower taxation, stimulating rapid business growth. Whatever the case may be, a financial atmosphere of tremendous supply combined with demand for some desirable asset, be it stocks, real estate, or even rare tulips, gives birth to the speculative bubble.[17]

At each juncture, the increase in speculative activity generates new mechanisms to speed exchange. The history of economic change is littered with the development of new financial and investment products, which generate interest and spread throughout the economy. The passages below could easily be re-written for the dotcom bubble, which appears eighty years later.

> The New York stock market's speculative fever in the late 1920s had been world wide news and had made the public much more aware of the increasing variety of marketable securities, as was shown by London's own speculative outbreak in 1927-28. This bubble – exploited mainly by promoters in some of the new industries – burst so quickly that it served mainly to prompt an overdue revision of the Companies Acts, and rather confirmed the high standing of new issue houses in the neglect of home industry.[18]

The vehicle that accelerates the bubble is powered by the desire to accumulate wealth, without necessarily having to endure the years of toil associated with the growth of it. The possibilities, which are related to the expansion of the bubble, invariably lead to a temporary suspension of regulatory codes and prudence that limit risk. The willingness to gamble generates a momentum that initially distances political self interest, a condition which encourages indifference and ambivalence from the architects of policy. Encouraged by the need to disguise responsibility, precisely at a time when caution and management is required, the bubble inflates further and widens the negative consequence of a collapse. The noise of the 'hot' investment or 'bubble' conceals the warning of its inevitable bursting. The clamour to be involved silences and blinds the crowd to the inevitable. The cycle of the bubble:

> describes the entire event: the rush to an unsustainable peak, followed by the equally dramatic collapse. A bubble implies the price of an asset, or an entire market, is no longer in balance consistent with the underlying fundamental value. A crash deals only with the sudden collapse, the disintegration in the prices of assets.[19]

The history of bubbles confirms that a collapse in an investment does not lead to a permanent exodus of investors from all forms of speculation.

> After a bubble inflates it takes a couple of bear markets before stock prices begin to return to the area of their intrinsic values. But if markets learn they also forget. The composition of the market changes constantly, old money managers retire, people die, and new investors enter the market. It is not so much that people forget what they learn in a bear market, but that they have not been educated by the bear.[20]

A review of the extensive literature relating to bubbles demonstrates both their longevity and different features. The selection of texts listed below adds insight into the broader debate on the theory of speculative advantage. Charles Mackay's *Extraordinary Popular Delusions and the Madness of Crowds* and Joseph De La Vega's *Confusión de Confusiones*, which appeared respectively in the nineteenth and seventeenth centuries, are two investment classics that have relevance to contemporary speculation and its consequences. Fridson's preface to the contemporary edition, which sees both texts published together, separates the two authors and highlights the following differences. Mackay seeks to understand the bubble and its outlandish volatility through the periodic outbreaks of mass hysteria and the folly of crowds. In contrast, Joseph De La Vega is viewed through the lens of a Machiavellian camera that captures red-handed the cunning behind the unnatural convulsions operational in the market. He depicts price fluctuations as the handiwork of scheming speculators,[21] which accelerate or frustrate speculative advantage.

Adding further insight to one of the best-known speculative bursts, Mike Dash's book *Tulipomania: The Story of the World's Most Coveted Flower and the Extraordinary Passions It Aroused* (2000) traces the Tulip bubble in Amsterdam to its origins in Central Asia and its effect on society and trade. The book follows the interest in the flower within the Ottoman and Holy Roman Empires and its import into Dutch society. The animated trade in tulip bulbs is related to the manic need to covet the bulb for advantage and speculation. The tulip boom and bust in the early part of 1637 leads Dash to reflect on the legal context of speculative activity and the need for regulation.

As mentioned above, the eighteenth century included a major speculative burst in the guise of the South Sea Bubble in which the national debt of England was recycled through the stock of the South Sea Company. Inspired by the tumultuous financial events of 1929, the events that rocked the eighteenth century are returned to and studied in a sophisticated fashion by Viscount Erleigh. Erleigh's *The South Sea Bubble*, written in 1933, is one of many texts inspired by the beauty and destruction of bubbles. The scheme to refinance the national debt of England through the stock of the South Sea Company acts as a reminder of previous bubbles and their similarities to contemporary debacles such as Enron.

Hogarth's classic reflection on the South Sea catastrophe captures the infectious melody and melancholy of speculation.

See here of causes why in London
So many men are made and undone
That Arts and honest trading drop
to swarm about ye Devil's Shop (A)
Who cuts out (B) Fortune's Golden Haunches
Trapping their souls with lots and chances
Sharing 'em from Blue Garters down
To all blue aprons in the town.
Here all religions flock together,
Like tame and wild fowl of a feather
Leaving their strife, Religious bustle
Kneel down to play at pitch and Hustle (C)
Thus, when the Shepherds are at play
Their flocks must surely go astray.
the woeful cause yet in these times
(E) Honour, and (D) honesty are crimes.

That publickly are punished by
(G) Self interest and (F) Vilany;
So much for monys magick power
Guess at the rest, you find out more[22]

Robert Sobel's *The Big Board: A History of the New York Stock Market* sheds light on the development of the New York securities market and its contribution to American economic growth. The book opens with an account of the New York Stock Market in the early eighteenth century, and illustrates the development of the stock market with economic growth in America.

Early investments in North America consisted almost exclusively of land. The few securities holders lived in cities, where informal markets grew, with most trading carried out in the street and in coffeehouses. Banking, insurance, and manufacturing activity increased only after the Revolution. In 1792, 24 prominent New York businessmen, for whom stock and bond trading was only a side business, met under a buttonwood tree on Wall Street and agreed to trade securities on a common commission basis. Five securities were traded; three government bonds and two bank stocks. Trading was carried out at the Tontine Coffee-House in a call market, with the president reading out a list of stocks as brokers traded each in turn.[23]

The penultimate event in the New York Stock Exchange, the 1929 Stock Market Crash is covered expertly by Galbraith in the well known *The Great Crash 1929*. The book is filled with warning signs to investments and governments on the destruction of speculative advantage and the weakness of policy to ensure its creative and constructive development.

A Monetary History of the United States, 1867-1960 by Milton Friedman and Anna J. Schwartz (1963) adds to a vein of classic literature in the discipline of economic history. Money is currency of life. With an in-depth account of the Great Depression the book offers a series of case studies including: the contrast between 1879-1896 and 1896-1914 in terms of the behaviour of the price level; the contrast between World War I and World War II in terms of the behaviour of the price level; and the impact of restrictive actions taken by the Federal Reserve system in 1937.

The above work is incisive in relation to a consideration of price level fluctuations that arise from the fear of a terrorist attack:

because lessons are learned about what moves markets, and the history 'which rhymes' in events will not rhyme in price movements because the big market players know what it should do and people trading off the back of it is factored in to the price movement – i.e. 9/11 sent bond prices through the roof. By the time a light aircraft went into the Pirelli tower in Milan a few months later most traders had realised that the right thing to do in reaction to a terrorist incident is to buy bonds and sell stocks (yes I know we're sick!) However, so many people knowing this and jumping on the bandwagon makes the price action slower, as the first thing people do is pull their bond offers/stock bids, as they know they will get run over. In light of no bond sellers/stock buyers, the prices can only move so far.[24]

Focusing on the key and influential investor Jessie Livermore, Edwin Lefebvre's useful, *Reminiscences of a Stock Operator* (1923) highlights the vulnerability of investors engaged in the options markets, who find themselves manipulated by the key players in the speculative casino.

Adam Smith's *The Money Game*, written in 1969, presupposes the Enron debacle and infers, unlike Sobel, that the stock market and all other equity markets are just a game. The power of the new, its hype and wide communication ensnares investors seeking to win without realising the winners have retreated from the game well before its conclusion. This is seen more and more frequently in the markets today when economic indicators are released. On the big movers the price action is not exactly as it should be, and looking at the action pre- and post-figure it seems clear that the information has been 'leaked' and profit taking occurs for the big players so quickly after the indicator is released that the rest of the market loses out, because the move has already happened. This is also similar to gamblers who sell their odds before a race i.e. buy the odds at 14:1 for 1 pound, before the race they are at 5:1, so sell them at 6:1 for the same price to someone else. In this way you have covered costs if you lose, but if you win, you pay 7 to the person you sold to, and keep 8 yourself – thus a totally hedged bet, and the winners all acted early.

Speculation predates the Internet, of course, and Enron existed before Internet mania took hold. But in its hubris and attending hype, in its focus on earnings instead of ethics, in its insistence that it is unique and unprecedented – in touting its innovative use of technology – Enron stands as the quintessential Internet company. And its fall, like the bursting of the Internet stock bubble, has been spectacular. One of the characteristics typical of a bubble, and especially typical of the Internet bubble and Enron, is blinding arrogance. Enron called itself the 'world's greatest company' (or sometimes just the 'world's leading company'), while the media raced to pile on the superlatives, dubbing Enron the 'most innovative' company in America, one of the 'fastest growing,' one of the 'most admired'. Small wonder that Enron's meetings with outside investors have been compared to revival meetings.[25]

The Money Game is a valuable text that makes clear the financial context in which games are played. It includes an account of the technicalities of investment that remains useful.

Other key texts from the 1960s include *The Go-Go Years: The Drama and Crashing Finale of Wall Street's Bullish Sixties* written by John Brooks (1969). Brooks' *Once in Golconda*, a study of Wall Street between the years of 1920 and 1938, contributes enormously to the perspectives of speculative culture and continues to be relevant on a range of fronts. On speculation, Brooks suggests:

> Speculation, trading for the principal purpose of taking a chance on a gain at the risk of a loss has gone on in stock exchanges since the day the first of them was organised in Amsterdam in 1602. This need shock no one; by its nature a stock exchange rivals a racetrack or a roulette table as a natural medium for taking risks, and furthermore, speculating in commercial goods, rather than in pieces of paper representing stores of goods or the hope of acquiring them, had gone on centuries before 1602. Most people if asked to account for the urge to speculate would certainly reply that it is rooted in human venturesomeness, acquisitiveness, and love of risk for its own sake.[26]

In a more contemporary setting, Michael Lewis's *The Future Just Happened* captures the excitement and excesses of the technology boom. The dotcom whirlwind is further addressed in Lewis' (1999), *The New New Thing*. The subsequent rise and fall in the communications and media bubbles will ensure the literature will continue to expand: an industry itself inflated by fear and fashion.

The Model of Bubbles

Uncertainty is the ever present companion of investment. Indicators may infer a particularly buoyant or negative trading environment that may or may not materialise. The degree of risk attracts particularly investors and reveals the psychology of investment. Risk means different things to different people, a factor which helps to expand the variety of positions available to an investor. Research limits risk but it does not eradicate it. A scenario where risk was eliminated would result in a non-market.

In a similar manner, it is widely perceived from outside the organisation that the performance of a company and the ownership of shares by its senior management is a prerequisite for guaranteeing a successful return. It would appear, however, that senior management, who are in a prime position to know the 'real' value and market price of their company's value, cannot beat the market consistently. Either with the knowledge retrieved from a study of the order books or access to confidential information, which may indicate a potential merger, acquisition or disposal, management should be able to judge the current or future performance of the company.

The purchase of their company's shares by company directors has traditionally been a good indicator of future market activity. Despite the availability of 'inside' information, company directors do not always beat the markets, selling shares before a rise and buying on the crest of a fall (the directors of Marconi bought shares for £1 and watched them fall to virtually nothing).[27] There is always the possibility that some variable in the market and the wider economy will change and alter the expected outcome. Like other indicators, the trades in directors' holdings should be treated as a guide to the performance of the stock and sector.

The networks and clusters that management engage in on a daily basis to circulate and receive information generates a wide degree of knowledge related to the businesses activities. The wider and often unrelated influences that affect the markets cannot be continuously *managed*; they are outside the control of management. A fortuitous set of relationships may produce a positive trading environment which can be manipulated successfully, but the risk that it may be undermined cannot be eradicated. Traders, analysts and the financial media tend to have their business favourites. Any investment pulls together a network of supporters; invariably each works, explicitly and implicitly, for organisations with a vested interest in seeing the investment rise. On the one hand, the words by John Flynn that 'the game of speculation is one played by some three or four thousand insiders and some half a million outsiders on terms of complete inequality' perhaps is as incisive today, as when it was written, but insider knowledge may beat the market or more accurately the crowd.

The industry charged with prediction and analysis is multifarious and extensive. For example, in seeking to predict the movement of the markets, Ali Mostofi's Citystats offers one-hour, clear, *accurate*, verifiable intra-day astrology trading forecasts for day traders, speculators, and futures traders.[28] Astrology, physics and Zen and the Art of Motorcycle Maintenance may highlight what appear to be related phenomena in the investment decision process, but success is not determined by it, it merely makes a connection, which may not otherwise be noticed. Various tools may limit the risk, and procure an advantage in certain circumstances, but the 'system' is not foolproof nor can it be. The complexity that surrounds speculative advantage does not subdue a long search for a model of bubbles. It does however make a bubble conditional on the context in which it occurs.

The first serious attempt in the twentieth century to explain the bubble effect was by Walter Bagehot, the former editor of *The Economist* in 1917. According to Bagehot the problem begins with an abundance of money and limited investment opportunities. He describes how originally surplus money was invested in land. The amount of land had not changed. Though the value of land had increased, it was less than the volume of money available for investment. The surplus was, in an ill-considered manner, directed to the variety of companies listed on the stock market.

The model highlighted below incorporates ten phases that provide the foundation of the primary analysis relating to bubble activity. An early idea relevant to the bubble scenario is the theory of successive market stages outlined by Schabacker (1934) in *Stock Market Profits*. This theory highlights six stages of a market crash. Stage one, recovery from fear and forced selling, in which prices recover fairly quickly after the market has been driven to low levels during the last cycle. Stage two, when prices respond to improvements in business and earnings, and are, for a short period, quite realistic. The third stage is over-enthusiasm, when prices rise higher than the perceived value. This is followed by the fourth stage, when the downturn begins. In the fifth stage the prices fall further, leading to the sixth and final stage, in which panic sets in forcing prices to equally unrealistically low levels.

With openings for investment scarce, anything that 'promises' a return becomes attractive. People begin to buy for speculation and 'so long as such sales can be effected the mania continues; when it ceases to be possible to effect them, ruin begins'.[29] This ruin, explains Bagehot, depends on the involvement of credit. If people have invested their own money then the consequences to the economy as a whole are not widespread. If borrowed money is used (leveraged investment) then the results are more likely to affect the economy as a whole, as the credit cannot be repaid.

Dalton, writing in the 1993 book *How the Stock Market Works*, comments that Black Monday in 1987 would have been far worse were it not for the legislation passed after the 1929 Crash, a view of keen interest to the authors. The damage to economies from the flight of investor confidence resulting from bubble activity is raising the spectre of regulation in corporate America and beyond. Perhaps the most notable bubble model that addresses the issue of economic deterioration and its wider destruction is based on Minsky's financial instability hypothesis, constructed in 1982, which aims to explain why a depression takes place.

The hypothesis includes the stages that occur in a boom and bust situation, beginning with the economy in steady growth, following a recent decline. Initially banks will only invest in projects whose predicted cash flows exceed their debt repayment commitments. This leads to a situation where all ventures are successful, meaning that less 'conservative' projects are then invested in. Until the pattern becomes established and new entrants seek quick profits, the ascent is reasonably controlled by existing conventions. The acceleration of investment generates further attention. At this stage the 'euphoric economy' arises, where people become convinced that all ventures will be successful. This confidence pushes up prices, and what Minsky terms 'Ponzi financiers', or speculators who borrow heavily in order to buy assets, become involved. The Ponzi method of investing means that debt commitments eventually exceed investment income. The assets must then be sold to repay debts. This means that the Ponzi investor's initial position is flawed and the pressure is to end up selling assets at a loss. An atmosphere of fear and panic is established. Sensational stories associated with the collapse explode in the various media. The hype fuelled by the speculation evaporates and unleashes a destructive force, which is rapidly communicated throughout the investing community, a situation leading to bankruptcy and panic by other investors. It is at this stage that the bubble irreparably contracts, as asset prices collapse and investment ceases.

The model constructed by Minsky was modified by Kindleberger and ordered into eight phases, which can be seen in Figure 1.1. (Phases one to eight). Cohen further develops the model by adding two more phases to Kindleberger's model, plus a further ten; added features which can be seen to occur alongside the original ten. See Figure 1.1.[30]

Phase	Description	Added Feature	Description
1	Trigger event	1	New securities emerge
2	Cheap credit	2	New financial innovations
3	Inflation in asset prices	3	Irrational investor arrives
4	Overtrading and speculation	4	Inadequate financial authorities
5	Gullible public joins in	5	Leverage increases
6	Nagging doubts form	6	Frauds and tricksters appear

7	The selling flood	7	Firms and institutions fail
8	The panic sell-off	8	Consistent patterns occur
9	Onset of debt deflation	9	Massive retracement in bubbles
10	Base-building in recovery	10	Base-building in prices/indices appears on the charts

Figure 1.1

Phase one, the trigger event, continues its consequences in waves throughout the growth of the bubble. It is exhausted only by the intervention of an alternative view that explodes with impact, leading to a sudden and dramatic crash. The book by Malcolm Gladwell, *The Tipping Point*, adds further insight into the sudden and often spectacular change in a product or service. Gladwell maps the flows of epidemics to explain change of any kind, particularly sudden, erratic bursts.

> I'm convinced that ideas and behaviours and new products move through a population very much like a disease does. This isn't just a metaphor, in other words. I'm talking about a very literal analogy. One of the things I explore in the book is that ideas can be contagious in exactly the same way that a virus is. One chapter, for example, deals with the very strange epidemic of teenage suicide in the South Pacific islands of Micronesia. In the 1970s and 1980s, Micronesia had teen suicide rates ten times higher than anywhere else in the world. Teenagers were literally being infected with the suicide bug, and one after another they were killing themselves in exactly the same way under exactly the same circumstances. We like to use words like contagiousness and infectiousness just to apply to the medical realm. But I assure you that after you read about what happened in Micronesia you'll be convinced that behaviour can be transmitted from one person to another as easily as the flu or the measles can. In fact, I don't think you have to go to Micronesia to see this pattern in action. Isn't this the explanation for the current epidemic of teen smoking in this country? And what about the rash of mass shootings we're facing at the moment from Columbine through the Atlanta stockbroker through the neo-Nazi in Los Angeles?[31]

The study by Gladwell provides insight into a key part of bubble development at the initial stage. Key individuals play an important part in attracting others to an investment.

The model accords closely with the points listed by Bagehot. The difference, however, is that Cohen's late version is the first to put the stages into short, numbered phases, rather than explaining them in greater detail. When relating historical bubbles to the model later in the book, Cohen occasionally leaves phases out altogether. It is necessary to rescue the links and detail to demonstrate the subtle intervention associated with power.

The first two phases and added features are quite straightforward, and are interconnected. The 'trigger event' is the site of rapid and enthusiastic exchange, which begins the bubble. Most commonly this would be associated with the introduction of new securities or financial innovations – something that captures the investors' imaginations. The 'cheap credit', which can be as a result of a thriving economy, can refer either to credit given to a company involved in the bubble, or to leveraged investment (added feature five). 'Retracement' refers to the loss of value of the stock involved in the crash, a fall that is not guaranteed to recover.

Added feature six is concerned with frauds and tricksters. Bagehot also discussed the term and popularised the term 'fraud', claiming that it is a consequence of high returns. Bagehot adds that this is because people are credulous when they are happy, and the money makes them happy. They will believe anything for a while, allowing the nature of the bubble to change, largely without detection.

Finally, phases five, seven and eight, and added feature three are possibly the most relevant factors in assessing the input and flights associated with crowds; the common denominator being the swelling and bursting of the bubble, a condition repeated in the struggle for speculative advantage.

The Role of Power in Bubbles

The remarkable developments in information technology and the establishment of global communication systems that occurred in the latter part of the twentieth century led to a proliferation in accessibility to information. Information is the crucial commodity, which is fundamental to sophisticated market economies. The idea of money without frontiers is reflected explicitly in the integrated global environment. The ambiguities of globalisation may not have been resolved, but the world is contracting towards a multi-layered network that resembles John Burton's famous web model.

Money continues to be accumulated and distributed unevenly throughout the world. The speed of exchange may have accelerated exponentially, but not all sectors of the global community have direct access to the electronics empire, although they may feel the consequences of its activities and its gaze. On the one hand, transactions are exchanged in a nanosecond. Outside the electric freeway, goods and services move in similar patterns to those recognisable one hundred years ago.

The hierarchy of power active in the global political economy, supported by wealth, tradition and the nexus of influential circles, manipulates the markets and influences outcomes in the political, economic and social domains. The view that the world is run by 500 or so key individuals does not derive necessarily from the domain of conspiracy theorists or financial terrorists. Speaking on wealth and US foreign policy, Noam Chomsky, professor of linguistics, suggests the 'rich are not ordinary persons, they are immortal and powerful, and they demand national treatment a right that no flesh-and-blood person can demand'.[32] The power that is exercised through small circles of influence is a continuum of history.

The major figures in financial history (the Rothschilds for example) have used and exorcised power in the markets to shape their investments. This is not a new phenomenon. The rich burghers and aristocracy influential during the Tulip Bubble benefited from and swelled the bubble, through subtle interventions, rumour and coded criticism.

The opportunity to expose the power relations active in the bubble scenario is related to the decisions of key investors, which can be studied. Whether influenced by individuals or privileged groups, key actors in the global political economy need to be identified in the growth of investment and speculative bubbles.

> Historically, power has been invoked most by conflict theorists. In the view of these theorists, there is usually someone or some groups who are thought to have power and to use it for some purpose. In contemporary debates, especially those that centre on the work of Michael Foucault, this assumption is not made. There is somehow power in the system or in the culture we have inherited, and that power controls us, sometimes in deleterious ways.[33]

The deleterious influence on bubbles is inflated by the input from authority, professionals and so-called experts. These interventions are often subtle. The coded nature of power is propelled by the opportunity to take an advantage from a privileged position, which is given credibility through its exposure in the various media. To assess the nature of power active in the arena of speculative advantage, a wider view of the socio-economic influences on investment needs to be considered.

> The tradition of political economy, as defined here, is distinguished from economic liberalism primarily through its treatment of power in economic life.

Economic liberalism regards the market, first and foremost, as a system of decentralised power and individual or organisational autonomy. Concentrations of power are one possible consequence of market exchange, but in no way a necessary feature of the market. For the tradition of political economy, by contrast, power is a core structure of economic life which determines economic objectives and the distribution of resources between social groups. Whereas economic liberalism treats concentrations of power as deviations from the norm, political economy sees power relations as a constituent feature of the way social groups produce and distribute goods in pursuit of their interests.[34]

In seeking to 'drill down' to the core relationship between power and bubble activity, the book uses a steer from the work of Steven Lukes. Lukes' ideas on the operation of power and its influence are incisive. The three dimensions of power outlined by the author – persuasion, manipulation and force – identify the categories that help in the study of bubbles. Historically, as subsequent chapters will demonstrate, speculative booms and busts are related to the power of force and manipulation inherent in the development of bubbles. In the media and information driven society that is typical of sophisticated market economies, the power and influence associated with persuasion and manipulation is raised as a key factor in the outcome of possibilities, financial or other.

The material that follows will seek to define a model of fundamental prices that is related explicitly to power. The notion of power as the key detrainment in the movement of markets will be viewed historically.

Economic and Business Cycles

The construction of a model to assess the development and demise of speculative activity cannot be separated from the range of political, social, economic, cultural and legal developments occurring in the wider economy. Economic indicators take account of the various sectors, for example, the macro-economic and investment climate through analysis of domestic data (GDP, inflation, budget, unemployment) and external data (trade and current account balance, debt reserves, foreign direct investment). It is clear that:

external factors also have a bearing, and the current geopolitical environment means that prices are constantly on the up due to uncertainty – people pull their money out of stocks and invest in bonds as they are a safer bet in a war/terrorist climate. The same is true for Gold, which is also currently trading high. Every time there is any war related announcement – Hans Blix speaking or today

Bush saying he'd give the weapons inspectors 3 weeks before starting military action, we see an immediate hike in prices.[35] One could therefore speculate that when the war concludes, presuming the outcome is satisfactory, that could be the start of the big burst of the bond bubble.[36]

Economic forecasts invariably reflect and influence a range of factors such as interest rates, consumer spending, unemployment and the general performance of sectors: service and manufacturing. The results from forecasts influence decisions through their circulation in the various media, examples include: daily papers (the *Financial Times*), Sunday papers (*The Business*), specialist magazines (*The Economist*), trade publications (*Leisure Management*), press cutting agencies (ICC data cards) and media monitors (PR Newswire), tip sheets (Penny Share List), radio and television (In Business and Working Lunch), investor relations blurb (company Intranets), brokers reviews (Jordens) and sector reports (Euromoney), and annual and interim statements (various companies). Numerous websites exist to check information in the public domain. Number Watch, for example, is a site dedicated to the monitoring of the misleading numbers that are generated by single issue fanatics, politicians, bureaucrats, quasi-scientists etc.[37]

The performance of the economy, from an investment context, informs decisions and actions throughout society, whether it is the choice between equities and bonds adopting - long or short term - strategies, or retreating into cash.[38] In an integrated financial system animated by the mobility of capital, macroeconomics is rendered a fluid environment that evades the rigid national application of policy. 'On the other hand, governmental regulation of the enterprise has proliferated, adding to the complexity of business activities.'[39]

The development of a bubble is noticeable in regard to a particular stock, sector or commodity through a persistent increase in its market price. The media led 'noise' or 'hype', related to the wide object of interest, creates a further separation between its price and underlying value, a development that generates distortions throughout the markets.

The effect of financial markets on the real economy goes back further than the Enron fiasco. The US economy had an unbroken 10-year expansion between 1991 and 2001. With the exception of the short-lived 1987 mini-crash and a couple of minor hiccoughs, Wall Street also saw an exceptionally long bull market from 1984 until 2000. Economic historians will debate whether the piercing of the tech stock bubble in 2000 was the main trigger for the 2001 recession; but it is clear that it played a major part.[40]

Whilst financial and economic data provides an insight into the health of the real economy, it should be noted that the movements in the markets can be deceptive and propelled by a variety of causes, some ambiguous. During a boom period, which can be gradual, all aspects of the economy are generally in a positive cycle. At this stage, the architects of economic policy are reluctant to intervene, anticipating the political damage which may result from bad news associated with intervention in any form. The general concern of governments is to be distant from the economic contractions that result from scandal, corporate exuberance and flaws in economic management. As the boom separates into several bubbles, the effect on resources and investment becomes increasingly asymmetric leading to serious fluctuations that create uncertainly and turbulent markets in all sectors of the economy. The need to intervene at this stage is palpable: policy needs to be implemented to curtail the ever increasing bull speculation and volatility. History suggests that this is unforthcoming until the wider consequences of a collapse have been felt.

The indicators that are derived from various statistical data are produced by a range of statutory and commercial organisations. The Office of National Statistics,[41] for example provides data on various sectors in the UK. Up-to-date US economic data is available from the Economic Statistics Briefing Room of the White House.[42] The indicators are increasingly transparent and are available to the public. Ironically, at a time when the discipline of economics is being criticised for failing in its understanding of the everyday business of life, the Internet has presented a platform where full information is a realistic possibility.

A brief review of the changing nature of the markets and its impact on the wider economy illustrates the complexity of pressure and resistance. It is crucial to assess an industry business cycle and the factors that determine its development. Periodic changes in the economy are traditionally related to the internal degree of consumption, investment and unemployment.[43] These are influenced by patterns over time. For example, *Seasonal variations* that register fluctuations in demand according to the time of the year are predicable but do contain anomalies. Seasonal companies record levels of activity: increased sales in retailing for example during Christmas (a shift from pre-Christmas activity to the sales in January is a recent trend); more sunglasses sold during warm weather. Trends within seasonal variations are important and illustrate the need to identify the appearance of countertrends. For example in tourism, typically seasonal, more retirees will seemingly be travelling off-season, spreading travel evenly throughout the year and eliminating the cyclical peaks and valleys typical of the industry.[44] This is compounded further with changing demographics: aging populations with disposable income. This view may be flawed however with the poor performance of stocks and the impact on pensions. *Cycles* are related to variations in business activity as a result of booms and slumps in the economy as a whole. Fears relating to a housing bubble or fear of redundancy impact on consumer spending. Cyclical companies react strongly to changes in the economy. Defensive companies such as pharmaceuticals cope relatively well with economic downturns. *Shocks* are typified by random shocks and unexpected events in the economy. These may occur in general or a particular market in which the business operates. The consequences of the attack on the World Trade Centre had an immediate and negative effect on the aviation industry. Correspondingly this reduced the revenue produced by tourism and business travel, which affected other sectors of the economy. *Trends* are influenced by favourable or unfavourable structural changes that cause longer term movements in a particular market. The issue of demographics is again relevant as are fashion tastes, which can spread throughout an economy and alter its preference and tastes (the loss of market share by the British retailer, Marks and Spencer, in the 1990s is an example of the havoc that can ensue from a flight in fashion-related tastes).

The multitude of variables active in a market and the wider economy renders any analysis conditional. Operational and management science is a sophisticated area of investigation, particularly in the development of analytical programmes and scenario planning. The collation of data is a crucial stage in the research process. Issues such as bias in the construction of quantitative studies and the process of conducting the survey need to be assessed to highlight difficulties relating to exclusion arising from religious, ethnic, class or gender prejudice. This is particularly relevant in international surveys.

The opportunity to succeed in extreme competitive environments is conditional on the availability of value-adding information, timing and execution. This is particularly relevant in the international context, where entering new geographical areas can damage the existing activities of the organisation.

It has been noted above how national economic policy makers are limited in the animated arena of macroeconomics. The state can of course intervene to limit fluctuations. but this can create associated threats and dangers.

> Black Wednesday reminded us of two things: one the size and the power of the foreign exchange markets, and two, the amounts of money that can be made by well capitalized, well informed, and pro risk traders.[45]

The political consequences of Black Wednesday continue to this day to haunt the British Conservative Party. The negative backlash in the economy and its continued effect on the electorate is one explanation for the financial prudence associated with New Labour, along with the efforts of the cautious chancellor.

Still swimming against the market tide, it was announced in the afternoon that interest rates were to be raised to 15%. The market ignored the politicians and continued to sell the pound, with the ERM band finally breached at the end of the day. With the Bank of England's reserves depleted by £17b on the 16th alone, the Government bowed to the inevitable. It suspended its ERM membership with Lamont stating that 'the interests of Britain would best be served' by the decision. The rate hike to 15% was promptly reversed. Having been devalued just days before, the Italian lira was expelled from the ERM on the same day. Sweden, Spain, Finland, Ireland, Portugal, Denmark and France all suffered market turmoil with their respective currencies, too. Between September 1st and September 22nd, the pound lost around 11% of its value against the US dollar and the German Mark. The ERM eventually disintegrated in 1993, with Lamont suffering the political consequences of Black Wednesday the same year (and Major in 1997). However, while arguments still rage over whether the country should have joined in the first place, Britain was indeed 'best served' by the ERM exit, as a series of interest rate cuts in late 1992 revived the economy. Certainly the stock market thought the ERM exit was in the country's best interests: it jumped 4.4% the very next day. Indeed, after touching a low of 2,281 a few weeks before the trouble, the FTSE 100 has never looked back.[46]

The limitations of government intervention have been widely studied by authors in business and political economy, for example Kenichi Omhae and Susan Strange respectively. The niche nature of government intervention is increasingly subtle in the integrated market environments of the twenty-first century. The 'realities' of sophisticated market economies, therefore, necessitate a sensitivity to a multi-disciplinary approach that seeks to unpack key trends and make clear ambiguities, which are associated with the booms and busts in various investments.

Pascal's Wager

'God is, or he is not. Which way should we incline?' The answer can perhaps be considered on the quality of the historical information, its thorough assessment, and consideration of all the possibilities. Hedging is a useful defensive strategy, which does not necessarily respond to questions but limits the potential repercussions. The choice, in the context of speculative advantage and minimising speculative loss, is related to the nexus of trades that shape supply and demand. Other factors such as the influence of the various media, the circulation of information through other means, and generic hype, accelerate the positive and negative flow of the investment. The market cannot be beaten, but it can be doctored.

Notes

[1] Domain Economics, Oxford Reference on-line:www.oxfordreference.com.

[2] Oxford English Dictionary (1989).

[3] Campbell and Bonner (1994) p.3, *Media, Mania and the Markets*.

[4] Shiller (2001) p.3, *Bubbles, Human Judgement, and Expert Opinion*.

[5] See the book by Edward Chanceller (2000) *Devil take the Hindmost*, for a trek through the booms and busts, starting with Rome, 200 BC, and including the Tulip Bubble Mania, the South Sea Bubble, the Railway Mania of 1845, the 'panics' at the end of the nineteenth century, the Crash of 1929 and the collapse of the economy in Japan. For a study on the boom and bust in the United States, see Robert Sobel's (2000), *The Money Manias: The Eras of Great Speculation in America 1770-1970*, which includes the Vandalia land debacle, the failed canal building schemes, the disastrous Florida land boom and the corporate exuberance of the late twentieth century. *Wheels of Fortune: The History of Speculation* (2002) *from Scandal to Respectability* by Charles Geisst straddles the scandalous occurrences in the markets and the limitations of regulation to control them.

[6] A prospectus brochure extolling the virtues of the non-existent kingdom of Poyais appeared and was widely circulated, creating a sensation. Based on the outpouring of public interest in this exotic country, and with the sponsorship of a former Lord Mayor of London, Gregor raised a loan of L200,000 ostensibly intended to develop his American territories, the subscribers' investments being secured by the purported riches of the gold and silver mines located in Poyais. For further details on the scams of liars and hucksters see: http://www.newint.org/issue168/liars.htm.

[7] Francis (2001) p.102, *Chronicles and Characters of the Stock Exchange*.

[8] See *The Gambler*, for in-depth figures and trends in the gambling industry. Mintel report www.mintel.com.

[9] Clapson (1992) p.20, *A Bit of a Flutter*.

[10] Rowling (1987) p.139, *Commodities*.

[11] Anon, email communication, 15 July 2002.

[12] www.clarity.net/~jake/bubble.htm.

[13] Campbell and Bonner (1994) p.26, in *Media, Mania and the Markets* add 'by definition of logic, when demand is at its peak, when something is most in fashion, when the crowd all want it, then this is the time when a sober view of the future suggests that it will not continue to rise in favour, but fall. There are no more willing buyers. No more people who will jump on the bandwagon. No more money waiting to flow into the market and drive prices up even further'.

[14] Ecclesiastes (II:I-2) *Book of Ecclesiastes*.

[15] BBC Timelines, 5 February 2003: When the South Sea Company had been set up in 1711, it was hoped that it would one day challenge the financial strength of the Bank of

England and the East India Company when it came to providing loans for the government to support the national debt. The company had a monopoly on trade with all Spanish territories, South America and the west coast of North America. In 1713, the company received the right to supply slaves to the Spanish colonies. In 1720, the government encouraged investors to trade governments stocks for South Sea Company shares and as these boomed, more and more people speculated in them (forcing the share price higher). In July 1720, with company shares at a vastly inflated, unrealistic and unsustainable level, confidence collapsed (as did the share price). Investors lost considerable amounts and some even committed suicide. Despite the Bubble bursting, the company survived into the 1850s.

[16] www.historic-uk.com/HistoryUK/England-History/SouthSeaBubble.htm.

[17] www.clarity.net/~jake/bubble.htm.

[18] Sayers (1967) p.51.

[19] Cohen (1997) p.4.

[20] Message board, http://boards.fool.com/message.asp?

[21]Frison, Mackay/De La Vega (1996) p.2, *Extraordinary Popular Delusions and the Madness of Crowds.*

[22] William Hogarth (1720) *An Emblematic Print on the South Sea.*

[23] Review by Gail Owens Hoelscher, (15 November 2000) from *Turnarounds and Workouts.*

[24] Anon, email communication 15 July 2002.

[25] www.emfguru.org/past/bubbles.html.

[26] Brooks (1967) p.79, *Once in Golconda.*

[27] The directors of registered companies in the UK are not allowed to deal two months before results are published. These so-called 'close periods' are monitored. Citywire provides a daily service that analyses the dealings of directors. View at: www.citywire.co.uk.

[28] Citystats subscription service provides minute-by-minute financial astrology forecasts for all time zones up to five days in advance. Unique intra-day trading signals predict movements for all major stock markets, such as: Australia AS-30, Japan Nikkei 225, Hong Kong Hang Seng, Singapore Simex, India Mumbai, Germany DAX, France CAC-40, Italy Mibtel, UK FTSE, Brazil Bovespa, US Nasdaq, US Dow Jones, Canada Toronto, Mexico Bolsa, and Argentina.

[29] Bagehot (1917) p.54.

[30] Cohen (1997) p.4.

[31] Gladwell interviewed: www.gladewell.com/books2.html.

[32] www-tech.mit.edu/V119/N8/Chomsky.8n.html.

[33] Honderich (1995) p.709, *The Oxford Companion to Philosophy.*

[34] Holton (1992) p.108, *Economy and Society.*

[35] Correspondingly, Turkey's currency and leading stock market index fell heavily in the first day of trading since parliament narrowly failed to approve US troop deployment in the country for a war on Iraq. The lira dropped about 5% against the dollar, trading at about 1,660,000 lira. The National 100 index of leading Turkish shares slumped 12.5% to 10,129 points. The falls prompted the central bank to hint that it might intervene in the financial markets, which helped the lira to recover some of its losses. BBC Front Page (3 February 2003), www.bbc.co.uk.

[36] Anon, email communication, 19 February 2003.

[37] www.numberwatch.co.uk.

[38] The difference between a blue chip company (a large and relatively secure company with steady growth) are less risky than 'speculative' stocks (small fast growing companies), which may be found on markets such as the alternative investment market (AIM). Some

blue chips companies are former growth stocks that have matured and consolidated. Others have disappeared, some like Marconi are disappearing. The distinction between income and value stocks is that the former does not experience rapid growth but pays generous dividends, whilst value stocks record favourable growth (these may be picked up from someone who has lost interest in the company or need the cash).

[39] Morrison (2002) p.85. *The International Business Environment.*

[40] Yorgos Papatheodorou (2002) p.80 *Accountancy.*

[41] http://www.statistics.gov.uk/.

[42] www.whitehouse.gov/WH/html/handbook.html.

[43] See www.ilo.org/stat/ and www.bls.gov.

[44] Anon, (2003) p.34, *The Futurist* January-February.

[45] www.ex.ac.uk/~RDavis/arian/lindaemu.html

[46] Black Wednesday Remembered (2002):
www.fool.co.uk/news/comment/2002/c020916b.htm.

Chapter 2

Fear and Risk: Without a Net

Introduction

In the pages below, the generic nature of risk in the various stages of the bubble cycle will be considered. Risk can be insured against but it cannot be eliminated. In some cases risks are incalculable. Whilst measures can be taken to insure against exposure, a risk adverse market represents a dull investment environment. The industry that assesses the vagaries of risk is immense. It includes a vast information gathering, the assessment of probabilities and application of financial instruments such as options, which allows risk to be managed more easily than outright buying and selling.[1]

Risk and Investment

Risk assessments and models vary between private investors, investment banks, trading houses and other investment-related institutions. Methods of calculation also differ between day trading and long-term investment strategies (in the trading profession the prevailing view suggests that there is more 'safety' less risk and better gains to be made in day trading than in long-term 'view-taking' speculation).

Despite the introduction of strategies, and the introduction of new agencies to regulate the investment environment, innovative steps are taken to attain high returns. For example, people previously got around risk rules by trading on open outcry markets, which are generally believed to be transparent and fair.

> In open-outcry trading, exchange members stand in pits making bids and offers, by voice and with hand signals, to the rest of the traders in the pit. Customer orders coming into the futures pit are delivered to floor brokers or dual traders who execute them according to the order's instructions. For example, a 'market' order tells the broker to execute the order immediately at the prevailing price in the pit; a 'limit' order specifies the price (or better) at which

the order can be filled; and a 'stop' order tells the broker to execute an order at the market price if a certain price is reached. Other types of orders specify the time of the trade (e.g., at the market's open or close) or allow a broker discretion in the execution. Orders also can indicate the period for which they are valid, e.g., a day, a week or until cancelled.[2]

Outcry markets have of course been largely replaced by electronic trading platforms (although they are favoured during volatile periods).[3] In the contemporary trading environment subtle deferrals from acceptable practices are taken to strengthen positions and limit an exposure, which necessitates the need for relatively close supervision. The investment environment is imbued with a culture of risk taking. It should however, be considered risk, which does not eradicate the player or the institution he, she or they represent.

On the one hand, the euphoria related to inflated returns associated with a bullish investment constructs a belief that the bubble will continue indefinitely. The fear of being 'left out' or 'missing the boat' fuels anxiety and contributes to the dismissal or poor appreciation of future risks. The warnings associated with risk issued during the rapid rise of an investment can be ignored. The consequences of a fall can however, be intense and dramatic. It consumes all that have failed to take appropriate precautions, particularly if investors are too distant from the market to take proactive steps to limit the exposure, a common occurrence with private investment. The images of traders leaping from buildings during the infamous Wall Street Crash present a picture, mythical or not, that dramatises the full nature of risk in speculative communities; people literally lose everything. Investors can find protection from malfeasance, but erratic trading decisions are generally outside the remit of official controls.

It is generally accepted in sophisticated market economies that widespread restrictive measures implemented by the state will damage the market, but that transparent and subtle interventions assist in its everyday activities – the debate between Keynes and Hayek continues unabated.

In the context of investment bubbles, speculators are encouraged to take risks, but taught that restraint and professionalism can be undermined through an obsession with spectacular gains. The government of the day may intervene to limit the political fallout from a particular stock, but intervention is fraught with danger. From the investors' point of view help is never sufficient when problems occur: investors tend not to be fully compensated. The collapse of Railtrack led to political intervention, but risks of some kind are part of the investment package. Losses, as well as gains, can be incurred.

The state may no longer be the autonomous entity that determined its future through the unchallenged manipulation of economic policy, but it does have influence with the business community and the markets through the construction and implementation of regulation, a factor that encourages an active response from a range of interests to limit the destructive consequences associated with it.

Risk Models and Speculative Activity

Risk models related to speculative activity have been further complicated by the increased influence of the following: 1. The ambiguous nature of risk that has proliferated in the twenty-first century. 2. The political, economic, social, cultural, ecological and legal arena has become imbued with uncertainty and turbulence. 3. The application of statistics in risk assessments has been replaced by a more holistic approach that widens the analysis to include normative approaches.

Psychological factors influence the operation and presence of risk. It is clear some people are not adverse to risk but are risk takers. Investors do not consistently behave rationally, a condition shaped by culture and experience. This may however be the result of poor or misleading information. The risk arising from mistakes and errors can be recognised but it is difficult to measure accurately. Therefore, models need to reflect the chaotic nature of markets, or the fuzzy logic that informs elements of speculative activity.

Experience or habit is a condition of speculative activity. The activity can be monitored to discern patterns, but it needs to be studied in context. Signs and signals are issued and acted upon, but the embedded manipulation should not be ignored in the investment decision-making process, an area under theorised or appropriately considered.

We get daily charts from a lady called ... * ('... charts') which state resistance and support level prices in the bonds we trade. Clearly if *... states (e.g.) 100.03 is a resistance level everyone puts sell orders there, presuming the price will bounce off it and go back down, thus we buy it back cheaper. However, this then creates a large order quantity which is hard to break – again, a self-fulfilling prophecy.

As soon as everyone realised how ludicrous the profit projections were for say Microsoft, which was at one time valued around 300, the prices collapsed quickly, and of course the bubble bursts rapidly because too many sellers and few buyers means the price has to keep going down. This again I see daily in my job, where you have to offload something you end up hitting 'best price', hopefully quicker than the next person, i.e. your sell order is matched to the nearest buy price available. If everyone tries to sell best price there are insufficient orders to buy there and so you sell at the price below – and so on.

There is also a famous 'shorter' (person who makes his money from selling stocks which she/he believes are going down and buys them back cheaper later on). When people knew what she/he was selling it had the reverse effect to the chatroom rampings – suddenly anyone long on the stock wants to offload it, and anyone not involved either shorts it also or steers well clear.

Everyday (pretty much) we see new highs in the bond markets we trade, and it is a matter of speculation that, whilst they go up and down all day, when certain levels are broken on the way back down the price will dump.[4]

Despite the complexity that accompanies risk, categories can be identified, measured and ranked using various tools and models. The relationship between a variety of risks and its probability of occurring is not an exact science; deviations from the norm in investment are possible – it is perhaps surprising fluctuations do not occur in more frequently in erratic patterns.

Each approach should be considered with an awareness of the generic picture, which may indicate countertrends and anomalies.

The term *risk* and *uncertainty* are often used interchangeably but it is important to distinguish between the two. Risk describes future outcomes for which objective probabilities can be identified – risk is the concept relevant to much of the work of insurance companies. Uncertainty relates to outcomes whose prior probabilities are unknown and unknowable.[5]

The work conducted by Shiller is helpful in making the distinction between risk and uncertainty. Drawing on the work of Frank Knight, Professor at the University of Chicago, Shiller indicates:

Risk...concerns events whose probability law is known, and that has quantifiable probabilities. Uncertainty concerns events that are essentially unpredicted in nature, whose probability must be judged by thinking, by analogy and induction, by thinking globally rather than specifically.[6]

The fear produced by financial wrongdoing and mis-reporting in corporate organisations, falling stock prices, and the uncertain political, economic and environmental structures, has contributed to a system that follows the 'noise' prevalent at the given time, a condition accelerated by the commercialisation and popularity of business news in the various media. For example CNN's *Moneyline*, CNBC's *Business Centre* and *Squawk Box* debate, influence and react to market moves.

Within the investment industry, poor practice and lapse monitoring generates a serious loss in confidence. The publicity associated with 'laugh out loud' investments, which hood-wink clients and investors into believing that certain stocks are more valuable than they actually are, generate an overly suspicious atmosphere, which is not in the interest of the industry long term. Some Merrill Lynch and Citibank traders have been admonished publicly for this form of practice.

In considering 'the habits and customs [institutions] of men which make up the money economy'[7] and their influence on the business cycle and 'the markets', the inherent power relations reoccur in successful and failed investments. The structures of power that impress on the processors that facilitate the attainment or denial of speculative advantage need exposure and consideration, particularly in a society driven by electronic information and the media in its various forms.

The exchange of information, which is filtered through electronic empires, necessitates the demand to look at the role of power and its impact on social and economic systems, investment decisions and choices. It is not an academic endeavour to investigate the coded nature of power, but a strategic move to illustrate the relationship between the interventions of implicit and explicit manipulation, and its effect on the decline and growth of the bubble.

Fear of Losing out in a Bull Bubble

The attraction of taking part in a spectacular investment is not a new phenomenon. Speculation associated with Ancient Gods, crusades, specie, gold rushes, and in a more recent setting, the scramble to provide finance for the plethora of research and technology initiatives, have attracted investors seeking spiritual and material rewards. Each advantage includes a degree of risk potential: loss of health, family, country or fortune. The bubble momentarily provides a snapshot of a fortune, which is difficult to capture.

The location of bubbles of hope such as the rewards on offer in sunset strip provide the currency feeding mini-dreams, which offer insight into the engagement with the bubble psyche. It is the prevailing atmosphere which conditions the degree of engagement, a condition that transfers to investment bubbles.

The short span of human life and its inherent struggles accelerates the need and desire to take risks. Risk is fundamental in enterprise, innovation and the everyday business of life.[8] Speculation generates activity that would not otherwise take place. The generic progression of wealth demands the facilitation of chance: it is better for a cycle to burst than a cycle never to begin. The removal of a favourable investment environment damages the economy as a whole, and allows political forces to manipulate desperation.

> It is often said that political freedom is meaningless without economic freedom. This is true enough, but in a sense almost opposite from that in which the phrase is used by our planners. The economic freedom which is the prerequisite of any other freedom from economic care which the socialists promise us and which can be obtained only by relieving the individual at the same time of the necessity and of the power of choice; it must be freedom of our economic activity which, with the right of choice, inevitably also carries the risk and the responsibility of that right.[9]

The ability to gather, exchange and transfer information into knowledge is a key determinant in acquiring speculative advantage and in limiting risk. The previous chapter indicated the value of clusters and networks in using information to procure gain in its varied form. Without doubt:

> markets feed off information, and networks are one of the most important media through which information travels. Markets are awash with information; people in firms hear all kinds of news, rumours, and reports whose veracity may be doubtful...having a relationship with someone, or having a connection with an organisation, helps to create access to reliable and credible information. Being told the truth is no good unless you can be sure that the message is true, and for this it helps to be dealing with a source you can trust.[10]

Whilst trust is conditional, Fukuyama citing the work of Aaron Wildavsky in the book *Trust* makes an important point both in assessing the influence of networks that are reliant on a degree of open co-operation between the various parties.

> Most people are simply habituated to a certain degree of honesty. Gathering the necessary information and considering possible alternatives is itself a costly and time-consuming process, one that can be short-circuited by custom or habit...this is true even for the seemingly sophisticated political choices made by educated people living in advanced societies. People form attitudes toward risk – for example, which is dangerous: nuclear power or contact with people with AIDS? – not from any rational analysis of the real risks involved in either case but based on whether they are broadly liberal or broadly conservative.[11]

Deception is a clever and damaging intervention. A communication derived from a credible source may be plausible, but it may not be compatible with the prevailing reality. The proliferation of electronic fraud and mischief in digital chat rooms increases the risk that information may be flawed.[12] Power is again exercised through the resource platform, which allows for a degree of authenticity to be gleaned without substance, a condition that improves the success of a subsequent decision.

There is a lot of discussion within the industry (though not insider trading, more like tips on horses etc) about good stocks. Around 1999 industry insiders were (and still are) kind of middle-men as far as the investment ladder goes. What I mean is if we presume that banks and the companies themselves ramped the stocks they probably got out as the industry insiders got in as private investors. They were then followed by private (virgin and otherwise) investors, thus whilst a lot of them eventually did lose, it was on a sliding scale, so at least their own knowledge of get-outs, gleaned from their professional stop limit knowledge, meant they lost less than the virgins.

The people I have spoken to theorise in hindsight that the banks lent money to the tech companies and thus needed to ramp them in order to get back their investments. Word on the street is that in most cases whilst the stocks still seemed fresh, new and a good buy the banks then sold their debt on, covering themselves and meaning they couldn't lose. Enron definitely did this.

The next stage was financial chat rooms such as www.hemscott.net and www.motleyfool.co.uk. These chatrooms are mostly known to industry professionals, though can be used by private investors. Here people exchange tips on good stocks etc. Around 1999 a phrase came about 'ten-bagger' (bag as in £1000 – typical trader Londonism!) to describe a stock which 'couldn't lose'. There was one particular female investor who would regularly list 5 or so ten-baggers and was always right, so the more she ramped a stock the higher it went. As pointed out by one investor I have spoken to, this in itself is a self-fulfilling prophecy.[13]

In periods of rising markets, the manipulation of solid information or rumour dictates the success or failure of a given trade. The reckless nature of numerous trades fuelled by hearsay, which underpins many ramps, resembles in its micro-operation, the tragic-comic approach to chance set out by the novelist Luke Rhinehart. In the book, *The Dice Man*, the everyday life of the central character is determined by the throw of the dice. In the passage below, which would have amused Pascal and Chevalier de Méré, Rhinehart,[14] the novelist considers the relationship between the dice and fate.

That afternoon the dice scorned all sorts of exciting options and steered me instead to a corner drugstore to reading matter at random. Admittedly, browsing through the four magazines chosen – *Agonizing Confessions; Your Pro-Football Handbook; Fuck-it* and *Health and You* – was more interesting than my usual psychoanalytic fare, but I vaguely regretted not having been sent by the dice on a more important or absurd mission.[15]

The choice to invest or not to invest ought to be considered on what may be lost rather than on what can be gained. The fear, however, of losing out or not being part of the initial stages of a bull bubble outweighs the caution. The mistake grows from that point.

A speculative bubble occurs when people become obsessed with a particular investment. Fear plays a large part in the bubble's build-up, with investors desperate not to miss the boat and willing to buy at any price, completely disregarding logic.[16]

Trow's point stresses the suspension of reason which is a key feature of irrational investment driven by the determination not to miss out at any cost. Harrison adds to this momentary loss of reason, which consumes the individual and the crowd, with reference to chaos associated with the final stages of the bubble and its collapse. It is recognised that:

One of the most worrying aspects of stockmarket investment is the tendency of professional and the private investor alike to behave like lemmings under certain economic conditions. Mass hysteria can trigger a dramatic fall in equity prices and even a full-scale crash.[17]

Harrison and Trow both make reference to the public's involvement in deepening the severity of the fall. This behaviour is not unique – it can influence the actions of market professionals:

The persistence of bull markets long after the fundamentals could support them, and then the sudden, extreme corrections, can be explained not by faulty slide rules or computers but by the collective, consensual psychology of the City and other financial markets. Keynes rather kindly called this 'animal spirits'.[18]

The first way in which the public inflates the bubble is through a wave of virgin investment. Schabacker writes extensively on this subject, and warns of the dangers of assuming that investing in stocks and shares will automatically result in consistent profits.[19] He claims that losses experienced by amateur investors are the stock market's method of justice – 'Why should the stock market pay back so much more to this individual in profit than he has put into it in study, in energy, in thought and in careful analysis?' The view perhaps suffers from its time, but not radically. The democratisation of information is not a guarantee of returns. It certainly helps, but the movements of the financial and investment markets are not uniformly transparent, particularly when deducing cause and effect.

The second mistake the public makes is hysteria. 'Calm, sane and unruffled judgement is necessary in most any business but it is especially important in market trading.'[20] The 'Madness of Crowds' discussed by Mackay recognises the almost pathological attraction of bubbles. The hysteria to buy in the first place, which inflates the bubble so greatly, and the panic selling which bursts the bubble, is influenced by similar external factors.

It is the market insiders (the key players close to the investment) who begin to swell the bubble – often well aware what they are doing. The bubble, inflated by the noise of its benefits, fuels the trading activities of the crowd who will inadvertently, be responsible for its final rapid growth and burst. The dotcom gold rush was noticeable in this effect.

The most famous case in the UK was the ramping by the Daily Mirror. It was noted in court that reporters working on the paper's column, City Slickers, bought shares in advance of recommending them. Most shares they ran 'buy recommendations' went on to go 'through the roof'.

Banks were putting out buy recommendations and selling to the private individuals who rushed to buy on their advice. One institution ran a buy on a company called 'Infobank'. This company turned down a reported takeover at £12 per share from Microsoft and were trading in the £40-£50 by the end of the bubble. The buy recommendation was with a target of £90-100 per share. In December 2002 these shares were trading below 40p and are now suspended due to investigation by the serious fraud office.

The attitude of a lot of private investors is that banks created the bubble to punish private investors who had stopped investing via fund managers etc, those who had taken the chance to play the markets via the cheap online brokerage companies.

People didn't know how to value this new generation of companies. All stocks having IPOs were a case of 'free money'. Stories were abounded of banks giving the opportunity of pre-IPO shares to favoured customers only. Everyone wanted in on the act – the Freeserve IPO highlighted that – it was really the first opportunity members of the general public in the UK had to become involved in an IPO during this bubble. It therefore became massively oversubscribed and extremely profitable for everyone involved.

A big highlight of this bubble that had not been experienced in a market like this before was the internet chatroom. The most popular in the UK were hemscott.net, motleyfool.co.uk and iii.co.uk. The term ramping was born.

People would work as a group to buy some obscure stock with some sort of IT background. Then numerous people would bombard the various chatrooms with constant positive messages about that stock. It was a tactic that

worked very well for months. There appeared to be so many people on these
bulletin boards with little or no knowledge of the financial markets, but they
were having a go with their own money. This was probably because all the
newspapers were full of stories of shares going up, not just by percentages but
by multiples.[21]

The ramping caused by the positive noises made by the 'experts' in the
various media thrives on investor gossip, which often occurs 'outside the
office' in restaurants, bars and cafés close to trading centres and financial
institutions. Small moves are noticed and talked about. An anonymous
trader illustrates below how the initial change in an established trading
position, which includes a common signal that is gradually communicated
through the investor chain presents opportunities.

> I was working for an investment bank at the time dealing in equity futures as I
> recall a lot of the life insurance, pension funds etc had been shorting equity
> futures for several weeks before the bubble actually burst.
>   When the stocks fell it was unbelievably quick, inexperienced people had
> been consumed by the fact that they couldn't lose with their investments; the
> saying 'rabbits in headlights' couldn't have been more appropriate. They were
> staring at big losses on their savings (or in worse cases on borrowings) and
> either panicked, dumping everything 'at market' (whatever price they could sell
> for), or what turned out to be the more foolish move – they held thinking
> everyone else was panicking and that when that initial wave was over then
> some stability would return into the market. Infobank, who I mentioned earlier,
> came off from £50 to £20 in what seemed like a week. At this stage I remember
> seeing quotes on Internet bulletin boards such as 'I was happy to buy these at
> £40, I am delighted to be doubling up at £20' and 'I never thought I would get
> the opportunity to buy some at these prices again'.[22]

The boom in American technology, which propelled the US beyond its
normal lead over the rest of the world, continues despite repeated falls, to
provide a range of investment opportunities. The speculative colossus and
the relationship between the Pentagon and commercial enterprise secured
and deepened the United States advance over all other countries in terms of
information technology. The technologies of the future, which are currently
being developed in Silicon Valley, should provide a new environment for a
speculative bubble. In the 1990s, the Valley went through a well-known
spectacular boom: money, graduates, everyone wanted to take part and be
part of the adventure. That is where Cisco, Intel, Yahoo and most Internet
icons, were born. These firms are currently less quoted. In some cases ex-
managers are unemployed and most start-ups have faded away. But Silicon
Valley is still at the forefront of innovations and evolutions, together with

Microsoft from Seattle. The fear that investors will miss the next bubble due to the absence of speculative activity is unlikely; the miscalculation is essentially determined by timing.

Kindleberger and Cohen highlight the involvement of the public in the bubble scenario. Although it is suggested that public involvement aids the rapid inflation and bursting of the bubble, they are not complicit in it. The point at which the 'professional' traders exit in volume signals to others that the turn is coming. The exit from the bubble reflects both a prudent move and betrayal. Like breaks in concentric circles, trading against the bubble damages those furthest from the countertrend and its initial momentum.

In riding against the herd, the 'contrarian' investor measures risk in a slightly different way, ignoring the psychological considerations that underpin particular booms and busts, preferring to trade against trends. The strategy adheres to the theory that:

> There are several human traits, which explain why the crowd is often wrong. They include: habit, custom, imitation, fear, emotion, greed, hope, credulity (and its opposite, incredulity), susceptibility, irritability, pride-of-opinion, wishful thinking, impulsiveness and conceit. Some of these traits are evident in bull markets and others in bear markets. But at all times [suggests Humphrey Neil in The Art of Contrary Thinking] the public mind is subject to 'suggestibility' and 'contagion' that causes it to act in a herd like and emotional, rather than rational, manner.[23]

The early play against a bubble is a high-risk strategy unless the investor relies on solid information to the contrary, an insight that allows positions to be hedged and opportunities realised in accordance with a formulated and well-executed strategy.

Fear of Losing in a Bubble Crash

In the aftermath of the boom and bust cycle, it is common for the negative financial penalties to be apportioned unevenly. The disruption that follows a sudden crash produces desperation, a memory that lingers and momentarily cautions against the wider allure of speculation. People fear similar losses. The 'enormous suffering and despair in the wake of the ultimate collapse'[24] accelerates intervention to limit the loss and insure against future losses. The social repercussion of investment loss can be found in the chapters of literature, which are imbued with tales of hardship; stories captured, for example, in the pages of Balzac's *The Rise and Fall of*

Cesar Birotteau, which is part of The Human Comedy series. William Thackeray's *Vanity Fair* includes the lines 'the great Calcutta house of Fogle, Fake and Cracksman', which 'failed for a million, and plunged half the Indian public into misery and ruin', correlates with the reality of the bubble burst leading to individual despair and collective harm in a nation-state.

Investors who own dumped stock and are distant from the performance of their holdings suffer enormously from falling prices. An investor may need to respond in seconds to divert disaster from a portfolio, but incessant monitoring may be impossible (a strong argument for a fund manager or broker with the responsibility of a stop/loss).

The sudden dumping of stock can be traced to several causes. Accounting irregularities, profit warnings, fraud, major world events, business confidence, hit shares hard, although unevenly.

Legislation and intervention to prevent bubbles is implemented by government and its agents to limit and control the diverse range of problems that can follow a sudden and widely damaging investment collapse. Correspondingly, government policy needs to be cautious that it does not exaggerate existing bubbles. For example, Eddie George, referring to successive interest rate cuts, suggested that the policy 'had to be careful not to exacerbate house market boom', which had consumed the housing market in Britain.

Commercial property and residential bubbles, equities bubbles, pension bubbles and bond bubbles need to be considered separately but each share in the eagerness of the investor to take part in active investment opportunities.

In reaction to the turbulent equities market that followed the entrance to the new millennium, investors have turned their attention to gold and bonds, particularly bonds. The degree of complexity in the bond markets is causing traders to reassess strategies and trading behaviour.

> It is clear that bond prices are too high, there is no value in buying anymore, but you cannot be short. It is a difficult market to trade at the moment. I guess this supports the theory of a bond bubble in practice, and it suggests that it may be about to burst.[25]

The sudden dearth of losses amongst investors creates animosity and repercussions, which are damaging to the industry. The need to complain about a piece of investment advice from a professional is often delayed or not initiated. From a general review of the financial press, it would appear that smaller clients are intimidated by their own advisors and allow losses to continue without criticism or intervention.

I am aware of small investors who have 'lost' a significant amount of money to fund managers, and are tempted to give them more money. In some cases it is prudent to initiate an investigation from the Financial Services Authority. If people don't question their professional advisers, and keep pouring good money after bad that creates a large market share in a bad market in itself. When it implodes, it creates wider problems and may drag prices down in good markets.[26]

Whilst on the one hand it would appear that democracy is expanding throughout the world, more regulation and less liberalism appears to be the trend in financial markers. The international business and financial environment has changed rapidly. Financial analysts and/or bankers (e.g. from Citigroup, Merrill Lynch, Morgan Stanley and Wall Street institutions) have to respond to the new demands of media dominated business news loops and uncertain markets, which do not neatly follow the existing predictions of models.

Risk Adverse Strategies: Stop/Loss and Safety

It has been noted that the uncertainty associated with any investment and the complexity inherent in risk, necessitates the consideration of the strategies to limit loss and reduce exposure.

As a general rule you should not lose more than about 8% of your 'pot' in one day, or one position. This goes more for day trading than the longer term, but it is still valid for hedge funds etc, so if 100k is invested in a stock and you sustain an 8k loss you should really get out of the position. Apparently back in the days of trading on the floor this was supposed to be the rule for each trader, but the way things worked you noted down your trades and runners would come around every so often to collect your cards and process the trades. According to one of my friends who used to work on the floor, when people had lost too much they would sometimes keep their cards in their pockets, claiming not to have traded, until they (hopefully) made back the losses over the course of the day, in order to avoid being stopped out. This technique allegedly brought down a couple of clearinghouses when people went so far over their limits and didn't make it back.[27]

The development of IT generates rapid trades in a deeply integrated and animated environment. The ability to monitor trades closely is necessary to curtail reckless mavericks: traders who can win or break the bank; this places demands on management in balancing the need for creativity and innovation and risk adverse precautions that limit high exposure.

On one occasion so many traders were bankrupted in one day that all the traders in that pit agreed not to put their cards in, essentially cancelling all the trading they had done with each other so that the day was essentially void. Clearly this would not work now because trading occurs on screens with people anywhere in the world.[28]

Risk management necessitates the need to adhere to agreed procedures. Although rigidity may need to be sacrificed on occasion, it needs to be verified through flexible processors, which result in secure success under managed conditions.

A trader predefines the amount of capital to risk on any given position. This is achieved with the use of stops and/or other instruments (options, etc). For example, if one enters the market with a purchase price of 100, it is predetermined that a price of 95 or lower creates too much risk – and a stop is placed at 95. Thus, in most market conditions the risk is limited and losses of 30, 40, 50% or more on a single trade are no longer possible.[29]

Companies themselves do stop traders out, but it tends to be a bit vague as to when. This is dependent on the culture of the organisation and atmosphere of the trading conditions.

It seems to me that *my* company will let you risk any amount that is in your account – i.e. one person here lost a quarter of a million euros in one day which was what he had made so far in the year. Whilst the risk managers did repeatedly talk to him throughout the day he was too stubborn to get out, and the losses were only really hurting him as that was the money he would be getting as a bonus. I believe that when he had gone into losses his account could not cover he would have been stopped out. It also depends on how much a trader can make in any given period i.e. my best day before the war [*Iraq 2003*] was about 10k euros and when I took a loss of that in one day I was told to stop. Then 3 consecutive days during the war I made about 20k euros, and consequently was not stopped a few days later when I got to the same amount of losses.[30]

In individual trading and private investment, the general rule of thumb is to stand only what can be lost without breaking into other accounts. If longevity is a prerequisite, a risk-all strategy ought to be avoided. Risks can be taken and should be of course, but heavy losses resulting from speculative trades should not result in a total flight from the market, unless of course a defensive retreat to cash or an alternative investment is a prudent move necessitated by the wider investment environment.

On an individual trade a trader should have an idea of the profit they would like to make and a stop. In my company there are 'rules' that we should not lose more than 3 'ticks' or 3 x our clip size (the size we are trading) on one trade, however sometimes this is unavoidable and not much can be done about it. Obviously trading an outright position is the most risky thing you can do, which to relate back to the bubble scenario, is where a lot of (virgin) investors go wrong. Professionals very rarely hold an outright stock position without hedging it in another market. For example, if you are long on x number of greatco.com shares you could also take a long position in bonds, as they usually go in the opposite direction to the stock market. Thus the profit you take is the difference. Private investors tend not to know the set techniques, or even to use them when a trade is already offside as damage limitation. So they hold and hold and see the only options as outright profit or taking losses on their own 'stops'.[31]

The decision on how much to invest depends on the financial resources available and the need to cover immediate losses. To reiterate, the guide is to never invest more than 10% of one's capital on a single trade. If however the trade moves in a positive direction, the danger lies in the pull of the trade, which can lead to an unnecessary gamble.

There is almost nothing worse than seeing a winning trade turn into a loser. Successful traders predetermine when they will adjust their stops to protect gains (right, the risk management stop that was placed upon entering the trade). If, from our example, the share price moves from 100 to 105, the stop would be raised from 95 to 100 to protect against loss. [32]

The point above is particularly relevant to the issue of bubbles as most people see a small profit and keep holding out because of the assurances that there is so much money in this trade. The loss of control introduced by greed leads to a general loss, which either wipes out previous gains or results in negative capitulation.

The Regulatory Regime in a Domestic Context

Regulation is a disputed area. Financial regulation is concerned with financial stability. Whilst regulation is commonly intended to respond to a particular flaw or loophole, it is not free from anomalies and uncertainty. The degree to which regulation is applied depends on the economic necessity and need to limit the misleading signals that are embedded in sophisticated markets. The need to standardise the various mechanisms and models related to finance and investment, to improve transparency to the consumer and provide a relatively stable investment environment led governments to create institutions to meet the varied explicit and implicit weaknesses in the markets.

> One of the risks in harmonizing the rule book is that the legal system (which is used to provide a framework for the banking and insurance sectors in most countries) could be confused with the disciplinary framework (which forms the basis of regulation and the conduct of business in capital markets and other financial services). This is an argument for having one regulator for banks and insurance companies and another for capital markets and other financial services. This is the 'twin peaks' approach taken by the new Australian and Canadian regulatory regimes. There is a risk of confusion in systems like the new UK one, which combines the disciplinary and criminal approaches to market abuse.[33]

Regulation, its development and application, cannot be separated from its contemporary historical setting. In the United Kingdom, Polly Peck, British & Commonwealth, BCCI, and Robert Maxwell's Mirror Group News International were active in the boom-to-bust decade of the 1980s. These companies reported spectacular earnings but ended the decade in ruins. Poorly managed business practices and unscrupulous methods plagued a string of corporate failures, which damaged investor confidence and undermined the development of solid markets.

> It was in an attempt to prevent the reoccurrence of such business failures that the Cadbury Committee, under the chairmanship of Sir Adrian Cadbury, was set up by the U.K. stock exchange. The committee, drawn from representatives from the top level of British industry, was set the task of drafting a code of practice to assist U.K. corporations in defining and applying internal controls to limit their exposure to financial loss, from whatever cause. The resulting report, and associated 'Code of Best Practice', published in December 1992, has generally been well received. Whilst the recommendations themselves are not mandatory, all accounts of U.K quoted companies (i.e., listed on the U.K. stock exchange) must now clearly state whether or not the code has been followed and if not, these companies must explain why.[34]

The response of the committee to corporate wrongdoing pre-empted a more serious wave of business regulation, a development that engaged with the plethora of new financial instruments, and the acceleration of financial business achieved through the integration of electronic financial networks.

> Corporate business seeks, in the face of determined pressure for change, to avoid, at all cost legislation that will change the way that it conducts its affairs. A clear example of this was the implementation of the Code of Best Practice

put forward by the Committee on Financial Aspects of Corporate Governance (The Cadbury Committee) from within the Stock Exchange structures in 1992. It was an attempt by business, acting in a voluntary mode to pre-empt legislative action by government. It was a successful attempt that has changed the pattern of relations between the business community and government in the United Kingdom for a generation.[35]

In improving standards, the Cadbury report ten years ago, said this body should be composed entirely of non-executive directors and that the majority should be independent. Within the UK, the Accounting Standards Board[36] has worked to limit ambiguities and set national standards. It is clear, however, that rapid change and financial innovation undermined the ability of regulators to avoid the collapse of Barings in 1995. The debacle, involving the trader Nick Leeson, highlighted both the failure of senior management within Barings and the absence of co-ordinated supervision between regulators in operating in more than one country.

Market or current value accounting is increasingly necessary as the basis for decisions. The tension that exists between a company's desire to retain a degree of confidentiality in its financials affairs and its responsibilities to the various regulatory bodies is not an easily resolved dilemma.

The lines between fraud, transparency and confidentiality[37] are complex areas that demand, in reality, a case-by-case approach. Despite the need to respect the client's request for confidence, a degree of transparency is required to ensure that wrongdoing is not encouraged either intentionally or by accident.

The legislative and regulatory framework has not eradicated the operation of fraud in recent years. Robert Maxwell, Nick Leeson and Ernest Saunders, to name a few, were able to manipulate fraudulently and recklessly a range of opportunities. The revelation of fictitious balance sheets, with assets swapped from one to another and artificial profits created by fake transactions, is not a new phenomenon.[38] The regulation environment in the UK continued to develop throughout the 1990s.

The new UK system of financial regulation follows the US model in separating the job of prudential control (which has gone to the FSA) from the responsibility of financial stability and the lender in the last resort facility (which remains with the Bank of England). This division of responsibilities is a feature of other financial systems, including the German one. It has nevertheless been criticized on the grounds that systemic stability and prudential control are indivisible. On the one hand, prudential control is essentially for stability, while on the other systemic support can be undertaken only by lending to solvent banks, which can be identified only by the prudential regulator.[39]

The role of the FSA has been further complicated by the repeated financial irregularities that have occurred outside its sphere of influence but which impact on it nonetheless.

The State and the Regulation of Investment Activity

The Financial Services Authority (FSA), the independent non-governmental body, was given statutory powers by the Financial Services and Markets Act 2000 to co-ordinate the domestic regulatory bodies into a single authority. It reflects the need of government, consumers and the investment industry to have a relatively stable and transparent financial market environment. The need to ensure that transparent information is available from a variety of sources is, along with the demand of monitoring overlapping markets, which were once segmented by industry classification, a key strategic objective. This point is crucial and impacts on the development of bubbles. In response to the volumes and complexity associated with the securities markets, the regulatory regime works to limit the damage to the investor and the markets. It is crucial to the investor to know that he will be treated without prejudice and the investment is relatively safe. To ensure that best practice is established and maintained, the Financial and Market Act sets out its objectives. These are listed below:

- Maintaining confidence in the UK financial system. This is achieved by, among other things, supervising exchanges, settlement houses and other market infrastructure providers; conducting market surveillance; and transaction monitoring.

- Promoting public understanding of the financial system. The FSA helps people gain the knowledge, aptitude and skills they need to become informed consumers, so that they can manage their financial affairs more effectively.

- Securing the right degree of protection for consumers. Vetting at entry aims to allow only those firms and individuals satisfying the necessary criteria (including honesty, competence and financial soundness) to engage in regulated activity. Once authorised, firms and individuals are expected to maintain particular standards set by the authority. The FSA monitors how far firms and individuals are meeting the standards. Where serious problems arise, the FSA investigates and, if appropriate, disciplines or prosecutes those responsible for conducting financial business outside the rules. The body can also use its powers to restore funds to consumers.

- Helping to reduce financial crime. The work focuses on three main types of financial crime: money laundering, fraud and dishonesty; and criminal market misconduct such as insider dealing.[40]

The authority needs to balance several variables. Competition needs to be encouraged and defended. Regulation that damages the competitive position of the United Kingdom is avoided within the legal context and demands Policy is founded on principles with punishment implemented for non-compliance. From a compliance perspective, the principles are listed as follows:

1. Integrity
2. Skill Care and Diligence
3. Market Practice
4. Information about Customers
5. Information for Customer
6. Conflict of Interest
7. Customer Assets
8. Financial Resources
9. Internal Organisation
10. Relations with Regulators

Investor protection is structured through the following:

1. Licensing (wide/private investors)
2. Individual Authorisitation (fitness competence/above board)
3. Capital Adequacy (large exposures/counterparty risk)
4. Client Asset Segregation
5. Conduct of Business Rules

The FSA's inquiry into the split capital industry has focused on allegations that some trusts colluded to prop up share prices by investing in each other. The Financial Services Authority probe, for example, of Aberdeen Asset Management followed a year-long inquiry into the mis-selling of so-called split capital investment trusts, and possible collusion by split capital fund managers. Aberdeen Asset Management is the UK's biggest split capital investment manager, with responsibility for 19 split capital funds. Split capital trusts are specialist funds which issue different types of shares offering different types of returns.

Investors can choose to buy shares which aim to provide either a steady income, or take a riskier bet on products which yield higher returns. But stock market falls have reduced the value of some trusts by up to 90% over the last three years, leaving many investors with heavy losses.[41] It has also looked into whether some investors were misled over the level of risk associated with their investment. As a result of the FSA's investigation, Aberdeen's shares fell, partly because of fears that it might face fines. The allegation may not be upheld, but the damage to the firm is immediate.

The FSA analyse statistical returns, research and produce reports and conduct interviews to identify financial and economic risk throughout the sector. The FSA have been active in examining the bonuses paid to analysts amid concerns that this might influence investment recommendations.

> Regulated financial services firms can be broadly split into two categories. Those that carry on investment business and are subject both to prudential regulation and conduct of business regulation; and the rest are subject only to prudential regulation. The latter are mainly banks, building societies, friendly societies, credit unions and general insurance companies, although many such firms also carry on investment business and so are subject to conduct of business regulation as well.[42]

The rapid growth of unauthorised investment firms with names such as Globeshare and World Trade Financial Corporation continues to expand further complicating a complex and crowded investment market.[43] The scams associated with unauthorised investment firms are commonly related to extremely persuasive sales pitches, which influence the investor to purchase useless shares.

> The firms operate out of a number of countries – popular choices being China and the South-east Asian countries – to get around UK regulations. Often by the time an investor realises that no money is forthcoming the operation has shut up shop, closed down websites, disconnected phone lines, moved on and changed its name. The latest scam uncovered cleverly lures investors into selling their original shares for an upfront 'administration fee' if they have found them difficult to sell through other avenues (not an uncommon occurrence). However, what investors find is that once the 'fee' has been handed over they never hear from the firm again and are stung twice, having lost both their original investment and the fee.[44]

The FSA have few tools available to limit the practice because the companies involved are generally outside its jurisdiction. It is able however, to inform investors of the scams and encourage a cautious attitude to investment and the risk involved.

The Challenge to Regulate

In the aftermath of the Enron and WorldCom scandals, and ongoing investigations in companies such as Ahold, the UK trade minister Patricia Hewitt released a report setting out ways of restoring confidence in corporate accounts.[45] The need to examine the operation of Chinese walls was highlighted to reveal the conflict of interests where firms provide both auditing and consultancy services to companies and clients.

The need to produce fairer figures is required to limit the misleading or selective performance of the company, which can be used in various advertising promotions to mislead investors. The ability to measure the degree of risk in a particular investment is related to transparency and accurate performance figures. Historical information provides a benchmark, but the standard presentation must inform and not manipulate the financial position.

The emergence of the FSA into a single entity reflects the increasing complexity of the finance industry, which needs to maintain confidence in its range of financial products and services.

The powers of the FSA are different to those of its predecessor bodies, incorporating for example, civil fines regime, a single ombudsman and compensation scheme and considerable flexibility over rule making. The scope of the regime will also be extended to cover professional firms and the Lloyd's insurance market. The Treasury will also maintain the ability to change the scope of regulation further without resorting to primary legislation. All of this, though, comes with extremely important new responsibilities to consult widely the regulated industry and to publish consultation documents when rule changes are proposed. Importantly, the FSA also has to publish analyses of costs and benefits of any proposed rule changes.[46]

The authority continues to face a number of challenges in relation to the fast-moving connected environment of electronic platforms, which are increasingly integrated between exchanges and countries, Euronext being the obvious example. It is essential to investor confidence to ensure fair play and transparency where possible, without being dictatorial in approach.

Further Policy

There are three key areas of concern to the investment industry. Transparency needs to be maintained in asset valuations. New policies such as FRS17 are being introduced to improve transparency in accurate valuation of assets in the balance sheet.[47] In a move to support the initiatives by the FSA, the Fraud Advisory Panel, funded by The Institute of Chartered Accountants of England and Wales (ICAEW) is seeking to encourage best practice through the transparent application of the basic skill of professional scepticism in the construction and execution of audits.

The markets for derivatives should also be an area of concern. The FSA Code of Market Conduct (the practical embodiment of their statutory powers over market manipulation) is incisive in its contemporary regulatory view of the dangers posed by derivatives.[48] The 1994 bond bust and the further instability caused by the punting of derivatives may be repeated.[49] In its basic form:

> Options and futures are the instruments traded in the highly complex world of 'derivatives'. Options give their holders the right to buy or sell shares or other securities for a set price by a specific future date – but they are not obligated to do so. Futures are contracts committing holders to buy goods or securities at a set price on a future date. Both of these instruments involve players taking risks on future market movements. Options on offer include those for individual shares and for share indices like the FTSE 100. Futures contracts can be bought over physical commodities like oil and wool, and over financial securities like bonds and currencies.[50]

The concern rests not with derivatives *per se*, but the general investment atmosphere where an ever increasing norm of tight margins encourages risk taking.

The final point addresses the issue that, despite the various initiatives to address fraud, the reality is that a vast number of cases will not be investigated. The demand on resources is too onerous to defeat the problem. The Serious Fraud Office, the Department of Trade and Industry, the Treasury, the Crown Prosecution Service and a host of other agencies, professional bodies and financial institutions are seeking to manage the situation, but with limited success. The development of cyber crime and the professional nature of the agents of the financial misdemeanour are making a complex problem considerably worse.

Notes

[1] The theory of probability owes more to Laplace than to any other mathematician. From 1774 on he wrote many memoirs on the subject, the result of which he embodied in the classic *Théorie analytique des probabilitiés* of 1812. He considered the theory from all aspects and at all levels, and his *Essai philosophique des probabilitiés* of 1814 is an introductory to the general reader. Laplace wrote that 'at the bottom the theory of probabilities is only common sense expressed as numbers', but his *Théorie analytique* shows the hand of a master analyst who knows his advanced calculus. Boyer (1989) p.492, *A History of Mathematics*.

[2] See www.theifm.org/tutorial/professionals2.htm.

[3] The introduction of new screen-based systems for trading securities and futures contracts has led to the emergence of a market for markets, and exchanges, broker-dealer firms, and market data vendors are competing to offer trade execution services that will attract customers and trading volumes. This competition is favoured in the United States by regulatory bodies such as the SEC and the CFTC, which have taken steps such as encouraging the listing of equity options on multiple exchanges and approving the applications of screen-based systems for designation as contract markets.

[4] Anon, email communication 25 February 2003.

[5] Ferguson et al (1993) p.103, *Business Economics*.

[6] Shiller (2002) p.12.

[7] Schumpeter (1986) p.1134n, *History of Economic Analysis*.

[8] See F.H.Knight, *Risk, Uncertainty and Profit* (2002) and the analysis provided by Schumpeter (1986) p.894, on vision, risk and enterprise in *History of Economic Analysis*.

[9] F.A.Hayek (1993 [1944]) p.75, *The Road to Serfdom*.

[10] Carruthers and Babb (2000) p.66, *Economy/Society: Markets, Meanings, and Social Structure*.

[11] Fukuyama (1995) p.36, *Trust*.

[12] See the article 'Digital Security: How to Worry Wisely', (2002) p.13, *The Economist*.

[13] Anon, email communication, 20 February 2003.

[14] In 1654, in the correspondence between Pascal and Chevalier de Méré, the questions of the throws of dice and probability were first raised.

[15] Rhinehart (1972) p.63, *The Dice Man*.

[16] Trow (1996)

[17] Harrison (1998).

[18] Koch (1997).

[19] Schabacker (1934) pp 23-25.

[20] *Ibid* (1934) p .59.

[21] Anon, email communication 29 April 2003.

[22] Anon, email communication 28 April 2003.

[23] Chancellor, E. (2003) 'Why does Contrarianism Work for Investors?' Multex investor, Reuters, www.multexinvestor.com.

[24] Cohen (1997).

[25] Anon, email communication 25 February 2003.

[26] Anon, email communication 27 February 2003.

[27] Anon, email communication 25 May 2003.

[28] Anon, email communication 25 May 2003.

[29] The May/June 2003 edition of *Traders*.

[30] Anon email communication 10 September 2003.

[31] The May/June 2003 edition of *Traders* magazine.

[32] The May/June 2003 edition of *Traders* magazine.

[33] Spencer (2000) p.243, *The Structure and Regulation of Financial Markets.*

[34] http://www.eqe.com/publications/revf94/risk.html.

[35] Crispin Michael White (2002) *Investment Ethics*, research paper.

[36] http://www.asb.org.uk/

[37] http://www.transparency.org/

[38] For example, the collapse of New Globe at the end of December 1900. The similarities between the collapse and the turbulence of one hundred years of corporate America are striking.

[39] *Op cit*, Spencer, p.244.

[40] http://www.fsa.gov.uk/.

[41] 'MPs were most critical of the firm's claims that zeros, the capital growth part of the investment trust, were 'low risk' – compared by one executive at the height of sales to government gilts'. *Accountancy Age*, 12 July 2002.
   http://www.accountancyage.com/News/1129893

[42] Balls and O'Donnell (2002) *Reforming Britain's Economics and Financial Policy*, p. 112.

[43] See www.fsa.gov.uk/consumer/fcs/index.html for advice on unauthorised investment firms.

[44] Mary O'Hara (2003) 'Don't get roped in by the off-shore cowboys', *The Guardian*, 3 May.

[45] http://www.dti.gov.uk/sectors_financial.html.

[46] Balls and O'Donnell (2002) p.131, *Reforming Britain's Economic and Financial Policy.*

[47] FRS17 defined benefit scheme assets are to be measured at fair value. Surpluses and deficits in defined benefit schemes are to be recognised as assets and liabilities by the employer (in most circumstances). Changes in the defined benefit asset or liability are to be analysed into various components, some of which affect earnings (as pension costs or finance costs) and some of which bypass the profit and loss account.

[48] www.fsa.gov.uk.

[49] See Gambling on Derivatives for further notes of caution on this high risk area of speculative activity: http://www.ex.ac.uk/~RDavies/arian/scandals/derivatives.html.

[50] http://news.bbc.co.uk/1/hi/business/the_economy/224146.stm.

Chapter 3

Action and Reaction:
The Psychology of Bubbles

Introduction

The analysis and mapping of motivations that underpin the individual and collective actions and reactions have become increasingly sophisticated in a range of disciplines. In psychology, the study of group behaviour has been particularly animated and sheds light on a series of interdependent social triggers that are relevant to this study. The intention of the material below is to critically reflect on the entrance to and exit from investment bubbles. The section is fundamentally about the psychological triggers operational in bubbles. Why do private investors, largely acting in clusters, appear to flock to a particular stock and create a bubble? In opposition to collective synergy, why, in the context of investments, is 1+1 often less than 2, and sometimes a lot less than one? Is negative information more salient and influential than positive, which may explain the quick 'get out' and the slow 'up take'?

It is proposed that a range of factors inform and affect investment decisions. The intention of the analysis is to add further depth to the view that bubbles are in some ways susceptible to manipulation, certainly by a privileged few that are able to use and act on information temporarily unavailable to wider onlookers.

The differences or similarities of investment decisions made by non-experts and experts are analysed to highlight the influence of the latter in shaping and encouraging trading activity.[1] The influence of psychological triggers within bubbles will be related to the markets themselves, which act in swelling and curtailing speculative activity.

Ahead and Within the Crowd

It has been referred to above that an investment of any kind should be undertaken with a dispassionate assessment of the possibilities and dangers.

The important factor is the degree of risk associated with the investment. Diversification needs to be considered in investment decisions. Emotional ties should be strictly limited and controlled, an attachment to a company can easily become a liability – mismanagement and the destruction of shareholder value does occur. Risk can be calculated using a variety of measures, but events can frustrate the most secure stock. Chance and coincidence should not be factors that inform the investment decision, variables that are prevalent in the casino (gambling may be part of the trader's psyche, but it needs to be tempered by a considered approach to investment). Investment, although not totally a science, draws on scientific methods (mathematics, scientific and probability models), to limit the failure of trading and maximise the gains.

Rupert Brown, in the influential book *Group Processes*, made the point that in early studies of crowd behaviour, notably by Le Bon and McDougall, the crowd possessed a 'group mind' that precedes the preferences of its separate parts. In fear, anxiety, or paranoia, its destructive nature was unleashed, overcoming individual preferences for restraint. This lemming like behaviour can be discerned to a degree in the resulting turmoil that accompanies financial panics. It is, however, largely descriptive and does not get to the phenomena that initiates the change itself. The overwhelming negative nature of crowd behaviour was however modified to include the operation or presence of goal orientated behaviour that could be recognised in both positive as well as negative terms.

In essence, a crowd can be defined as:

a gathering of a considerable number of persons around a centre or a point of common attention. This criterion of polarisation distinguishes a 'crowd' in the psychological sense from a crowd in the sense of a mere aggregate of people in the same place at the same time, as in a 'crowded street at the rush hour'. The definition, however, pulls together two types of groups of this ephemeral kind [or joins, unites], which it is convenient to keep apart: the crowd and the audience.[2]

The material below is concerned with the 'crowd' and not the audience. It is, however, recognised that the generic crowd contains various elements of social activity that is not conducive to generalisations. Where possible the aim will be to unpack and analyse the differences.[3]

The excitement associated with a bull-run in a particular stock or sector demonstrates the 'group mind' at work. In markets where a trailblazing stock can be identified, upgrades can be initiated to the projected outcome of the investment, which can be unrealistic. The stock itself may continue with the addition of investors keen to participate. The progression can be moderately sustained – and may involve several rallies – before it eventually breaks and fractures with unerring speed.

The important ingredient in operating successfully in a vibrant and bullish stock is knowledge of the sector and an informed assessment of the sustainable performance of the stock. The need to be informed is a crucial element in investment. The history and direction of a particular company or stock should be analysed before a decision is taken to invest. There are no crystal balls in trading, although good positions can be taken to maximise gains and minimise losses.

The trader representing a financial institution draws on information produced from a variety of professional and peer-related sources.[4] There are also informal networks where traders exchange knowledge and information with the wider business community. It is common for companies to speak to the analyst community to appraise the perspective of the investor. Similarly, businesses are visited by traders and financial analysts to assess the position of the company, its growth strategy or deployment of its products and services. The visit stimulates relatively reliable information that provides indicators in terms of performance and growth.

On the London Stock Exchange, traders are kept informed through the Stock Exchange news services. Private investors, despite real gains in the access to financial information, are slightly behind real time in trading terms.[5] News media such as Reuters add further insight to the 'big picture' and other specialist financial-related agencies supply information in a variety of forms.[6] For example, verbatim transcripts of Chief Executive Officers (CEOs) communications with the various media can be studied to identify hints in a change in strategic direction. Press clipping agencies and media monitors track current affairs and related items for clients keen to be informed of developments.

The advantages of institutions over the private investor are narrowing but there are clear benefits in the ability to draw on the advice and knowledge of investment and business analysts. This must be qualified with a note of caution. The advice analysts give may not be in the best interests of the client. The analyst is required to present information on areas such as investment analysis, research, bond analysis, economic modelling and chart analysis. Whilst they are invariably used as a guide, the numerous technical papers they produce support positions or underpin trends, which may or may not be thoroughly understood. The work of the analyst is valuable and without it decision making would definitely be more speculative. Despite positivism, it must be kept in mind that expectations can be inflated to meet previous estimates, a condition that can generate problems.

Analysts are active within investment management departments. A specific industry sector, a geographical area (still relevant in a borderless world) or a list of specific companies may be under review at any point. The key is to provide insight into the potential performance, growth rate, sensitivity and vulnerability of a market, sector or company. The analysis of mergers and de-mergers, acquisitions and disposals, partnerships, products, the competition, technological development, government intervention through regulations are key areas that demand professional inspection.[7]

The analyst generally relies on a range of information to complement on-going research and analysis. The picture that is formulated by the professional analyst is derived from largely empirical sources. Trends and fluctuations are studied to distinguish between seasons, cycles, shocks and trends. Costs and prices are analysed through time series data to discern the wider positive and negative ramifications. Share values can be calculated by using a discounted-earnings model. The method allows future earnings based on analysts' forecasts and recent results to be estimated.[8] It then discounts (a figure of £10m profit now is worth more today than in five years) to the present to arrive at the current valuation.[9] The ValuePro approach uses a discounted cash flow (DCF) technique to value common stock. DCF techniques are used by investment bankers for merger and acquisition analysis, Wall Street traders to value all types of debt obligations, and Wall Street analysts to value stock.[10] Demand forecasting is undertaken to highlight shortfalls and excesses, which may provide insight to the wider trends in supply and demand. Issues relating to strategy, international business, economic and political environments are analysed and included in the picture. The outcomes may produce opposing views, but the process is related to an in-depth consideration of data.

It would appear however that other normative elements intrude and undermine 'common sense', the practical rationality that is codified and legitimised through the institutional framework is disturbed, particularly through the opportunities and threats produced by bubble activity. Institutional investors can also succumb to a heightening of emotionality. The key feature is:

> A lowering sense of responsibility, a diminution of our powers of criticism, and a slackening of normal controls. This has been put down to the 'impression of universality', the notion that so many other people can't be wrong.[11]

It would seem that deviations from the empirical script are largely motivated by the failure to attain full information or the recognition of embedded misinformation. It must be remembered, however, that the trader is trawling and waiting for a split second of action and is not adverse to reacting to an opportunity (this is no doubt why she or he was recruited in the first place). The difficulty of balancing instinct with tight instructions is open to advantage and error.

With any investment there is a degree of doubt. Once the stock is secured it needs to be monitored. The private investor can check the share price and study the various business and investment columns for indicators that infer the sector may or may not change. The institution relies on a network of business and social relations that produce clues to future outcomes. It is no accident that financial areas are well serviced with social and leisure amenities. Whilst being vulnerable to the misinformation associated with gossip and the decisions taken from them, there is a resource to access in this area. For example, information may inadvertently come to light, which may indicate the recognition of major selling by directors in a particular company. The alert may lead analysts to investigate underlying trends, both within the business and industry sector to highlight potential profit warnings (which can be repeatedly disguised or creatively explained away) or worse.

The Emotion of Motion: Psychological Triggers in Trends and Countertrends

The largely selective and conditional nature of human actions frustrates and complicates, regardless of the preferred methodology, the observation and consistency of decision making, which can only be temporarily purged through regulation. Bias, devotion expressed in various forms, or unwillingness facilitated by social convention, may produce behaviour that temporarily compounds, positively and negatively, the rational thing to do. This is no less the case in selecting an investment and trading stock.

> Psychological research has indicated that there are biases in decision-making. These biases have implications for the decision as to whether to invest in stock market related products, the extent of such investment, and the nature of these investments. The biases could cause investors to make poor decisions on their behalf.[12]

The emotional-scape that impacts on decisions and actions is an ambiguous terrain. In its extreme, it is a destination that may result in delusion, inspiring a series of actions without apparent reason. This is a key feature in bubbles. The setting here relates to the mistakes and accidents prevalent in bubbles.

> In the case of aggressive or destructive crowds, however, another factor seems to come in. People in the crowd are not only more excited, they are liable to behave in a way they themselves would consider reprehensible. The crowd situation seems to allow a release of motives, which are otherwise controlled, even if conscious, or to motives of which the actor may be unaware.[13]

This is the domain of reckless trading, a condition arrived at not necessarily with the explicit goal of fraud, but a miscalculation of the outcome and costs associated with it. Unchecked, speculation without control may, when dealings in large volumes are traded, lead to the collapse of the institution (the Barings debacle being the most obvious example). For the institution, the demand on management lies in maintaining the balance between the adequacy of controls and checks and the facility for creativity and risk taking amongst traders. Self-management, however, is not an end in itself it is a means to an end.

An explanation for the slow and gradual development of a particular stock would appear to be related to the caution associated with the 'too good to be true investment opportunity and returns'. Optimism may explain why individuals feel that they are more likely than others to experience positive events (such as being successful on the stock market). The rise in a particular stock can be relatively slow and modest. Its persistence, and the expectation for exponential development, widens interest but not immediately. One interpretation could be that negative events (i.e. losses in the stock market) are more salient than positive events (i.e. gains in the stock market). Therefore it may take a lot of positive information to influence individuals to buy (for positive reasons) but only a singular instance of a negative consequence (i.e. loss) for people to sell.

The flaw in the calculation is not difficult to identify. Its neat separation between success and failure is debatable. An investor may hold onto a falling investment in the hope that it may revive and soar to new heights – its fortunes are not guaranteed.

> Equally, unsurprising, therefore, that when love's young dream begins to turn sour – when those beloved shares start to fall; then fall again and again – we anthropomorphise [read Marconi] in a completely destructive way. Since our shares have committed the ultimate crime of betraying our most precious hopes, they must be punished; punished ruthlessly, remorselessly, ground into the dust.[14]

The link that ties emotion and risk in bubble investments is an important factor that needs to be explicitly recognised. Financial economics treats upside and downside risk as being equally weighted, but prospect theory suggests that people are more concerned with the downside. Prospect theorists have shown that people are risk-averse when choosing between a certain gain and a bigger gain – they will choose the certain but smaller gain – but not when offered a choice between a certain loss and a possible bigger loss.[15] Kahneman and Tversky (1979) developed prospect theory to remedy the descriptive failures of subjectively expected utility (SEU) theories in decision making.[16] The method of 'framing' (the way decision alternatives are presented) can be used to illustrate the importance of risk-avoidance over speculative gain.

Paul Rozin and Edward Royzman have explored the contagious nature of negativity. The themes raised by their hypothesis are: a) negative potency (negative entities are stronger than the equivalent positive entities), b) steeper negative gradients (the negativity of negative events grows more rapidly through space and time than does the infallibility of positive events, c) negativity dominance (combinations of negative and positive yield evaluations that are more negative than the algebraic sum of individual subjective valances would predict, and d) negative differentiation (negative entities are more varied, yield more complex conceptual representations, and engage a wider response repertoire). All these themes shed light on the intangibles which may inform or cloud a choice of investment. The condition the authors call 'negativity bias', infers that in most situations:

> negative events are more salient, potent, dominant in combinations, and generally efficacious than positive events. (There are exceptions to this claim, but they constitute a minority of cases and often involve special circumstances).[17]

In the debates on negativity effects, motivation and cognition, in the main exclusive influences, are generally presented to explain various actions.[18] In the context of investor psychology, it would appear that the motivation of investors to avoid negative outcomes is related to the desire to limit the potential losses involved (this is not necessarily the case in bubble investments). Thus the relatively seasoned investor would seek to 'insure' against loss with recourse to a diversified portfolio.

With an extraordinarily vibrant stock, the initial investment should be covered and directed elsewhere; a defensive position through positive action. Without pre-emptive intervention, a solid investment can be undermined through a rapid fall, a condition that leads to panic and idiosyncratic trading to limit exposure. Similarly, the cognitive element resonates with the fears and prejudices of investors who, acting on limited information, place a premium on negative information, a condition exacerbated by an intense media society actively interested in bad news. In both cases, the prevalence of negativity goes some way to explain the sudden busts as opposed to the staggered booms.

> In the purest condition, negativity dominance holds that the combination of events of equal but opposite subjective valence will be negative. Thus if losing $100 is worse than winning $100 is good we have an instance of potency. But if we find that losing $100 is as bad as winning $150 is good, that losing $100 and winning $150 is negative then we have negativity dominance.[19]

The positive basis in investor decision making should not be ignored. Rozin and Royzman cite Matlin and Stang, *The Polyanna Principle*, as a key text that illustrates the influence of positive words, positive experiences, and positive views of the world, and in other domains. This factor is clearly operational in stock picking. The proliferation of stock market commentary in the various media allows the communication of a particular recommendation, a condition that is self-perpetuating and prophesying through communicative action. Its popularity, despite falling markets, is influential.

> The stock market is more important than it used to be psychologically because people are so much more attuned to it. It has become, for many people, an everyday activity to check the market. Now because we're thinking so much more about the market, I think, that this so-called 'wealth effect' – which is the effect of the stock market on our decisions to spend – might arguably be stronger now than it was in the past. But it's not just a simple 'wealth effect' – which is that you spend more because you have more wealth – I think the stock market value affects our whole view of the world.[20]

The above passage could easily inspire disagreement. The influence of the media is important to private investors particularly in stock picking. There are, obviously, exceptions; it may be taking place in the media but not in the share price. However:

> the stock market is a little bit like Sky News with all these 'breaking stories' there has to be a steady stream of them in order to keep us all interested. And because anyone can deal in a few seconds the market all tends to be the same way. And I think that's the important point – the same way. Basically that creates the runs both up and down, everyone is all buying together OR all selling together, nobody is stepping up to take the other side. How else can you explain that the biggest stocks in the world which were worth billions of $ or £

can suddenly go through a volume vacuum. Look at Vodafone the other day when it went down to 100.5p and then closed somewhere around 110p. This stock is worth billions and yet for a few hours in the morning, the whole crowd was selling. Now I don't get CNBC or Bloomberg TV etc but I'd bet my mortgage that this was the main story of the day, with them stoking the fire. Now I wouldn't say that the producers in the back had any devious motive, they were only doing their jobs and if they had run the story in the 'inside pages' then their viewers would have complained saying that it was the biggest story of the day and you didn't report it well because you were discussing say French Water stocks! So the investors/traders demand it and the media provides it. Or the media provides it and the investors and traders feed off it.[21]

With the proliferation of finance-related programmes and features in the various media, the cycle of boom and bust in a range of sectors and markets is increasingly quirky, with the bad news items generally swamping the good. Profits warnings, for example, of major companies are treated similarly to the declaring of conflict between states. The story is subservient to the headline. Seemingly:

in this day and age we all want the quick fix before we go onto the next quick fix. Now the media and market will follow a story for as long as it's hot so that might be a day or 2 or even a few years as was the internet bubble. As long as there's big money and big movement then it's news. That also applies to the downside as well but not as much because the money is normally made in rising markets. Yes the internet stocks still get press on the downside but maybe on a factor of at least 5-1 i.e. now if they go down they get 1 press report, if they go up they get 5 etc. So is it reckless, do the press report in a reckless way? Yes and no. Five years ago I would say yes, but now it's the way of the media 'Sensationalism'. And that doesn't matter if it's the Sun newspaper reporting on a football star or Bloomberg on a stock, we all want it NOW and before the next thing breaks.[22]

The underlying reality of the headline is rarely questioned. The dizzy seesaw of current affairs, movies, products, fashion, entertainment, lifestyles is all part of everyday life. With each new sensation, simplistically, somebody wins and somebody loses.

Experts and Non-Experts: The Leaders and Led Revisited

The availability of advice on investment and financial matters has become widely accessible through institutions providing a wealth of information and its spread in the various media.[23] This reflects, despite difficult trading conditions, the increasing popularity of investing in equities and related products amongst private investors outside the United States. Television includes specialist programmes that reflect and perpetuate an interest in the financial performance of companies, governments and markets, and the investment opportunities they generate. On the Internet, sites related to all forms of financial activity, such as chat rooms seeking easy profit (and on occasion generating mini investment bubbles), are accessible. Practical advice in the financial supplements of the broadsheets is generating a wealth of financial journalists who are increasingly meeting the demand for specialist magazines and trade articles. The availability of information to institutions and the private investor may have become relatively balanced, but the ability to make sense of the sheer volume of materials presents an advantage to institutions. They have the resources to analyse the vast array of financial data and information.

The big problem for private investor and small investment clubs is the degree of time needed in fully assessing investments and the time required watching share movements.[24] A private investor or club for example may have a floor, which may limit losses, but to work effectively someone needs to be watching the price continuously. A piece of news or information that indicates a lull or worse in profits can easily be missed and overvalued shares held with damaging consequences to the portfolio. A fall can occur at any time, so a floor strategy is advisable but difficult to maintain continuously. A stop-loss policy (shares are sold automatically if the price falls below a predetermined level) is an option, but to work effectively a broker will need to be instructed to execute this action and a commission will be charged.

There is also the issue of execution to consider, particularly for the private investor using email. It is often seen as a useful tool in capitalising on attractive share prices, but delays should not be ignored.

> To get from the sender to the receiver email passes from one computer, known as a mail server, to another. The server looks at the email address, similar to the address on an envelope, and then forwards it. It might get there in two seconds, it might get there in two days.[25]

The role of advisors, pundits, tacticians, and gurus are embedded in financial and investment history. In an article concerning the religion of market economics, Michael Prowse makes an incisive point when he suggests:

> We think of ourselves as freely choosing to do this or that. But life is more complex. In practice, we all accept authorities of one kind or another. We all

regard some set of principles or maxims as too basic to be questioned. We all, in short, worship something. The divine, properly understood, is thus an unavoidable aspect of human existence.[26]

In previous bubbles, some form of authority shaped the events that provided the investment opportunities, not necessarily intentionally. The influence of the Church, the wealthy (acting as a hierarchical strata of society) or the state were implicit in various social and financial lotteries.

Pope Urban II, opening the Church of Clermont on 18 November 1095, has been cited as the starting point of the crusades. The campaign included speculators of a kind, the Knight's love of booty.[27] In the plague-ravaged atmosphere of the Tulip Bubble, the elite burgers, aristocrats, and experts of good taste raised the aesthetic profile of the flower and facilitated speculation. During the wrangle that underpinned the South Sea Bubble, representatives of the state were complicit in sending prices higher.[28]

To elaborate on an earlier point, the media and entertainment-orientated society of the twenty-first century, revitalised with the digital power of the electronic medium, has elevated the message (which includes varying degrees of authenticity and credibility) to a wide audience. Authority and leadership is fragmented and ambiguous. Direction is identified through tenuously related links that may appear to be a trend, moving either in a positive or negative pattern. This is related to the sensationalism associated with stories, which are largely connected to the need to be heard in a crowded and rapidly changing news market.

...what makes news in the financial markets – quick profits and losses and in the information age today anybody with a £500 PC and modem is as switched on as someone in the bigger dealing rooms. Look also at how the news (non-financial) is gathered and produced. A big splash for a few days and then everyone loses interest because there's an even bigger splash from some other 'Breaking News'. It all has to be 'breaking' otherwise it's yesterday's news. So I think that the part that the media play is to continue to push these financial 'breaking news' stories whether on TV, print etc to keep us all interested. Now I or you can be sitting at home playing the stock market on our computers, click a few buttons and instantly make/lose big or small money. In the old days (say 5 years ago) we'd be doing this business via the phone and if our broker was out for lunch, it would be no problem, 'we'll catch up with him later'. Now later is too late, the money's been made or lost.[29]

The reports relating specifically to investment conditions, which occur throughout the trading circle, illustrate the range of fortunes, from exponential growth to the destruction of shareholder value, which can affect a particular stock. The crucial factor in the material discussed above is time and its acceleration in terms of markets and change.

The various snippets of information that can be gleaned from the various media present a picture that is, despite rigour, relatively impressionistic. 'We' get part of the story. The underlying political, natural, economic, technological factors demand tracking and analysis. These can be assessed through a range of resources.[30] Specialist agencies provide market research in a range of countries. It must however, be remembered that indigenous researchers recruited from a specific region may hold particular political and social views, which may distort the findings. No method is entirely foolproof.[31]

Despite the concerns highlighted above, pages of supporting data are required to provide substance to a stock's historic performance. To avoid serious losses and the destructive attraction of bubbles, this demands a degree of sophistication on the part of the investor.

Building and Following Market Speculation: Experts On and Around the Trading Floor

In assessing the subjective, private beliefs of investors and the role of experts and other sources (financial pundits) in the process of circulating investment speculation, it is necessary to consider the context in which the exchange of information occurs. Timing is the recurring factor that contributes to success or failure in the cycle of an investment. Again it is the quality of the information that underpins the decision. The operation of a conflict of interests can on occasion be recognised in some investments. Analysts can promote investment in companies while they may have possessed undisclosed and derogatory information about their financial health. Therefore, is the expertise of a trader a misleading guide? Do the majority follow advice from this source against its better judgement? The opposite is also no doubt likely, a trader may save an investor from an exposure to a loss or identify a particular option, which would be unforthcoming using other methods. The relationship between the 'expert' and the 'non-expert' demands attention: what are the expectations of both groups?

Shiller considers the strategies of professional investors and the representativeness heuristic, identified originally by Tversky and Kahneman (1974), when he suggests that:

> We can expect the same representativeness heuristic to encourage people to see patterns in stock market price changes, simple patterns like a bull market or a

bear market, even though such sequences of same-sign price changes are actually quite rare. Thus, the representativeness heuristic can encourage people to expect intuitively past price changes to continue, even if they know, from professional training, that they should not expect this.[32]

Whilst training and instruction are necessary to build confidence, the decision to act, and be successful, on a price chance is primarily shaped by experience. This may produce counter trends in the market: patterns may be identified. Correspondingly, certain variables may not be identifiable, resulting in a different outcome to the one predicted. A passage in Michael Lewis's *Liar's Poker*, hints at the value placed on experience on the trading floor.

Deep down, however, the stock market people didn't care much for book learning or school or anything except raw experience. Quotes from stock-market legend Benjamin Graham were wheeled in to defend their position: 'In the stock market the more elaborate and abstruse the mathematics the more uncertain and speculative the conclusion we draw therefrom...Whenever calculus is brought in, or higher algebra, you could take it as a warning signal that the operator was trying to substitute theory for experience'.

In trading, everything is important. The key elements are context and degree of influence; the sermon of elasticity. The same-sign price changes, spread between separate events and periods, may be superficially similar, but the outcomes differ through the operation of relatively unidentifiable variables. The traders' position in the market enables the access to 'better information', which can be applied to a range of previous financial situations to assess the potential of a particular outcome (this is particularly true with the often exclusive and incestuous nature of networks that operate between traders). Other methods would include charting.[33]

On trading floors around the world, there is usually a mix of traders with backgrounds ranging from recognisable qualifications, MBAs and Ph.Ds to non-academic traders, with qualities of tenacity and a nose for opportunity in abundance. Each has particular strengths and weaknesses.

The role of the analyst should not be ignored in this process. From the economic data, analysts upgrade and downgrade trading predictions. The analyst attempts to interpret the market and the stock under consideration. The results are not however without limitations, and private investors can on occasion make extremely successful and considered moves without recourse to institutional support.

The above throws light on how 'experts' use the information at their disposal to inform the investment preference, a process that is generally unavailable to the non-expert. The private investor may however accumulate knowledge through successive and successful incursions into the stock market and share such information and knowledge with others through investment clubs or financial Internet chat rooms. It is essential that investors monitor company information, recognise how a specific sector functions and assess how the company is performing in relation to others in the sector. A model or a strategy should be constructed to assess the performance of a company and investment. Relative price/earnings ratios, yield and past performance needs to be included in the primary analysis.

It has been raised how experts move between the arena of the institution and the business community with relative ease. The interesting point of reference is the degree to which this network shapes opinion. Three kinds of opinion comparison, the triadic model, has been used by Jerry Suls, René Martin and Ladd Wheeler to construct a theory to make clear the dynamics of opinion comparison. The view that we compare with others when we are uncertain is established, particularly with regard to an uncritical view of similarity. The authors suggest that the social comparison of opinion is best considered in terms of three different evaluative questions:

Preference assessment (i.e., 'Do I like X?')   ➔ Related preferences

Belief assessment (i.e., 'Is X correct?')   ➔ 'Expert' or similar

Preference prediction (i.e., 'Will I like X?') ➔ previously experienced X.[34]

The insight provided by either viewpoint informs the debate of actions and non-action of investors. Belief assessment:

> Is concerned with evaluating the truth of a proposition. The triadic model proposes that people should prefer to assess their beliefs by comparison with others who are more advanced or 'expert' with regard to the domain under evaluation. Level of expertise can be conceived in terms of standing on related attributes or background factors that permit the other to assess the situation and assertion more adequately. Conversely, comparison should not be preferred with others who are dissimilar by virtue of being less knowledgeable (or disadvantaged) on related attributes.[35]

The reference to the 'similar expert', infers that experts are listened to if they are perceived to hold the same basic underlying values to be influential sources of comparison. The common attribute may be the financial rewards from a particular investment. There is a degree of synergy in expectations. Those not sharing an opinion may view the advice less enthusiastically, the activity being an unconvincing investment not to be trusted. Despite this, in some situations, the absence in the general symmetry of underlying views may be temporarily overcome though something seeps through boundaries, in harmony – generating and expanding the development of a bubble.

The 'X is correct model' needs continued effort to sustain. Fashion and confidence direct beliefs.

The preference assessment introduces a substantial degree of subjectivity. A belief in a particular stock is arrived at through reference to the alternatives, which may result in a range of outcomes less enthusiastically received than the selected preference. The opinion is not necessarily shaped by analysis; the foundation is an emotional tie, which may be misleading. The performance prediction introduces a modicum of criticality. Performance can be measured through comparison and the results analysed to select a trend or pattern. The problem of context is not however overcome – 'X' may have been experienced, but 'X' may not be transferable to the new situation.

Mirrors and Reflections: The Emergence and Disappearance of Cycles

In the article, *The World Economy at the Turn of the Millennium Toward Boom or Crisis*, Robert Brenner highlighted the problem of over capacity and over production on a system-wide scale, for the repeated stagnation that has afflicted the world economy since 1973. The gradual shift in enthusiasm for big companies to small in the markets demonstrates that the challenge to sustain growth and limit over-capacity are continuing to be fundamental concerns for management and policy makers concerned with macroeconomic growth. Despite problems with productivity, however, it is a mistake to ignore the potential performance that can be achieved in large companies.

Whilst there are numerous versions of globalisation, the integration that pulls economies together through the expansion of trade and business is accelerating.[36] The picture is however uneven, with areas of underdevelopment remaining economically depressed.[37]

In 1999 the United Nations estimated that the assets of the world's three leading billionaires were greater than the combined GNPs of the world's poorest countries, the inhabitants of which number 600 million people. In the 1960s the richest fifth of the world's population had a total income thirty times greater than the poorest fifth's; in 1998 the ratio was 74:1. According to the World Bank, some 1.3 billion people now live in abject poverty, meaning on an income of less than $1 a day. And the way the world is going, the gap between rich and poor nations may widen further.[38]

Despite the asymmetries in growth within and between states, opportunities are presented in various forms.[39] The risks that permeate throughout the developing world can be discerned in emerging markets, a site for respectable gains. This is traditionally an investment area managed by professional investors acting for specific institutions. Bonds and IOUs issued by developing countries are imbued with risk, but insight into particular economic catastrophe and potential reform can result in positive returns.[40] The demands go well beyond country risk analysis; timing when to enter and exit the market is again a crucial factor.

The periodic fluctuations in the pattern of economic activity reflect in and are influenced by the performance of companies and stocks.[41] The long cycles in economic cycles, traditionally viewed with reference to Kondratieff cycles, have long been subsumed by short-term business cycle analysis, with reference scales between three to ten years.

The series and overlapping cycles, for example, capital expenditure, consumer spending[42] and unemployment, reflect the periodic fluctuations in the pattern of economic growth. In the markets, two key elements identify the rate of expansion or contraction of a market: the growth or decline of the end-user sectors into which the product is sold; and the technical, economic and social changes that are taking place that may affect the demand for the product in these sectors.[43]

A particular toy, a pop group, film merchandising, is increasingly a fleeting image or icon that has a short sell-by date (an example would be the mixed fortunes of the merchandising relating to the second Star Wars trilogy, a sustainable industry the first time around, and part of a lengthy bubble to the relatively independent and under-performing bubbles of the second trilogy). The animated realities of the various media contribute to the rapid rise and expiry of product portfolios.

Simply put I don't think that the media themselves create the bubble directly, but they do so indirectly. What I mean by that is, look round you in the life that we live (especially in the media) everything is so quick, we as humans want everything quickly and easy. We can't be bothered to cook so we buy supermarket TV dinners or snacks. We want that super body but instead of going to the gym for 1 hour every few days we buy those stupid muscle toning machines that mean that we'll actually get lean and mean while we're watching the quick 30 minute TV show etc etc etc.[44]

The 'what's in' and 'what's out' cycle, reflected in the annual 'basket' of goods and services used to calculate the monthly rate at which prices are rising, provides insight into the on-going changing nature of consumables.[45] For example:

> Ally McBeal has replaced the Oxo family as the model for how modern Britons live. Low-calorie, ready cooked meals for one are 'in' and the stock cubes needed to make traditional family dinners are 'out'... The clothes mangle has become the washing machine, infants' smocked frocks are Babygros and the humble gramophone record is now represented by the DVD and the recordable CD.[46]

There is a relationship between low interest rates and the speculative behaviour of investors, certainly in terms of volume and liquidity available to the market. The factors operate in tandem; low interest rates which in turn, although there are exceptions, accelerate capital expenditure and consumer confidence supporting the positive trends in the economy. Portfolio life cycles accelerate and investor activity is strong. With a degree of macro stability, consumer spending and debt become more excessive, leading to mini-booms in a variety of sectors.

Cycles and markets cannot be separated. The economy is made up of separate investments and exchanges. David Fischer, in the book *The Great Wave*, analysed the links between economic trends, social tendencies, political events and cultural processes to illustrate the range of influences on prices and the consequences to a range of social conditions. Drawing on price records, Fischer mapped the bursts of inflation to patterns of change in society.

Price records are also part of a story. Other influences are important. A passage from Carruthers and Babb makes explicit the social construction of markets:

> Markets, like all social constructions, do not appear or arise automatically. And they do not everywhere look the same. Markets are real in the sense that they have real and important consequences for human behaviour. But they are not something humans have no control over; they are not natural in the same sense that the weather, or human biology, is a part of nature. Rather, markets can be shaped this way or that in different societies.[47]

A range of exogenous and endogenous factors influence how markets are shaped and modified. For example, events such as the attack on the World Trade Centre, disruption in the Middle East or a series of political difficulties affect the markets, particularly commodities in the long term. The performance of the dollar, both its strength and weakness at various points, correlates into observable consequences in markets and economies around the world. Without strong alternative currencies such as the euro or the yen, investments such as gold emerge to meet the demand for a secure and temporary shelter.[48]

Confidence, positive or negative, whether it is the result of the interventions of a buoyant media or the collective unease of the markets, produce tangible effects on the order books of companies, a factor that needs to be included in the investment appraisal.

Trends can easily be interrupted and overturned. Events and moods are related explicitly to risk. High or low risk can be managed. In the well-known book, *The Risk Society*, Urick Beck argued that the risk society is embedded in the global condition. The proliferation of fear in society and the markets has led to the synthesisation of risk and insurance: fear is primarily a market, where the products of fear are traded. Nonetheless, confidence is a sensitive emotion: the fall in prices following September 11 2001 were dramatic. The recovery of prices was equally spectacular, an indication of the maturity of markets.

The ebb and flow market activity is reported to a wide audience on a daily basis. Major stories and events are reported and forgotten. The picture that is produced is a fragmented mosaic that is seemingly impossible to complete. Therefore, the view that prevails is a caricature of reality, a snapshot that is credible for some, and inaccurate to others. It is the difference that allows speculation to occur.

Pre-empting Bulls and Bears: The Investment Consequence Money Supply

The initial development of a bubble generates an ever-increasing demand on credit lending to meet the demands for investment. The availability of easy credit increases the willingness of the private investor to add to the frequency of bubbles, and creates a new phenomenon – 'baby bubbles' (or mini-bubbles). The introduction of additional credit initially creates opportunities, but adds, when the economic circumstances deteriorate, to turbulence in the markets. The bubble may be inflated by the media, but there is not necessarily collusion. A bubble, however, produces stories. Whilst some remain personal, others are the currency of the media. It is certain that:

> ...if they don't report it heavily they get complaints. What the real savvy traders have done since the beginning of news is to use it to their advantage and right now there's no better time for that. As it's hitting the front pages or is the

latest 'breaking' item they'll be normally going the other way, so if it's going up they'll be selling into it. The point to make about all of this is that you normally find the media getting involved well after a stock has started to move. So you might have ABC stock priced at 100p making a steady climb over a period of months to 150p (no real story there), then suddenly it jumps 20% in a day with reports that its found some new mine, or wonderdrug, or superchip etc, now that's a breaking story and then everyone jumps all over it – That's where the true pros are selling, they bought it months ago when nobody was looking, now they're selling it taking their profits and looking for the 'next quiet/small thing'. In the past stocks normally didn't move a great deal, a stock that moved up or down 100-200% in a year was right up there with the best performers. Now stocks can do that in a week or month. Therefore everyone has realised that in effect Rome can be built or destroyed within a day. So in effect if you're in the media you just can't afford not to jump on something, in the old days a week or so delay wouldn't really matter either way.[49]

It would appear that bursts of financial activity provide the opportunity for the proliferation of errors. Previous examples of investment losses are ignored in the rush to find the best return on investment.

The essence of a speculative bubble is a sort of feedback, from price increases to investor enthusiasm, to increased demand, and hence further price increases. The public memory of past high returns, and the optimism those high returns generate for the future generate the high demand for the asset. The feedback can amplify positive forces affecting the market, making the market reach higher levels than it would if it were responding only directly to these positive forces.[50]

Collective decision making is a common activity in speculative behaviour. Initially, low inflation, above average economic growth rates and a long bull market contribute to the impression that stocks can only increase and that dips are nothing other than buying opportunities. For example, the developments in technology that excited the public imagination created a parabolic rise in share prices (which had little relation to the underlying value of the companies developing the technology).

An activity that reflects the impression of the operation of crowd psychology develops into a mania and results in the over-valuation of shares. More and more people get involved and shares are bought with little or no knowledge of the business the company is engaged in. This creates a reinforcing dynamic in which the market is anything but rational, a condition that results in 'too good to be true' investment schemes promising impossible performance. Finally no more people are willing or able to buy. The high profile of the company is cajoled by rumour. The excitement induces panic and the stock crashes. At this juncture it becomes obvious that borrowing to finance share purchases has taken place on a massive scale.

In the surge of the boom, it appears that other factors are introduced that differentiate the bubbles from previous booms. For example, accompanying the IT adventure was a rapid change in the ways in which the stock markets operated. In the rush of IPOs (initial public offerings) that were notable in the dotcom boom, the new technology and telecommunications stocks temporarily replaced the old established companies in the Financial Times Top 100 share index (the FTSE 100). The prominence of the NASDAQ, run by the National Association of Securities Dealers, using the automated quotation system (thus NASDAQ) – origins lie in the 1960s – exploded in activity in the 1990s with the fast growing IT related industry surge. Technology enabled:

> private investors to deal directly over the telephone and internet much more quickly on an execution basis, that is by just placing an order and confirming that the price is acceptable. Many investors prefer this method, regardless of the cost savings they make, as they point to times in the past when a discussion with their stockbroker had deterred them from making a profitable investment.[51]

The technological developments and the social changes are apparent in bubble activity and will be analysed in subsequent pages. The above has opened up the discussion on the value of psychology in understanding the investment behaviour of investors. It is the operation of complex variables prevalent in the social sciences that has frustrated economists in the development of mathematical and statistical models, which explain economic behaviour using scientific tools. Although insight has been achieved, it is the social element that has not been thoroughly considered, particularly from the social and critical theory standpoint. Operational and management science has, with the development of hardware and software, succeeded in analysing large amounts of data. Decision maths, using matrices that are then multiplied, can be manipulated ad infinitum. It is, however, the quality of the initial research process, the methodology of data collection that needs further examination and critical reflection. There is a need to highlight and address the political and social anomalies that occur as a result of the potential of bias or ignorance: without doubt social norms and prejudices that undermine the outcomes of predictions in the investment process.

Notes

[1] Who are 'the experts'? The richest people – those who have the key information, the 'truth'?

[2] Sprott (1958), *Human Groups*, Pelican, p.160.

[3] A definitive definition of the crowd is controversial. Who are 'the public'? What is 'the crowd'?

[4] John Howkins's book, *The Creative Economy*, highlights the ideas business – the means by which new ideas and innovations are marketed and sold. The ideas emphasis mirrors the evolving nature of 'new economics' in economics, based on information and ideas.

[5] New figures released by the Association of Private Client Investment Managers (Apcims) estimate that there are now 370,000 private on-line traders in the UK. See: http://www.apcims.co.uk/.

[6] See: http://money.cnn.com/.

[7] Financial journalism does however provide insight. Literature in the form of Michael Lewis is incisive and adds to the general understanding of the markets. Peter Waine and Mike Walker's novel *Takeover*, for example, provides insight not readily available on hostile take-overs.

[8] See: http://www.quicken.com/investments/

[9] Patel, A.B. (2002), 'Perchance to lose: ay, there's the rub', *Financial Times*, 20 April 2002, p.4.

[10] See www.ValuePro.net.

[11] *Op cit, Human Groups*, p. 161.

[12] See Redhead, 'The Psychology of Personal Finance', *Company Accountant*, p. 26, October 2001.

[13] *Op cit, Human Groups*, p.162.

[14] Bearbul, (2001) pp 22-27, *Investors Chronicle*, 27 July 2001.

[15] Ferguson, N. (2001), *The Cash Nexus*, The Penguin Press, p.12.

[16] For a full description see the contribution on prospect theory in *The Blackwell Encyclopaedia of Social Psychology*, pp. 460-463.

[17] See Rozin and Royzman, 'Negativity Bias', *Personality and Social Psychology Review*, p.297.

[18] For an introduction to this debate see 'negativity effects', in *The Blackwell Encyclopaedia of Social Psychology*.

[19] *Op cit*, 'Negativity Bias' p.299.

[20] Robert Shiller, Radio 4 Analysis, Broadcast 15 August 2002.

[21] Alex Hoar, email communication, 20 May 2002.

[22] *Ibid*, Hoar.

[23] Check, for example: www.morganstanley.com.

[24] Potential investment clubs should consult: http://www.proshare.org/

[25] 'On-line on time?', BBC News Working Lunch
On-Line: http://www.bbc.co.uk/workinglunch.

[26] Prowse, 'The case for treating market economics as a religion', *Financial Times*, January 26 2002, p. 11.

[27] Hans Eberhard Mayer's book, *The Crusades*, suggests on p.22, that 'despite everything that that has been said about pilgrimages and holy war, it would be wrong to hope to explain the big part played in the crusade by the knights only in terms of religion, group psychology, and a professional ethos. Dry economic and social factors were also significant, more so indeed than is commonly allowed today…After all, at Clermont Urban himself had

promised that all those who went on crusade would enjoy undisturbed possession of the lands they conquered.

[28] 'The price of South Sea shares was talked up, not least by Government representatives, up to and including the King , from £128 to £1,050 in the first six months of 1720; and 85 per cent of the annuitants (by value) surrendered their claims in exchange for these shares', from Peter Jay's, *Road to Riches*, p.207.

[29] Alex Hoar, email communication, 29 April 2002.

[30] http://www.oneworld.net/.

[31] This actually highlights a major area of research that continues to be under theorised and researched.

[32] *Op Cit*, Shiller, p.4.

[33] Technical analysis incorporating previous moves in the market to predict future possibilities, useful complementary tool.

[34] Jerry Suls, Rene Martin and Ladd Wheeler, 'Three Kinds of Opinion Comparison: The Triadic Model', *Personality and Social Psychology Review*.

[35] *Ibid*, p.223.

[36] See the IMF World Economic Outlook: http://www.asb.org.uk/.

[37] For balance of payment information see: http://www.imf.org/external/np/sta/bop/bop.htm. As the web page explains: the Statistics Department of the IMF disseminates a wide range of information in the area of balance of payments. This information includes: the coding system used for balance of payments statistics; the annual reports of the IMF Committee on Balance of Payments Statistics; the statistical papers presented to that Committee; copies of newsletters issued twice a year by the Statistics Department, which cover issues of topical interest; information on balance of payments methodological and statistical publications; information on surveys on issues such as direct investment and portfolio investment; country experiences in the estimation of travel services; information on the IMF's guidelines and data template for the dissemination of data on international reserves and foreign currency liquidity; information on the statistical treatment of financial derivatives; and recent methodological developments for statistics on international trade in services. In conjunction with the Bank for International Settlements, the Organisation for Economic Co-operation and Development, and the World Bank, the IMF also disseminates data on external debt.

[38] Ferguson, N. (2001), *The Cash Nexus*, p.311.

[39] For political insight see International Simulations: http://www.lib.umich.edu/govdocs/intsim.html.

[40] Miller 'Emerging market bond funds: opportunity awaits but investors need steady nerves', *Daily Telegraph*, 15 June 2002, p. B6.

[41] For the United States see: http://www.doc.gov/Economic_Analysis/. For the UK check http://www.hm-treasury.gov.uk/.

[42] In 2002, the University of Michigan consumer sentiment index – which measures shoppers' willingness to spend fell to 92.4 in May, down sharply from 96.9 in April but revised upwards from the preliminary figure of 90.8
see: http://www.lim.com/newspage/michsent.htm.

[43] Hurd and Mangan (2001), *Essential Data Skills*, p.11.

[44] Alex Hoar, email communication, 29 April 2002.

[45] To assess the UK's retail price index see: http://www.statistics.gov.uk/.

[46] 'Goodbye, OXO Mum. Hello, Ally McBeal. UK's price index catches up with the times', *The Independent*, Tuesday 19 March 2002, p.3.

[47] Carruthers and Babb, (2000), Economy/Society, p.2.

[48] 'Rough Waters', *Forbes Global* (2002) p. 58-59.

[49] *Op cit*, Hoar.

[50] Shiller, 2002, p.3.

[51] For a brief review of changes in the stock market at the beginning of the twenty-first century see Brian Phillips (2000) 'The Stock Market – Friend or Foe?', *Company Accountant*, August, p. 19-29.

Chapter 4

Tulipomania: Bubbles, Mysteries and Cycles

Introduction

The series of chapters that follow are specifically related to bubble activity during the 'modern' era, beginning with the contested Tulip Bubble, 1634-37, which continues to advertise the full drama associated with boom and bust bubbles. Each event has been studied in a vast literature, but placing a series of seemingly unrelated bubble events in historical context allows an insight into the similarities and differences pertaining to the development and implosion of animated speculative activity.

The approach does not replicate similar studies faithfully. The material posited is viewed through the lens of political economy. Wealth and interests are analysed to assess the operation of power in both its explicit and subtle form.

A study that considers bubble activity ought to reflect on the micro and macro influences and consequences, assessing short, medium and long-term perspectives. It is recognised, however, that some bubbles contain unique characteristics, which are not easily transported or present elsewhere. The material included in the subsequent chapters will endeavour to identify such elements.

The review begins with a look at the infamous Tulip 'Bubble', which grew gradually over a long period, attracting investors from all classes, but collapsed spectacularly within a couple of days.[1]

The animation of investment is not separate from the economic, political, socio-cultural and religious developments, which impact on speculation in various ways. Furthermore, bubbles can collide, run at various points, and deflate unevenly: if one asset falls through disillusionment, expiration or the revelation of additional, perhaps derogatory information, with a subsequent deflation in price, the flight of liquidity seeks alternative assets, which through the transfer inflates valuations elsewhere. If the alternatives are limited, a potential bubble may arise. A point that needs to be made explicit: bubbles are generally underpinned by some element that counts as substance.

The opportunities and threats associated with speculative activity are related to the absence of perfect information, which may actually only be a temporary condition. With it of course, the Tulip Bubble may not have had such an infamous history.

A feature of the material included below is a concern with the timing and execution of an investment, the purchase or selling of a share. In the context of bubbles, the development is not generally determined by one single factor: it appears that a range of considered interventions, accidents and events influence the outcome; incoherent pulses which the 'stories' below aim to reveal.

The material below is considered in respect to a small booklet on the Tulip Bubble by Sautyn Kluit, entitled *De Tulpen-en Hyacint-Handel* published in 1865, which contains numerous sources and avenues of study, a book maintained by Euronext[2] in Amsterdam. Further sources were gleaned from Amsterdam's Historical Museum,[3] The Rijksmuseum, which houses a vast collection of important paintings relating to the Dutch Golden Age, adds insight to the development of the Dutch East India Company and the influx of wealth to Amsterdam. The vast secondary literature, which ironically forms a mini bubble itself, is considered with caution.

The Deception of Beauty

The Tulip Bubble continues to attract keen interest. Deborah Moggach's book *Tulip Fever* and its potential transfer to film by Steven Spielberg illustrates its interest to modern story tellers. The Tulipomania episode was used by the author Alexander Dumas in the search for the Black Tulip,[4] a dramatic piece that captures the fever surrounding the covetousness of rare flowers. This tale of financial corruption is based on the story of the execution of John and Cornelius De Witte, a true event, which occurred nearly 40 years after the episode of tulip mania. It is said that King William of Holland suggested to Dumas that he should use the fate of the de Wittes as the basis of a novel.

The speculative phenomenon of Tulipomania, which occurred in the early seventeenth century, fits into the annals of classic political economy. On the one hand, it was a boom that emerged in an economy enjoying the influx of wealth that had been obtained from the strategic gains arising from international trade and exchange. It was also influenced by urbanisation and political conflicts in the form of the Dutch wars of independence, the Thirty Years War, which began in 1618. The bubble followed substantial political, social and religious change (the emergence of Calvinism in the sixteenth century, which promoted the idea of visible proof in this world of preselection of the next)[5] cautioned against the deception in the speculative trade of Tulips. The warnings of the harm resulting from gambling were, however, tempered by the vast gains that could be made from trade in the flowers.

> The consequences of the Reformation, which was more than a change in the religious structure, led to the redistribution of power in trade and finance. In July 1572 the first 'free' assembly of the States of Holland was held in Dordrecht, which had recognized the Prince of Orange as its leader in the revolt. The Catholic Church lost ground in the region to Calvinism, hard work however overshadowing sobriety, and in 1579 following the capture of Amsterdam the Geuzen (Calvinist brigands), the Union of Utrecht was formed and an independent Dutch republic declared.[6]

Other factors such as the increasing acceptance of the protestant ethic, Dutch Independence since 1609, and the loosening of the grip of the Spanish Inquisition, Catholicism and King Philip of Spain,[7] contributed to the atmosphere of individual excess, and the need to enjoy life from the darkness of illness and political and religious repression. The wider context of political economy is relevant in assessing the generic and evolving atmosphere, in which the bubble occurred. At the end of the sixteenth century the Netherlands still occupied the minds of the Spaniards, who looked upon them indeed as their just prey.

> The archduke Albert of Austria, nephew of Philip II, and governor in the southern Netherlands, decided to continue the struggle against the northern provinces and in 1600 he was defeated decisively by Prince Maurice the stadholder, at Nieuport...In the field neither Maurice or Albert could gain any very decisive advantage, and Spain, through gaining a naval victory off Cape St.Vincent in 1606, was defeated by the Dutch fleet off Dover, and again in Gibraltar Bay in 1607. Spain's resources were now seriously weakened, and being tired of war, she concluded a treaty with Holland in 1609...In 1648, by the Treaty of Munster, Spain was forced to renounce all claims on Holland.[8]

The political and military atmosphere allowed trade to continue, and with an end to the difficulties in sight, the Northern provinces developed wealth, commerce and trade relatively unhindered.

> For the Dutch republic...the Treaty of Münster was the prize for a century of struggle. The northern Netherlands were recognised as fully independent from

Spain and were permitted to retain any conquests which had been made overseas, mainly at the expense of Portugal. The Dutch Republic was not even required to guarantee religious toleration to its residual Catholic population, although in practice repression would not have been in the interests of internal stability.[9]

In the tulip market, the demand for the rare varieties appealed to both the growers and the increasingly wealthy merchants who were also keen to elevate their status. The tulip was initially prized as a grandiose fashion accessory, the new colours and varieties being highly prized commodities for decoration. It was the prized item in the aristocratic garden. The decade of 1610-1620 became:

> the 'classical period' of Dutch costume. After the angular affectation of the dress of the previous decade we have the character of jovial freedom of movement which is customary to associate with the Dutch habits of their 'Golden Age'. The whole is characterized by a broadly genial grace, combining the grandiose with male elegance, good temper, and humour, symbolised by the wide sweep of the large hat with its waving plumes.[10]

The influx of wealth that circulated added to the demand prevalent amongst the upper classes for special delicacies and items that advertised privilege and status during a period of increasing affluence.

> Only a deeply bourgeois culture, it is implied, could possibly have selected the humble tulip – rather than, say, emeralds, or Arabian stallions – as a speculative trophy. But there was nothing suburban about tulips in the seventeenth century. They were, at least to begin with, exotic, alluring and even dangerous. It was precisely at this point at which their rarity seemed capable of domestication for the mass market that the potential for runaway demand could be realised. It was this transformation from a connoisseur's specimen to a generally accessible commodity that made the mania possible.[11]

The wealth that had increased the resources of the rich produced a keen interest in extravagances and luxuries. The shift in taste that accompanied change in the political and religious structure was felt throughout society.[12]

> The demand for tulips of a rare species increased so much in the year 1636, that regular markets for their sale were established on the Stock Exchange of Amsterdam, in Rotterdam, Harlaam, Leyden, Alkmar, Hoorn and other towns. Symptoms of gambling now became, for the first time, apparent. The stock jobbers, ever on the alert for a new speculation, dealt largely in tulips; making use of all the means they so well knew to cause fluctuations in prices. At first,

as in all these gambling manias, confidence was at its height and everybody gained.[13]

Wealth accumulated in Amsterdam whilst elsewhere throughout Europe political and economic entities struggled with growth and internal unrest. The interest in the riches of nature was not confined to Holland.

Nearly ninety new shrubs and trees were persuaded to grow in English gardens and parks during the sixteenth century. Contracts with Turkey led to the naturalization of lilac and tulips. Hyacinths, anemones and crocuses joined the long familiar roses, marigolds and violets. Professional nurseries were established to satisfy the amateur demand for imports of plants and shrubs...In 1612 Emmanuel Sweert's catalogue of what was available in Amsterdam to feed the current tulipomania listed some hundred varieties.[14]

The Northern provinces built their affluence through the increased activity derived from international trade, which saw an animated transport of various commodities and the methods underpinning the transport of them. The political and religious refugees that had escaped in intolerance and repression from 1492 onwards played an important part in the fortunes of the Dutch republic. The influx of various peoples including Jews,[15] seeking relief from persecution contributed fresh ideas and trading enterprise.

By 1622, it was estimated that 33 per cent of the population of Amsterdam were immigrants. While the proportions were higher elsewhere, reaching 51 per cent at Haarlem and 67 per cent at Leiden. Their contribution to the Calvinist congregations and to the economic 'miracle' of the Northern provinces was immense. Over half of the 320 principal depositors in the Bank of Amsterdam after the first two years after it had been founded (1609-11) came from the South.[16]

It was shortly after tulips were introduced to Western Europe from Turkey that those with a rare infection, which created a striped pattern on the petals, became coveted possessions and important commodities.

Bargains were made for the delivery of certain roots; and, when, as in one case, there were but two in the market, lordship and land, horse and oxen, were sold to pay the deficiency. Contracts were made, and thousands of florins were paid, for tulips which were never seen by broker, by buyer, or by seller. For a time, as usual, all won, and no one lost. Poor persons became wealthy. High and Low traded in flowers; sumptuous entertainments confirmed their bargains; notaries grew rich; and even the unimaginative Hollander fancied he saw a sure and certain prosperity before him.[17]

The changing political and social structures allowed wealth to disperse throughout the region. New opportunities appeared daily. The Amsterdam municipality had direct influence on the main financial institutions, specifically the Amsterdam Exchange Bank, the *Wisselbank*, which needed to be added to and developed to meet the increased demands placed upon it. It is not an exaggeration to claim that Amsterdam:

> was the greatest port in the World, controlling at least half of the entire trade of the United Provinces, Amsterdam now further increased its population and its wealth. By the time Rembrandt had settled here [summer 1631] the number of its inhabitants had reached two hundred thousand and its boundaries had been extended far beyond the medieval core on either side of the Amstel river.[18]

Trade expansion, financial leverage and employment in a range of capacities, at all levels, fuelled growth and expectations. In response to the developments overseas and in recognition of the animation in the ports, the circumstance necessitated the creation and stretching of duties in financial, trade and political institutions.

> As a result of the flight of talent from Antwerp in the previous century, Amsterdam was now the economic capital of the West. The Dutch East India Company had been founded in 1602 to beat the Portuguese at their own game in trade with the Far East. To promote the development of the economy the government had founded the Amsterdam Bank in 1609. The bank offered long-term credit, issued bills of exchange and banknotes, and generally facilitated mercantile expansion as Dutch fleets brought riches of East and West to Europe to be re-exported in the famous *fluytship*, the extraordinary short-haul cargo vessel invented by Dutch shipbuilders. The ship and the bank together made Holland the import-export capital of Europe.[19]

The riches gleaned from contact with the East multiplied the rich merchants and burghers residing and trading in Amsterdam. The stock exchange set up to trade in East India Shares necessitated a stable financial system.

> In 1611 came a second institution, the new exchange. Originally a market for commodities, whose prices often determined those for much of the world, it became the scene of purely speculative dealing. By the middle of the century there developed the traffic in 'futures' and in options to buy or sell which meant that fortunes could be made and lost by speculation in goods that never existed at all. Efforts made by the States General to prevent these aspects of capitalist activity had not much success.[20]

Joseph De La Vega's idiosyncratic but extremely informative *Confusión de Confusiones* captures the fortunes of the Dutch East India Stock.

> Gradually the company developed to such an extent that it surpassed the most brilliant enterprises which have ever been famous in the history of the world. Every year new shipments and new riches arrive, [the proceeds from] which are distributed as profits or are utilized in expenditures in accordance with the stipulations of the administration. (The dividends are sometimes paid in cloves, sometimes in [promissory] notes, at other times in money, just as the directors think fit).[21]

The increasing wealth flowing into the region facilitated speculation in a range of goods and services. The burgeoning nature of trade and commerce created a business and commerce-driven environment, which built with it the trinkets and decadence of economic success.

> Shipping, trade and financial services were brought together at the Amsterdam *Beurs*, or Exchange, which from the start of the seventeenth century superseded the exchanges at Bruges and Antwerp to become, 'the nerve centre of the entire international economy' until well into the nineteenth century. The merchants and brokers who gathered in the arcades of the 1611 *Beurs* building 'traded in literally everything known to that society'; their deals included all manner of commodities, financial instruments (shares and government bonds), sea insurance, freighting, and foreign exchange. Within a stone's throw of the *Beurs* were *Wisselbank* and the VOC, enabling merchants to enjoy unrivalled business opportunities.[22]

At the beginning of the seventeenth century, the Bank of Amsterdam was created to limit the disruption of the various types of coin in circulation; the stable *gulden florjn* was introduced and became the currency of choice within and beyond its borders. Wealth continued to be accumulated through trade. The United East India Company (Verenigde Oostindische Compagnie, or VOC)[23] and the West India Company (WIC) can be recognised as early multinational corporations (MNCs). The VOC extended trade throughout India and the Far East, whilst the WIC manipulated the slave trade and plantations in the Americas.

> The Dutch set out to make money by commerce. They found a world where trade was bound to force. No spice could be bought without the benevolence of the local ruler or his agent, who had his own living to worry about. No buy was sure: local rulers would sell the same crop twice. The political rivalries of the region were complex and ephemeral – Muslims vs. Infidels, petty chiefs who would be king or sultan, loyalists vs. rebels, with the one becoming the other and then back again.[24]

The fortunes of the VOC were initially mixed, but with strong financial resources and a close relationship with the Dutch political leadership, the debts incurred by wars inspired by grand economic aggrandisement, particular in Asia, were manageable, although the nerves of investors were tested. The strategy of the VOC was deeply immersed in international affairs, as the passage below demonstrates:

> The VOC could not consolidate its control over the spice trade of the Indonesian archipelago, without also monopolizing the trade in cotton cloth from south-east India, which was the commodity most in demand in the spice-producing areas. Under the aggressive governor general of the Dutch East Indies, Jan Pieterszon Kohen (he held office in 1619-23 and 1625-9), the company expanded its operations in Asia by a deliberate act of policy ('we must have more men, ships and money'). The executive committee of the VOC made it clear to Kohen in 1622 that there were limits to his policy of 'maintaining trade everywhere with power and armed force'...war was viewed as an instrument of company policy.[25]

The passage above illustrates the extraordinary enthusiasm for developing trade and commerce. It also recognises the strong overlap between wealth and power, which was repeated in various sites throughout the world. In Amsterdam the vortex generated by wealth accrued by trade and the finance associated with it sought new avenues for the creation and direction of capital. Expectations were unrealistically increased, a common trait in all bubbles. Trade in all possibilities was considered.

> The late 1630s witnessed the most spectacular jump in VOC share values on the Amsterdam Stock Exchange of the entire seventeenth century...A similar phenomenon occurred in the large houses in Amsterdam. The prices of rich men's houses actually fell in the early 1630s, but then shot up in the late 1630s, undergoing one of the two steepest rises of the seventeenth century (the other was in the late 1650s). The initial boom in tulip horticulture, and the speculation in tulip bulbs, were signs of the growing sense of ease with the achievement of security and returning prosperity, combined with the rapid accumulation of large surpluses amid restricted investment opportunities. Rarities up to around 1630, in the mid-1630s cheaper varieties of the tulip were widely marketed and tulip-fancying rapidly pervaded the middle strata of Dutch urban society.[26]

It has been established that during the initial stages of the bubble ever widening numbers had access to credit. Inflation was occurring due to silver from the Baltic, a development financing Dutch trade. The bubble was underpinned by leverage through credit, the increasing use of futures,[27] and the animated environment of Dutch finance, which introduced options to widen speculation.[28] In terms of generic growth, the development of institutions to support trade and exchange dominated the increase of wealth.

> The real point about precapitalist markets, then, is not that they were protected, artificial monopolies – though many of them were. Instead, it concerns the underlying structural reason for this latter circumstance: the mechanism of mercantile surplus accumulation which was being fought over lay in control of the circulation of commodities (not their production); and competition of all kinds – military, technological, organisational – therefore concentrated in the realm.[29]

The search continued enthusiastically for the unique flamed flowers commending high prices. Production was initially confined to estate producers and gentlemen horticulturalists, and was sold in large weights. With increasing demand, lots were broken up and speculation ensued. Before the democratisation of beauty, the unfamiliar, the exotic and the scarce were hunted to elevate standing and position; the Semper Augustus bulb becoming the key item of desire and status.[30]

Tulips were soon exclusively acquired for speculation – buying with the intention of selling quickly at a higher price. With heightened excitement to be part of the tulip investment, fundamentals were ignored. The basic fundamentals of all asset prices are expectations about the discounted value of future cash flows from investment (not a wide financial notion applied in the seventeenth century by virgin investors).

Between 1634 and 1636, rising tulip prices seemingly fuelled a rapid bubble, which attracted investment from all levels of society. It has been widely reported that at its peak a single Semper Augustus bulb (which was particularly rare) cost the equivalent of £500,000 today. Ferdinand Braudel captures the mania eloquently and expands on the novelty of the bubble:

> What was new in Amsterdam was the volume, the fluidity of the market and the publicity it received, and the speculative freedom of transactions. Frenetic gambling went on here – gaming for gambling's sake: we should not forget that in about 1634, the tulip mania sweeping through Holland meant that a bulb 'of no intrinsic value' might be exchanged for a 'new carriage, two grey horses and a complete harness.'[31]

Tulip auctions and the wheeling and dealing of bulbs in futures markets caught on in the taverns and cafes, which widened the market and attracted new investors. The establishment of option markets increased the ability of ordinary people to speculate on bulbs. Amateur horticulturalists appeared through various trades keen to be part of the speculative furore. Futures in all commodities are high risk and are generally exercised by specialists; perishable goods such as tulips being particularly susceptible to uncertainty.

> With a long period to delivery, it was inevitable that buyers should be tempted into an interim deal, selling again to a new buyer and realising a profit or else upgrading their own stock. They did so, of course, without ever laying their eyes on the blooms or the bulbs, and before long buyers approached potential sellers whom they knew had not had possession of the stock. They in turn offered a 'paper' price contingent on delivery, meaning to pass their 'paper' sale on to yet another third party. As prices based on expectations raised with the impending spring, so the turnover of what was in effect a trade in tulip futures quickened.[32]

In the rush not to miss out on rapidly increasing stocks, novices entered without a full consideration or realisation of the potential threats. Tulip exchanges were gambling markets. During the period when new investors are willing to enter the market, the investment is self-fulfilling. Financial rewards are occasionally gleaned from the investment that realises its gain and exists in the market, which is positive publicity in itself. When the bubble bursts however, there are few new investors willing to enter the market. This creates the flight of liquidity throughout the chain resulting in non payment and default.

Despite the wide desire to pursue the tulip investment, the product itself, and the success related to it, was largely related to a momentary investment opportunity. Whilst those close to the bubbles recognised its flaws, distant investors and traders ignored the vulnerability of the bulbs, and continued to trade regardless of the warning signs (for example, a marked decrease in new investors). New methods of attaining credit were being made available, a 'service' that added volatility to a booming speculative product, regardless of its nature.

The increasing participation in the tulip markets generated extensive ill informed speculation; loans were taken to fuel trades. Other factors, for example the depletion in human resources lost to the plague in the previous bubble paradoxically improved the wealth of the remaining labour.[33] The impact of the plague and the lip-service given to the sweep of Calvinism deepened the Tulip Bubble. Scare labour pushed up wages, allowing relatively low paid workers to be part of the investment bubble. Braudel records the impact of the plague in everyday life, which increased the premium on scarce labour.

Plague occurred in Amsterdam every year from 1622 to 1628 (the toll 35,000 dead!). It struck in Paris in 1612, 1619, 1631, 1638, 1662, 1668 (the last). It should be noted that after 1612 in Paris 'the sick were forcibly removed from their homes and transferred to the Hôpital Saint-Louis and to the Maison de Santé in the faubourg Saint-Marcel. Plague struck London five times between 1593 and 1644-5 claiming, it is said, a total of 156,463 victims.[34]

The peak of the bubble throughout 1636-1637 resulted in a speculative fever that was attractive to new investors. The wealth that flowed into Amsterdam from trade continued unabated, a condition that makes speculative dealings favourable and necessary.

Grotesque details of Tulipomania at the peak have secured it a central place in the annals of irrational investor behaviour. How could a bulb that sold for over 5,000 guilders in 1637 be worth only one-tenth of a guilder in 1639, and still be rationally priced? This type of pricing behaviour seems impossible to explain if we assume market fundamentals are driving up the price. However, there is another side to this story. A rare tulip bulb is not the same kind of asset as a common stock or even a unique Rembrandt painting. It has to be compared to the pricing of any similar self-producing asset with a premier breeding tag. Prize bulls, thoroughbred horses, pedigree dog breeds and growers of quality plants all belong in this same category.[35]

The opportunities became widely popularised and new investment flowed into the tulip trade. Futures markets became commonplace with speculation and nature sharing uncertain characteristics.

The Sound of Traffic: Listen to the Flowers

The investment was fuelled in part by borrowing and swap investments, which pushed up the general price of tulips through the introduction of new money.

The crash occurred in a flourish. The market peaked in February 1637, with no new investors willing to push up the prices in the auctions. In Haarlem, traders were shocked when bulbs failed to meet predicted prices.

The growers in Haarlem were becoming anxious that they would soon be left with worthless stock. According to *Samenspraeck*, confidence cracked on February 3. By the next day, markets in Haarlem were in full retreat. A meeting was held in Utrecht on the 7th, which prepared the way for a full confidence in growers at Amsterdam on the 24th. The confidence attempted to enforce all new season contracts at 10 per cent of the price agreed, but in a devastated market, even 10 per cent would not hold. In Haarlem, the reckless buyers were instructed by the Mayor and the Governors to put up three and half per cent, but most, it seems, paid nothing at all.[36]

Rumour spread rapidly generating panic and a fear of sudden crash, a self-fulfilling prophecy if the rational act of executing the removal from the investment is operated (the crash occurring in days or hours is a feature of bubble decline, a fact that requires emphasising). Traders who held bulbs ordered by buyers found that clients refused to pay, as the agreed prices had fallen so quickly.

The consequences of the negative noise on tulips led to the accelerated abandonment in stocks, pledges and commitments related to tulips. Talking down investments is as precarious as talking them up.

The chronology of key events relating to the stages of tulipomania, filtered into Cohen's model below, demonstrates the rise and the decline of the investment:

Phase	Description	Added feature	Description
1	Viruses emerge on tulips	1	New varieties of tulip bulb
2	Holland had access to credit	2	Futures and options
3	Inflation (silver from Baltic trade financed Dutch trading)	3	Irrational investors
4	Overtrading and speculation	4	Inept authority intervention
5	Most adults joined in	5	Leverage and futures
6	Nagging doubts in Harlem	6	98% retrenchment
7/8	Instant panic sell-off	7	Tulips almost worthless
9	Onset of debt deflation		

Figure 4.1[37]

When applying the events of Tulipomania to this model, Cohen omits some phases altogether, for example the activities of fraud and tricksters, which were however limited by the establishment of investment committees in the taverns (an early form of regulation introduced to formulate an accepted code between traders).

It is the case that the Tulip Bubble was not without inputs of creativity from speculators of all kinds seeking an advance on their investment, a common factor in bubbles.

Whilst the tulip crash ruined individual investors, it did not fundamentally damage the growth of the major institutions of the day.

The Response of the State

The Government had realised that there was a bubble before it collapsed and acted, albeit tentatively, to limit the potential economic damage. Concerned that the prices for the tulip bulbs were unsustainable and that the hysteria might destabilise the economy, the Dutch authorities intervened in January 1637. In order to dampen speculation, the authorities announced that prices could not be sustained without direct penalties to the investor. These were designed to be ambiguous; the move was intended to curtail speculation without obvious interference. Almost immediately, as a result of this intervention, prices began to fall. It is clear, like the Dotcom Bubble centuries later, that the Government contributed to the crash.

> In any event, the magistrates of the Dutch towns saw the niceties of equity as less pressing than the need to de-intoxicate the tulip craze. Their intervention was hastened by the urgency of returning the genie speculation to the bottle from which it had escaped, and corking it tightly to ensure against any recurrence.[38]

The intervention added to the nervousness and prices began to fall. In the aftermath, the courts heard claims on contracts, guarantees and promises, but in an atmosphere that the losses were largely self-inflicted through what appeared to be a series of exuberant gambles; investors did not find satisfaction. It was held that the investments were gambling debts, which could not be enforced by law. Without liquidity, which had taken flight into assets elsewhere, or had fallen into the pockets of the 'smart' who could fund an alternative speculation elsewhere, contracts were declared obsolete by the States of Holland, damaging confidence and harming expectations, although not irreparably, in the wider economy.

Borrowers who had expanded their dealings with speculation through the access to credit realised the full extent of their losses. The collapse led to social unrest and accusations.

The appearance of sudden speculative activity is a dilemma for any government. On the one hand, speculation fuels an entrepreneurial spirit. The need to temper its exuberance can be met with disdain; unnecessary intervention damaging growth and expectations. The other extreme produces an investment atmosphere which can lead to a rapid boom. In this situation, a sudden collapse, without a warning or intervention of some kind from government, encourages criticism that action should have occurred earlier to control the rapid rise.

The response of the Dutch authorities was to 'regulate' the futures markets that had appeared during the tulip speculation. The term regulation is perhaps misleading; it certainly was not the type of regulation familiar in the twentieth century which is underpinned by strict legislation and punishments in law, although rules of the game were established and in part adhered to. Strict requirements were introduced, but gradually other less disabling financial measures were introduced to allow finance to support enterprise.

The public finances of the States of Holland had been managed competently, a factor that held to sustain the Golden Age beyond the tulip crash.

> In their fiscal policy, therefore, the States of Holland showed their readiness not only to overcome established differences between cities and countryside, but also to combat local 'particularism'. Despite the failure of the attempt of the provinces of Holland and Zeeland in 1579 to centralise the 'common means' as 'general means' for all of the provinces at a national level, this 'centralisation' was a remarkable success at the provincial level. It counters the claim that the combination with a strong national centre is indispensable for successful state formation.[39]

The form of governance in the States of Holland limited damage to the wider economy from the reckless investment in tulips. The policy towards the wider economy allowed commerce and trade to flourish.

> The new type of provincial government set up between 1572 and 1600 bore little resemblance to patterns of provincial government in Habsburg times. In effect, the Revolt not only created a new confederate state and central institutions but also shaped provinces, as coherent administrative entities, as well. The Revolt made Dutch provincial government stronger, and more efficient, but only because the provinces were now the organs of a partially federal state which required greater collaboration, and heavier taxation, than could be conceived of before 1572. Holland was the driving force behind the new union.[40]

The temptation to overstate the direct correlation between the collapse of Tulip Bubbles and the end of the Dutch golden age should be resisted. The bankruptcies, recession and the pressures placed on the national treasury from damaged tax revenues, led to a withdrawal of funds previously directed to maintaining the strategic demands of foreign policy. This cannot solely be attributed to the Tulip Bubble – other costs associated with maintaining a large naval force to secure and protect foreign trade were also a strain on resources.

In fact, the Dutch economy slowed down to a degree in the 1640s before putting on a tremendous spurt from 1650 to 1672, which extended especially to luxury housing, civic building, and paintings, the market for the last collapsing with the French invasion of 1672. [The French would call it 'liberation', not 'invasion.'] At the height of the boom there was 'mania' for clocks and clock towers.[41]

It is important to remember however, in the context of the operation of war and the finance of it, that:

It was the Dutch who first perfected the techniques of war finance capable of sustaining an enormous army almost indefinitely...The key to this effortless financial power was, in part, the enormous wealth of Amsterdam, which by 1650 was the undisputed commercial and financial capital of Europe; but it was equally the good faith of the Dutch Government, which always paid interest and repaid capital on time.[42]

In the years immediately following the bubble, the international trade that had become a rapid source of growth and economic development led to conflict between established and emerging powers, the development of commercial centres increasingly being the concern of foreign policy.

One effect quickly appeared in the much greater attention paid to commercial questions in diplomatic negotiation from the later part of the seventeenth century and the fact that countries were prepared to fight over them. The English and the Dutch went to war over trade in 1652...Governments not only looked after their merchants by going to war to uphold their interests, but also intervened in other ways in the working of the commercial economy.[43]

Ultimately, the overseas colonies could not be sustained without new investment, resulting in a seismic shift in the balance of power. The incredible wealth enjoyed by the City of Amsterdam built by the trade and entrepreneurialism began to wane from the beginning and throughout the eighteenth century, a casualty of naval wars and the escalating costs associated with them. The earlier Tulip Bubble did create difficulties for investors, but its implosion did not directly damage the wider economy (it appears that the reasons behind the mania lies in the development of a bubble; verging on psychological issues in Dutch investors' minds). Holland would, however, continue to be a cultural and influential force: tulips being a commodity of substance.

In the debris of the collapse, it would perhaps surprise the investors who had lost in the fall to learn that the flower industry in Holland had over the centuries developed and maintained an international reputation for its blooms. Tourists continue to flock yearly to view the Aladdin and China pink tulips, and the gladioli, lilies and hyacinths in the Vogelenzang, Keukenhof and Bloembollenstreek.

Notes

[1] There is an immediate note of caution. Peter Garber's thought provoking book, *Famous First Bubbles: The Fundamentals of Early Manias*, which provides a refreshing reality check, infers it was not a bubble. It is clear, however, some form of speculative fever did strike in the formative years of the Dutch Golden Age. Myth, fabrication and artistic licence are a common feature in bubbles, a point made in the book review by John Cochrane on the very same book. The review goes on to suggest that 'Many of the stories are completely implausible. Would a crafty Dutch merchant leave a $10,000 tulip lying around for a sailor to touch, let alone eat? Why would anyone trade a complex list of household goods for a tulip future? Why do we pass on such stories?' (Cochrane 2001) p.1154.

[2] Check the Euronext web page for information on the Exchange: http://www.aex.nl/aex.asp?taal=en.

[3] See http://www.ahm.nl/.

[4] See http://www.few.eur.nl/few/people/smant/m-economics/tulipmania.htm.

[5] Calvinism is the branch of Protestantism founded basically (although preceded by Zwingli and others) by Jean Calvin (1509-64). The distinctive doctrine of Calvinism is its [emphasis] of predestination which states that God has unalterably destined some souls to salvation to whom 'efficacious grace and the gift of perseverance' is granted and others to eternal damnation (Pears Cyclopaedia 2000-2001, Section J8). The important point is the impact on social economic relations. The Catholic Church to a certain extent considered the idea of predestination, but the Calvinist turn went further.

[6] Driesum (2000) *Amsterdam*, p.16.

[7] Philip II was put in charge of the Netherlands, Naples and Milan by his father Charles V, on 25 October 1555.

[8] Marriott (1935) p.515

[9] Lee (1991) p.69.

[10] Van Thienen, (1951) *The Great Age of Holland*, p. 11.

[11] Schama (1987) p.350.

[12] The authorities of the City encouraged tolerance to a degree and promoted trade.

[13] Mackay (1996 [1841]) pp. 117-18.

[14] Hale (1994) p.518.

[15] The philosopher Spinoza being one of them.

[16] Bonney (1991) p.163.

[17] Francis (2001) p.5.

[18] Hibbert (1986) p.118.

[19] Burke (1985) *The Day the Universe Changed*, p.153.

[20] Pennington (1970) pp 75-76.

[21] De La Vega (1996 [1688]) p. 149.

[22] Jay (2000) p.192.

[23] See http://batavia.rug.ac.be/.

[24] Landes (1998) p.141.

[25] Bonney (1991) p.451.

[26] Israel, 1995, p.533.

[27] These enable agents to buy, at a price agreed today, some product or asset which will be delivered and paid for at some time in the future.

[28] Euronext provides a succinct definition of an option: A contract that permits the owner (depending on the type of option held) to purchase or sell a security at a specific ('strike') price until a specified expiration date. An option to purchase a security is a 'call'. An option to sell a security is a 'put'. The price of the option itself is the 'premium.'

[29] Rosenberg (1994) pp 100-101.

[30] The price of one special, rare type of tulip bulb called Semper Augustus was 1000 guilders in 1623, 1200 guilders in 1624, 2000 guilders in 1625, 5500 guilders in 1637 http://www.few.eur.nl.

[31] Braudel (1982) p. 101.

[32] *Op cit*, Schama, p. 353.

[33] The plague presents a strange picture in Dutch life. It feels quite gothic, almost romantic. Those fiery tulips on a background of sick people dying of the plague in the gutters and the back streets; bodies dumped in the canals.

[34] Braudel (1981) p.88.

[35] Cohen (1997) p 19.

[36] Buchan (1997) p.112.

[37] Model adapted from Cohen (1997) p.20.

[38] *Op cit*, Schama, p.361.

[39] For an extremely informative of Dutch public finance in the sixteenth and seventeenth centuries, see Fritschy's 'A Financial Revolution Reconsidered: Public Finance in Holland during the Dutch Revolt 1568-1648.'

[40] *Op cit*, Israel, p. 291.

[41] Kindleberger (2000[1978]) p.110.

[42] Parker (1979) p.102.

[43] Roberts (1990) p.519.

Chapter 5

The South Sea Bubble: From the Mississippi to the High Seas

Introduction

The South Sea Bubble is best understood with reference to the Mississippi Bubble, which occurred in France a few years beforehand, as a consequence of the implementation of the economic ideas of the famous Scottish financier, John Law.[1]

The Mississippi Bubble would set in motion a series of speculative adventures, which would include frenzied action and messy politics. It continues to provide a rich site to mine for insight into the various factors that impact on and shape speculative activity.

The South Sea Bubble relates to the succession of financial projects associated with the appearance of the South Sea Company in 1711, which was introduced by Robert Harley as a Tory rival to the Bank of England with the intention of managing English trade with South America.

The idea behind the parent scheme was that the state should sell certain trading monopolies in the South Seas in return for a sum of money to pay off the National Debt.

The material below builds on the themes introduced in the previous chapter, which recognised the emergence of speculative behaviour involving large numbers of investors from various levels of society. It should be noted that in this period regulation remained in a crude form. Despite this, intervention arising from the officers of government led to substantial repercussions that on occasion produced unintended effects (a condition that continues in a modern setting).

The psychological dimension was considered in the previous chapter on Tulipomania, which inflated the prices of the flowers to an unsustainable level (this trait is repeated in the South Sea Bubble).

The key features of the Mississippi and South Sea Bubbles will be studied to shed further light on the nature of bubbles active within classical political economy.

The Mississippi Bubble: The Social and Political Aspect and Impact of Speculative Activity

The eighteenth century was a defining period for France. Throughout this turbulent century, finance and economics would play a decisive part in shaping the political and social struggles that exploded and shook European nations to their foundations.

The French economy under Louis XIV had stagnated with the aristocracy voluntarily incapable of contributing ideas and intellectual financial knowledge on how to re-invigorate the economy. The French turned to John Law, a Scottish financier who would apply his monetary theories in France through such institutions as the Banque Royale and the Compagnie des Indes.[2]

John Law believed that the replacement of specie coin by paper money would lead to the expansion of the quantity of money in circulation, which in turn would generate significant economic activity.

When Law came to France in 1714, he renewed his acquaintance with the nephew of King Louis XIV, the Duke of Orleans. The duke became Regent of France after the king's death in 1715. The regent served as ruler while the heir to the throne, 5-year-old Louis XV, was still a minor. The duke recalled Law's financial prowess and sought his advice and assistance in straightening out France's financial mess left over from years of reckless spending under Louis XIV. This association with the Duke of Orleans would ensure Law's place in history. Not only would Law advance the use of paper money, the French word millionaire would come into use as a result of his most famous scheme – the Mississippi Company.[3]

The Mississippi Bubble in France was the precursor to the extraordinary events in London, which followed the example of the optimism associated with John Law's Mississippi scheme in Paris.[4]

If it had not been for a series of extraordinary events in France the South Sea Company might have jogged on indefinitely as a respectable failure, living on an annual interest paid to it by the Government for having taken over £10,000,000 of debts upon its foundation. Inadvertently the French staged a dress rehearsal for the South Sea drama: more than this, the Paris performance introduced a novel twist which fired the imagination of the English directors.[5]

John Law was an enigmatic figure who held a keen intellect for financial matters and no less so for mischief. Nonetheless, Adam Smith in the classic 1776 *The Wealth of Nations* reflects favourably on the talents of John Law.

That the industry of Scotland languished for want of money to employ it was the opinion of the famous Mr Law. By establishing a bank of a particular kind, which he seems to have imagined might issue paper to the amount of the whole value of all the lands in the country, he proposed to remedy this want of money. The parliament of Scotland, when he first proposed his project, did not think proper to adopt it. It was afterwards adopted, with some variations, by the Duke of Orleans, at the time Regent of France. The idea of the possibility of multiplying paper money to almost any extent was the real foundation of what is called the Mississippi scheme, the most extravagant project both of banking and stock-jobbing that, perhaps, the world ever saw.[6]

Law created a system based on paper bills; promissory notes related to the value of land.[7] In return for delivering liquidity to the French economy, Law was awarded the franchise to manage the national debt by the Duc d' Orléans, who had executive power during the reign of the boy king Louis XV.

The opening decades had witnessed an expansion of geographical aggrandisement. The French had been the first of the European powers to covert the resources of the southern new world. Louisiana would become noted for its cotton, maize and tobacco, but initially it was desirable to the French for its gold and silver deposits. Although Louisiana was not well known throughout France, it took on a mythical character, rich in treasures and potential.

The Compagnie de la Louisiane ou d'Occident was established in August 1717 by John Law, a Scottish financial genius. The Compagnie was granted control of Louisiana. The Company's plans to exploit the resources of the region – the 'Mississippi Scheme' – captured the popular imagination. Believing that the region was a source of limitless wealth, people rushed to invest. Share prices opened at 500 livres, but rapidly rose to 18,000 livres. At this point, speculators indulged in profit-taking, causing a run on the shares. Confidence collapsed, causing a run on the company's capital and the company went bankrupt. Many individuals were ruined, not only in France, but throughout Europe.[8]

The flaw in Law's idea can be traced back to the issuing of additional shares and the increase in inflation. Without strenuous policies to stem the general level of prices, money and its paper derivative devalued causing political concern and social unrest.

There was no fear for the future, as 'panics and depressions' were unknown. There had never been a stock market 'boom' before; indeed there had never been a stock market. A small narrow street by the name of the rue Quincampoix had been a resort for men dealing in government securities; it now became the centre for the Mississippi speculation...They were up at eight o'clock in the morning, drums were sounded and the crowd poured in. From then until dark the street was a bedlam of surging, shouting people, eager to buy and sell. The owners of the houses along the Quincampoix did a thriving business by renting their property to brokers at exorbitant fees.[9]

Despite its initial success, Law made mistakes in addition to the issuing of new shares. The expectations of the riches to be discovered in the new world were unforthcoming. Word gradually spread back to France that the promised benefits were impossible to attain. The message gradually produced a negative view on the investment, which stilted favourable speculations.

His bank issued shares in the development of the French colony in Louisiana. The initial returns were poor; convicts had to be sent out to work in harsh conditions, and the promised sugar, spices and cotton failed to materialise.[10]

Ignoring the problems, the demand for liquidity continued to be insatiable and more paper money was provided. Whilst the Mississippi scheme had not immediately met expectations, it was still supported and produced strong interest. Bentham captures the mood eloquently, identifying two key aspects of bubble activity (a) peer pressure; and (b) psychological neurosis:

Call them *air bubbles* if you like; these bubbles acquire through custom a consistency which suffices to enable them to do service, until an unforeseen and sudden shock arrives to which they cannot stand up. The individual who has taken them does not accept them on the strength of the opinion on which he himself entertains of their solidity, but on the strength of the opinion which he sees or which he supposes in others. Such was the case in the Mississippi speculation; such was the case in the South Sea affair. Even if I believe that a note of £100 is not worth a farthing, I shall none the less be willing to give £200 for it, if I see other persons willing to take it from me, not only for the same sum, but for still a greater one.[11]

The attraction of paper money is widened by the promotion of initial gains, which encourages speculation from people not familiar or specialised in the investment. The lack of knowledge is most damaging during the final advance to the peak, when the smart money invariably departs when satisfactory profits have been attained. The delay in information, which reaches investors at various stages, results in the wide holding of falling stock; the ability to execute a buy and sell option at the right time being largely dependent on word of mouth and informed warnings.

Law devalued shares in the company in several stages during 1720, and the value of bank notes was reduced to 50 percent of their face value. By September 1720 the price of shares in the company had fallen to 2,000 livres and to 1,000 by December. The fall in the price of stock allowed Law's enemies to take control of the company by confiscating the shares of investors who could not prove they had actually paid for their shares with real assets rather than credit. This reduced investor shares, or shares outstanding, by two-thirds. By September 1721 share prices had dropped to 500 livres, where they had been at the beginning.[12]

In a speculative atmosphere, there are key moments when the action of a particular investor triggers a wave of consequences. For example, the news that the influential Duc de Conti, one of Law's major investors with connections to the throne, had demanded gold instead of paper generated panic.

The Government had printed hundreds of millions of paper money in order to give the people the means of buying shares in Law's company. This had caused appalling inflation. The price of all commodities had rocketed. Bread, milk and meat had risen six and seven times in cost. Cloth had increased 300 per cent.[13]

The attacks on Law became overwhelming. It was a radical idea that had rejuvenated the fortunes of France, but which also caused radical ruptures in the circles of the upper classes and social upheaval in the wider society.

The Mississippi bubble had burst. Law had been too impatient, taken on too much, failed to allow his fragile mechanisms time to work. He had helped to instigate a recovery in commerce and agriculture, but had gone too fast and had imperilled his own success. In the process he had made the notion of paper money feared in France, hindering economic reform in the future.[14]

The ideas of John Law would be copied in the infamous South Sea Bubble, a speculative foray that Adam Smith would label an outright fraud. The collapse of Law's system in May 1720, and the death of the Regent three years later, led to the return of the *rentiers*, a group Law despised. French finance fell into the hands of his business rivals and his reputation was repeatedly tarnished by Montesquieu and Voltaire, who disapproved of him.[15]

John Law, who had established a range of important connections, fled to Venice in 1725 and remained there until his death four years later. Louisiana as a territory was eventually purchased by the United States during the Thomas Jefferson administration by a treaty signed on 30 April 1803.

The South Sea Bubble

The temptation of employing money to make more money was rapidly becoming recognised as a fast way to increase wealth. In Britain, the fortunes of the Mississippi Bubble had been followed with astonishment. John Blunt of the South Sea Company had studied John Law's activities with keen interest. Blunt, the architect of the company, would become an instrumental figure who would realise his vision with the passing of the South Sea Bill by the House of Commons on 7 April 1719.

> Sir John Blunt was the projector of the South Sea Bubble, which, in 1720, produced such extraordinary effects in England. As the scheme did not at first prove successful, rumours were spread that Gibraltar and Port Mahon [Minorca] would be exchanged for Peru. The stock soon rose to 1,000 per cent, and the excitement lasted until September, by which time it had sunk to 150. Several eminent goldsmiths and bankers were obliged to abscond; and every family in the kingdom felt the shock.[16]

The South Sea Bubble began in 1720 after a long period of prosperity in the English economy. The debts accumulated by war, however, created economic strains for the nation that threatened to damage growth. The development of trade had rapidly led to a vast amount of wealth that required re-direction. Investment opportunities that gave a good return were in short supply. The monopoly status of the South Sea Company attracted investors seeking a strong return from future trade and development. Despite the opportunities, the bubble generated into one of the worst social and economic disasters in British financial history.

Establishing the Company: Legitimating Bubbles

The company had been given legitimacy through the South Sea Bill, passed by the House of Lords to lessen the costs associated with war with France, and address the serious debts that had been growing in the war of Spanish succession. Fundamentally, the rationale behind the patent scheme was that the state should sell certain trading monopolies in the South Seas in return for a sum of money to pay off the national debt (which stood at

£51,300,000 in 1719 when the scheme started).[17] Prior to the reign of Anne, the national debt had amounted to £16,000,000.

> The Government of King George I under Stanhope and Sunderland wished to reduce the tax burden necessitated by paying interest on the National Debt, and they promoted a scheme whereby 3/5ths of the Debt was converted into South Sea stock: i.e. all the Debt not held by the two other big financial corporations, the Bank of England and the East India Company.[18]

Fifteen years earlier the Bank of England had been licensed by William III with the intention of sustaining and managing the finances of the monarchy; the initial Tory investors considered it an option to counter the Whig national bank. It also provided an alternative to the financial influence of The East India Company, which lowered the cost of government borrowing.

> The financial interests that represented the Bank of England had enjoyed a more favourable return on their investments during the wars, and there was obviously room for greater competition between the nation's creditors. The Tory ministers of Queen Anne's reign had indeed encouraged the formation of the South Sea Company in 1711 with a view to providing an effective alternative to the Whig Bank...The South Sea Company's scheme of 1719 seemed well calculated to redistribute the national debt while offering better terms to the national Exchequer.[19]

The arrangement entitled the South Sea Company to set and develop trade between England and the South American coasts, a potentially lucrative opportunity that would establish new trading routes and increased trade in commodities. In assuming this debt, confidence in the company was secured, attracting a rush of investors. In reality, the move to establish gains in the region was beset by difficulties.

> The Anglo-Spanish Treaty of 1713 had given the Company a monopoly of the Spanish slave trade and a valuable share in the Spanish American market of European goods. In theory, this offered the most promising prospects. In practice, the difficulties of managing this far flung trade from London were to prove immense, and they were made worse by the often bitter conflicts between the British and Spanish governments. The trade could not have proved profitable in the short run, and even with time it could hardly fulfil the wild expectations raised by 1719.[20]

Despite the problems, the business was initially founded on relatively firm foundations. The furore associated with its introduction, however, included dubious promotions of unsound elements, which damaged confidence. The goal was quick returns from a careless market. Investors felt that the offerings were solid and continued direct funds to the purchase of stocks.

In April 1720 the company issued new stocks at £300 each, with an option to buy with a £60 deposit, and the remainder payable in eight instalments. This credit vehicle for purchasing shares generated massive interest, and the stock values kept on rising. Within one month the stock was worth £550. When the company issued more stocks for only 10% deposit and nothing to pay for a year, prices inflated rapidly to over £1000.

> Thousands of people imbued with the idea of getting rich quickly rushed to buy the company's shares, which rose from £100 to £1000. Other companies sprang up, some of them to promote the most absurd objects – to extract silver from lead, to import asses from Spain, to work perpetual motion machines, to trade in human hair, to make salt water fresh, and so on.[21]

In response to the eagerness of the public to invest, companies formed on the back of the South Sea Company. Each claimed involvement in a variety of activities in the same field, undermining further the credibility of the ventures. In the rush of speculation, bad enterprises appeared, blatantly slurring the reputation of the market. These companies were notoriously vague about their businesses, perhaps the most obscure being 'an undertaking which shall in due time be revealed'.[22] Bubbles have a mad, psychological dimension, which encourages irrational behaviour. The absurd nature of the speculative hype and rogue companies did not immediately drive out investors, who ignored the warning and continued to seek out advantageous positions, however tainted.

> In the four weeks from the 27th May to the 24th June South Sea stock rose from 500 to 1050 while the stocks of numberless other companies soared upwards with equal or even greater velocity. All roads led to the Alley, but those nearest to it, like Cornhill and Lombard Street, were impassable owing to the block of coaches, while the passage itself was congested by a seething throng of people of every sort and kind.[23]

All levels of society were involved in the speculative gamble. On the one hand, royalty, misguidedly but profitably, ventured into the market (like Tulipomania, this is an important feature in bubble activity, which is noted in the progression from chapter to chapter).

> The Prince of Wales himself accepted office as Governor of the English Copper Company in spite of the remonstrance of Robert Walpole and Speaker

Compton, later as Lord Wilmington to be famous in history as England's most obscure Prime Minister, who protested with justice that the Company's stock would be hawked about the City as the Prince of Wales's bubble. His Royal Highness's gracious wish to share in the pursuits of the people resulted in the addition of £40,000 to his private fortune.[24]

Bentham is again valuable in directing thoughts to the velocity of the eager speculation in rising stocks; the dimension of time is crucial in understanding bubbles.

When in the case of the South Sea Scheme an annuity that had been sold at £100, rose in the course of a few months at £1000, it was not by the combination of the actual possessors of property, but [by] a competition among those who, being confident that how high a price soever they should give for it, they should always be able to sell it at a higher, were continually anxious to possess more and more of it. When in Holland, at the time of the Tulip rage, a flower of that kind that might before that time had been had for a shilling or two, found purchases at 5 or 10 guineas, it was till not any combination amongst the growers of those superfluous ornaments, but the competition, the adventurous wager-laying competition, among the purchasers that was the known and real cause.[25]

The bubble continued and excitement spread. Investors directing additional resources to speculation, sought to attain credit to fund the gamble. In the gentlemen's clubs and in the common hostelry, stocks were debated, hawked and ramped.

But the paper fortunes of the investors were, unknown to them, already under threat. The sheer scale of the stock-market revolution the Company had created threatened its existence: it had, in effect, been too successful. Coupled with the new and emerging businesses, the South Sea Company's ascent gave the impression that the country was going through a financial revolution of the sort that Law had inspired in France; that a vibrant new energy was coursing through the economy, so that anyone with an ounce of business sense should climb aboard the new ventures or risk being left in the dark age of the old economic order.[26]

The arrival of a range of investment opportunities and the ability to speculate swelled the bubble and widened its influence. The introduction of widespread fraudulent practices is difficult to pinpoint, but the appearance of firms and stock without underpinning value increased in the 1720s. In response to the influx of speculative companies, few investors began to become wary, dismissing stories of theft and investment wrongdoing. The madness continued, attracting new investors keen to be part of the speculative adventure.

The Tempest: Bubbles Off Course

The end of the South Sea Company came about when news got out that the directors had sold their shares. The directors of the South Sea Company had initiated action against a number of companies without an official charter from the government. To a degree, the move was successful, but the losses that could be incurred from the investment became suddenly stark, contributing to panic involving both rich and poor.

> A swarm of bubble companies buzzed into life, including one for 'importing jackasses from Spain,' in which millions were pledged. But the directors overplayed their hand. It was impossible for ever to 'peg' the price of a stock not covered by assets, they overloaded the market, and struck the first blow at their own safety by getting the government to proclaim as illegal some eighty rival companies. A rush to realize those worthless shares spread the panic to South Sea stock.[27]

The picture was increasingly complicated by the numerous illegal second rank companies, whose losses wiped out gains elsewhere. Fear began spreading to more solid enterprises. Indebtedness added to the malaise, resulting in a flight of confidence that ushered in accusations of wrongdoing and a generic flight from the market. The price of all shares fell and the market collapsed.

> The collapse of the farthing-table bubbles had been a plain warning, if any had paused to heed it, that the Golden Age could not last indefinitely.[28]

It became evident that after selling the entire subscription of stocks, one owner made for the continent and was never heard of again. Stories of losses and financial woe spread apace, leading to heavy losses.

> Sheer panic set in, speculators struggled to sell with as much frenzy as they had expended a few weeks before in their efforts to buy, but now there were no buyers; one after another, they found themselves either involved in commitments which they were utterly unable to meet or, at best, in possession of paper suddenly stripped of all value. Fortunes melted and assets froze overnight.[29]

The collapse again illustrates the power at the centre of bubble activity over investors distant from the key developments inside the financial world. Further selling on the news of fraud and irregularities destroyed what confidence that was left.

> The impact of this wave of selling on South Sea stock was staggering. Both the Government and the directors had overlooked the fact that many speculators had shares in more than one company, and most of them were obliged to sell South Sea stock to meet their obligations. On August 17th South Sea stock had stood at 900. On September 28th it was 190. The crash had come with a vengeance.[30]

The key stages of the South Sea Bubble are highlighted below:

Phase	Description	Added Feature	Description
1	SSC given monopoly	1	SSC sells stocks
2	Shares available to buy on credit	2	Credit options available
3	Inflation in asset prices	3	Irrational decisions
4	Stocks bought for speculation	4	No financial authority
5	Public joined in	5	Leverage increases
6	SSC directors sell their shares	6	Fraudulent companies
7/8	Public sell shares	7	Shares became worthless
9	Long depression followed		

Figure 5.1

The South Sea Bubble fits neatly into Cohen's model. It incorporates the operation of fraud in a more complex manner, highlighting the role of insiders in taking advantage of the unfolding bubble. Despite the collapse in confidence in the credibility of vast returns, the South Sea Company continued until the 1850s.

The theory that the waves of the bubble follow a particular pattern, the first wave initiated by key individuals and institutions followed by a second wave including virgin investors, which swells the bubble encouraging the first wave investors to purchase more shares, is reiterated. The bubble continues to widen, generally swelled by assess to credit (a development noted by Kindleberger). The arrival of increasing numbers of virgin investors, which is in part triggered by the original investors withdrawing gains and attracting attention, replaces the investment, which has smartly sought asset growth elsewhere. The remaining stock fulfils its initial expectations, and new entrants may chance further investments, but the stage before the collapse is precarious although disguised. The strategic investment reversal is communicated through the financial networks and the various media, albeit it in a crude form (basically an exchange of information between groups), and animates a withdrawal from the bubble, a flight that may induce panic.

Government Response to the Collapse of the South Sea Bubble

In the aftermath of the collapse, the Government attempted to fix things and limit the damage. The Government tried to reassure people that the economy was solid, but the realisation that cabinet ministers had been involved in corruption added to the panic, which was already contagious. The crash resulted in a political crisis. It was rebutted with the suggestion that:

> the bubble was part of an international crisis with matching disasters in Paris and Amsterdam; it was not impossible to lay some of the blame on impersonal financial forces unconnected with individuals in the City or at court. In any event the king's ministers were, with the exception of two or three suitable scapegoats, permitted to get away with their crimes.[31]

Sedgwick in his study of the History of Parliament makes explicit the wide-spread anti-government feeling engendered by the collapse of the South Sea Bubble, which made the Tories so confident of the success of a rising that they did not think it worthwhile raising a fund for a general election.[32]

Throughout the early 1700s, governments had been slowly learning how to handle millions of pounds instead of tens of thousands. Although some knowledge had been gained of high finance, ignorance was still very great. In the confusion:

> the Earl of Sunderland pushed Walpole forward, for he was one of the few members of Government not involved in the scandal, though more by luck than judgement. There is no doubt too, that Sunderland hoped that Walpole's attempt to serve the Government and the Court would destroy Walpole's political capital.[33]

The financial victims of the South Sea Bubble clamoured for the guilty parties to be publicly revealed and punished. In an atmosphere of confusion and political intrigue, Robert Walpole would use the consternation to his advantage and against the odds manoeuvre to the highest political office. A favourable view promotes, albeit rosily, the action of the Government to contain the crisis.

> The Government did all they could for the country, and a number of ministers suffered for their part in the disaster. Walpole however, who had all along opposed the scheme, gained great popularity and was incidentally the first minister of state to receive the title of prime minister.[34]

Robert Walpole's initial act as prime minister was to protect the royal family, and members of the Government from scandal. In the aftermath of the bursting of the bubble, Walpole had 'shielded the most highly placed villains from parliamentary or judicial retribution, thereby preserving the court of George 1 from possible ruin, and advancing his own political career'.[35] Walpole's intervention did not however save John Aislabie, the Chancellor of the Exchequer and several members of parliament.

> During the winter attention was given to the punishment of those responsible for the disaster [the South Sea Company]. In this Walpole was agreed, but he saw the risks in allowing men's passions to run away with their reason. The government was in danger. Charges of receiving stock as bribes were brought against Lord Sunderland (£50,000), James Craggs, Sr. (£30,000), John Aislabie (£22,000), Charles Stanhope (£10,000), and others for varying amounts.[36]

The turbulence that had allowed Walpole to influence events was driven by uncertainly and confusion. The full extent of the damage caused by the implosion of the bubble remained unclear. It was a period of accusation and retribution. The need for strong leadership was essential. Walpole had:

> attained office by industry and exceptional attention to detail, ruthlessness, but chiefly through the luck of the survivor. In1720-21 the South Sea Bubble crisis had, in blowing up the Whig hierarchy, blown him towards power. Stanhope, and the two Craggs had all died; other rivals, like, Aislabie, had been discredited and driven from political life. As one of the senior Whig politicians unbribed by the South Sea Company (or whose bribes did not come to light) Walpole inherited power. Since the King's mistresses, and also very probably the King, were among those bribed by the Company, office could not be allowed to fall into the hands of intemperate men, who would press inquiry too far or give way to the public outcry for vengeance. Walpole came forward as 'Screen-Master General'; so far from being seen as a popular saviour, he was, at that time, 'the most execrated and despised man in public life, indeed far more intensely than Sunderland or the South Sea Directors'.[37]

To lessen the degree of agitation, the Riot Act was initiated to curtail the increasing ferocity of the protests. The measures introduced to restore confidence failed to remove the suspicion associated with paper money. In an atmosphere of mistrust, investment sought solid assets.

> Informal cartels permitted collaborative investment. The South Sea Bubble had left prejudice against the Joint-Stock company which was embodied in the Bubble Act of 1720. Subsequent scandals concerning public trusts, notably the Charitable Corporation and the York Buildings Company, drove prejudice still deeper. The temper of the age was deeply opposed to corporations.[38]

On the one hand, the Bubble Act limited the possibilities for investment in joint-stock companies. Each required a Royal Charter that rendered a company illegal without one. The directors of the South Sea Company had initially wanted the act to reduce the prevalence of fraud, which was becoming increasingly associated with the company and its operations. Shares in illegal companies would be invalidated without the Charter. In the first instance, the act provided a degree of confidence and investment continued, but with additional scandals and rumour the stock floundered and fell.

> The Bubble Act of 1720 put severe limitations on the creation of joint-stock companies, while the Usury Laws set a limit of 5 per cent on the rate of interest which could be charged for loans. The export of a number of goods was prohibited, and duties were imposed on the importation of a great many others.[39]

The act had been introduced to protect the interests of the South Sea Company. The attempt to limit the flight of capital into alternative assets related to the bubble failed, damaging its generic development. The combined effects of money shortage and prosecutions under the act:

> pricked the 'bubble' and share prices crashed. Few companies were able to weather the storm and for the rest of the century investors remained wary of promotions.[40]

The need to restore confidence and make the process appear transparent led to the regulatory interventions directed at the South Sea Company.[41]

> It was hoped that by confiscating the estates of the South Sea directors and others responsible for the fraud enough might be obtained to recompense the sufferers. As much as eight or ten millions had been mentioned. When, however, on April 17th, the committee appointed to inquire into the values of

the estates reported, the sum total available appeared to be only two million pounds.[42]

Julian Hoppit, in an excellent article 'Financial Crises in Eighteenth-Century England', puts in sharp focus the complexity of linking financial crisis to the progression of the economy as a whole.

Chalmers, for example, was struck in 1794 by the limited impact the bursting of the South Sea Bubble had on financial systems of the domestic economy in 1720, while Carswell in 1960 believed the crisis to be both deep and pervasive. Similarly, Clapman argued in 1944 that in 1763 'There was no true crisis', yet a little over ten years later Lovell firmly believed that there was.[43]

Despite the bursting of the bubble and the general suspicion of joint-stock companies, the economic health of the country was not impaired. As with the tulip mania, other influences and trends were at work.

The population in England had begun to grow more rapidly during the late 1720s; fortunately the revolution taking place in agriculture led by pioneers such as Jethro Tull helped to meet the demand for food, although the majority of families lived on a modest diet with little meat. Prices began to increase, which fuelled social pressures and discontent.

The prime mover of this price revolution was the increasing pressure on aggregate demand, caused by the acceleration in the growth of the population. In England, demographic historians Anthony Wrigley and Roger Schofield discovered that the rhythm of price-movements correlated closely with rates of population increase in the eighteenth century. After a long pause from 1660 to 1720, the population of England began to grow more rapidly during the late 1720s, at precisely the same moment when the price revolution also started. The correlation could not have been more exact.[44]

Coupled with the changes in demographics was the impact of inequality in the social structure. The rich were able to cope with the price increases, but at the lowest end of the social and economic spectrum, poverty became a noticeable feature, a condition that would result in the unleashing of revolutionary forces throughout Europe.

A positive consequence of the South Sea Bubble was the transfer of responsibility for national debt from corporate institutions to the Bank of England, which had avoided serious exposure to the speculative adventure, a move which further established control and confidence in the economy.

The latter part of the eighteenth century provided a glimpse of the rapid industrialisation and technological developments to follow, which would produce a series of mini-bubbles. For example:

Abraham Darby's discovery (1709) of a method of smelting the ore with coke, which, when it spread in (1760 onwards), freed smelting from its dependence on shrinking supplies of timber, and located it on coalfields instead of in the forests. Similar developments occurred in the forging side of the iron industry when improvements such as Henry Cort's pudding and rolling processes (1784) enabled vastly increased quantities of high quality iron to replace wood and stone in many sectors of the economy – to such a degree that the last decade of the century saw a veritable 'iron mania'.[45]

The overlapping technological, financial, economic, political and social consequences of the eighteenth century provided opportunities for investment and speculation. The industrial revolution, which began around the 1760s, would propel Britain forward. War continued to accompany the new British Empire. Whilst the South Sea Bubble and the Mississippi Scheme were held as examples, new 'impossible to fail schemes' were introduced, inferring that cautious investment is a temporary condition.

Notes

[1] French history taught in France does not elevate his status.

[2] For Le Musée de la Compagnie des Indes see

http://www.culture.gouv.fr/culture/archeosm/fr/fr-act-mus3.htm.

[3] For a further study of John Law and the Mississippi Bubble: 1718-1720 see the on-line publication for the Mississippi History Society:

www.mshistory.k12.ms.us/features/feature22'aw2.html.

[4] At that time, what is called 'Louisiana' was about 10 times larger than the current US state with that name, stretching all the way to current Toronto, throughout the central plains of the US.

[5] Cowles (1960) p.54.

[6] Smith (1776) p.417.

[7] See John Law, *Money and Trade considered with a Proposal for Supplying the Nation with Money.*

[8] www.mapforum.com/05/kop.htm.

[9] *Op cit*, Cowles, p.69.

[10] Baker, M. (2003) 'Law's paper revolution ends up as pulp fiction', p.B2.

[11] Stark, W. (1954) 'Jeremy Bentham's Economic Writings', pp 158-159.

[12] *Op cit*, www.mshistory.k12.ms.us/features/feature22'aw2.html.

[13] *Ibid*, www.mshistory.k12.ms.us/features/feature22'aw2.html.

[14] Pevitt (1997) p.276.

[15] Buchan (1997) p.131.

[16] Francis (2001) p.23.

[17] Entry Pears Cyclopaedia 2000-2001, L113.

[18] Williams (1980) p.415.

[19] Morgan (1984) p.364.

[20] *Ibid.* p.364.

[21] Marriott, J. (1935) p.508.
[22] Bagehot (1917) p.80.
[23] Erleigh, V. (1933) *The South Sea Bubble*, p. 77.
[24] Ibid, p.80.
[25] *Op cit*, Stark, pp 254-255.
[26] Balen (2003) pp 115-166.
[27] Feiling (1950) p.651.
[28] *Ibid*, p.111.
[29] *Ibid*, p.113.
[30] *Op cit*, Cowles, p.141.
[31] *Op cit*, Morgan, p.365.
[32] See Sedgwick (1970) *The House of Commons 1715-1754*, p. 64.
[33] Plumb (1950) p.59.
[34] *Ibid*, p.509.
[35] Langford, P. (1992) *A Polite and Commercial People*, p.22.
[36] Henderson (1975) pp 8-9.
[37] Thompson (1975), pp 198-199.
[38] *Ibid*, p.179.
[39] May (1993 [1987] p.38.
[40] Seddon (1966) p.125.
[41] All levels of society had joined in the gamble. The Committee of Secrecy set up by the House of Commons in December 1720 to investigate the company proved that there had been fraud and corruption embedded in the schemes. For a further and solid overview see: http://www.harvard-magazine.com/issues/mj99/damnd.html.
[42] *Op cit*, Thompson, pp 28-29.
[43] Hoppit (1986) pp 39-40.
[44] Fischer (1996) pp 123-124.
[45] Williams (1980) p.226.

Chapter 6

Bubbles in the Near Past

Introduction

This chapter considers the waves of bubbles throughout the nineteenth and twentieth century. The South Sea Bubble 'being the spectacular curtain raiser to the prosperity, vulgarity, and commercialism of the mid-eighteenth century',[1] was followed by successive investment booms. The technology, media and telecommunications bubbles, which flow into the twenty-first century, continue to draw attention. They will be studied in the next chapter.

The material in this chapter suggests that although bubbles are conditional on certain unique factors (socio-cultural, political, technological, legal and economic), particular common influences shape and frustrate the progression of bubbles.

The objective therefore, is to make clear which features can be identified in repeated bubble scenarios both chronologically and thematically. The presence of anomalies, ambiguities and accidents also form part of the study.

Nineteenth Century Bubbles

The nineteenth century in Britain was notable for rapid technological and economic development, notably from the benefits of the agrarian revolution started in the eighteenth century, a development that accelerated the progression of industrial capitalism (other investment environments were evident elsewhere in international markets, but the focus begins with the development of the industrial revolution). The former began an essential development in the feeding of the increased numbers attracted to the industrialising towns, increasing speculation and production.

The industrial revolution, which is generally dated between 1730 and 1850, provided Britain with its preponderance of coal and iron, and the technology and knowledge to transform basic materials through the process of industrialisation. The development of the great factories, driven by the mechanization of the textile industry, maritime trade, the demand and appearance of urban labour, and the burgeoning bourgeois class, were responsible for the boom in trade and wealth. Gentlemen's clubs sprung up in the major towns where ideas on engineering and finance were exchanged. Mining provided the fuel for the industrial revolution. Transport, in the form of canals, an innovation by Francis Egerton, was also a key factor in the development of industrialisation in Britain.

In Britain, the period was notable for its relative peace, the promotion of hard work and strict moral standards, an example led by Queen Victoria (1819-1901), Queen of the United Kingdom of Great Britain and Empress of India. The Napoleonic post-war gloom gradually dissipated with the ceasing of hostilities. The rise in industrialisation culminated in The Great Exhibition held in Hyde Park in 1851, which demonstrated the numerous advances in a range of technologies. The exhibition promoted Britain to the rest of the world – a world, in the words of Jules Verne's famous character Philias Fogg, 'getting smaller'.

Financial institutions were to be as powerful as states. England, France, Prussia, Austria and Russia were momentarily equalled in influence by the City-based Baring Brothers. The new industrial environment, however, was not equally generous to the human resources that fuelled the production and the army of disenfranchised resided outside the novels of Charles Dickens in everyday life.

In the later part of the nineteenth century, social conditions and unemployment worsened, reinforcing the view that something had gone wrong with the rapid industrialisation and economic growth, a flaw in the benefit of industrialisation to the working class.

> The upper classes profited immediately, and fairly soon a new educated middle class acquired some of the same privileges and advantages. Many men of humble birth and scant education but of inventive bent became the engineers and builders of the emerging technological age, while a whole new society of industrialists, merchant venturers and capitalists wrestled much of the political power from the established landowners...But for most people the fruits of this advancement were not enjoyed for several generations.[2]

The complexity of the boom and its demise are best summarised in Saul's important book, *The Myth of the Great Depression 1873-1896*, which imports a valid note of caution in isolating the trends and economic and financial events, which unfolded throughout the century.

Whilst there is plenty of evidence to claim that a depression occurred, it is too extreme to suggest that a bubble crash occurred in the 1890s.

Productivity raced ahead of demand. The difficult years followed the boom of the early 1890s, but its exact nature is open to intense debate.

> The events of the 1870s and 1880s, whatever the factors underlying them, caused a serious decline in business confidence. The unusual economic environment may well have lowered expectations and in this way reduced the level of industrial investment. It is an intangible influence, but contemporary accounts suggest it was not an insignificant one.[3]

Saul concludes, however, that the generic view of a 'Great Depression' is misleading, a caution to other interpretations of bubbles such as the Tulip Bubble in the early seventeenth century. The collapse of prices in one sector of assets need not be a catastrophe that pulls down all aspects of the economy. Hobsbawn makes a similar point in relation to the Great Depression.

> Historians have doubted the existence of what has been called the 'Great Depression' of 1863 to 1896, and of course it was nothing like as dramatic as that of 1929 to 1934, when the world capitalist economy almost ground to a halt. However, contemporaries were in no doubt that the great boom had been succeeded by a great depression.[4]

Fischer makes clear the enigma of turbulence present in the Victorian era, which unfolded under the superficial veneer of correct society. The age was steeped in structural change, within an atmosphere of considered resistance to it. Therefore, the range of mini-bubbles were largely unorganised and disparate.

> The equilibrium of the Victorian era was highly complex in its dynamics. Its underlying stability increased the visibility of many cyclical rhythms. There were harvest cycles in farm prices, inventory cycles in manufacturers, and commercial cycles of many different lengths. There were diurnal cycles, weekly cycles, seasonal cycles, annual cycles, generational cycles and perhaps a fifty year cycle. Many of these vibrations were highly regular in their complex cadence. As the equilibrium continued, the amplitudes of short-cycle movements (harvest fluctuations in particular) tended to diminish through time. This dampening process was typical of price equilibria in general, and very different from the expanding amplitudes that developed in price revolutions.[5]

New opportunities appeared for entrepreneurs and emerging industrialists, gambling and speculation ran parallel with growth, and fortunes were won and lost.

In 1807 and 1808, a general and feverish love of speculation was abroad. Joint stock companies were the feature of the day; canals, bridges, and life assurance being great favourites, which, if injurious to the speculator, were beneficial to the country. To this period London owes Waterloo and Vauxhall bridges, with many more of those public works forming to the foreigner objects of so much interest.[6]

Despite the equilibrium in some areas, Landes' *The Wealth and Poverty of Nations* infers how regulation in its basic form added to the costs on enterprise and risk taking. The role of government in bubbles is a recurring theme, which demonstrates the consequences of intervention in the markets.

In the nineteenth century, when things got costlier and risks greater, the most effective device for mobilising capital was the chartered joint-stock company with limited liability – chartered because limited liability could be conferred only by the crown or Parliament. These large, semi-public enterprises never made much use of long-term bank financing, because no bank was big enough. The Charter of the Bank of England provided that no other bank could have more than six partners. Not until 1826, and then only outside a sixty-mile radius from London, were non-note-issuing joint-stock banks permitted; and only in 1833 were non-note-issuing joint-stock banks permitted in that radius. Yet these new banks were little different in size and policy from their private counterparts, even the railway builders didn't need their help.[7]

The 1820s and 1830s are notable for the increased trade in foreign loans and stocks. The interest surrounding this expansion attracted investors keen to take advantage of quick gains, which were believed to be relatively low risk. Goods were exported to South America without full recognition of whether or not the markets could absorb them, leading to a flight of speculative investment.

By May, 1835, the market became overloaded; all were sellers; the price dropped; and on the 21st the panic commenced. Spanish stock fell at once sixteen per cent; the scrip went to three discount; and the lower the price; the more anxious were the holders to sell. Every one grew alarmed; and those who had bought as a permanent investment parted with all their interest. Private gentlemen, who had been tempted to buy, hurried with heavy hearts to their brokers; and the Stock Exchange may be said to have groaned under the burden.[8]

The wide collapse of foreign securities ensued, causing serious and widespread social disruption amongst investors. The dealing rooms at the exchange became animated with disagreements and accusations.

Establishments were reduced, families were ruined, delicately-nurtured women were forced to earn their bread. Death ensued to some from the shock, misery was the lot of others, and frantic confusion once more marked the alleys and the neighbourhood of Capel Court. Consternation reigned paramount, and almost every third man was a defaulter. All foreign securities were without a price, the bankers refused to advance money; the brokers' cheques were first doubted and then rejected; nothing but bank notes would be taken; and, with a desperation that will never be forgotten, the jobbers closed their books, refused to transact any business, and waited the result in almost abject despair.[9]

Railway Manias

Throughout the nineteenth century the railway began to play a crucial role in the development of economies. The American and Canadian railroads produced vast wealth, which did not trickle down evenly to the men who toiled to lay the tracks and build the locomotives.

The early railroad development in the U.S. is really a lesson in technology transfer. The initial innovation of the railroad in England in 1825 was copied by the Americans five years later, but the technology was modified substantially as it was successfully adapted to economic conditions in the U.S.[10]

Vast fortunes were made by the companies in the vanguard of the development, concentrating wealth and power in the hands of the few. The technology used by the Americans in building the tracks and locomotives generated a demand for its products, with related exports reaching as far as Russia.

From 1840 America's usable railway track was longer than that of all of Europe. Nonetheless it remained a predominantly rural society based on farming until well into the twentieth century. New York was the country's largest city, its financial headquarters and its principal port and point of entry from Europe, but it was not yet a world financial centre. America was poised for, but not yet in the throes of, the transport communications revolution based on the steamship, the railways and the telegraph which reached its apogee in the late nineteenth century.[11]

The railway in the United States entered into a rapid phase of development. Due to the vast stretches of distance to be covered, the costs were also astronomical. Initiatives to raise capital were not exempt from dubious practices.

A railroad allowed for an interesting choice between two kinds of larceny – robbery of the customers and robbery of the stockholders. The most spectacular struggle occurred in the late eighteen-sixties between rival practitioners of these two basic arts. At issue was the Erie Railroad, running from the New Jersey side of the Hudson River to Buffalo, in those days a deplorable and often lethal streak of rust. Cornelius Vanderbilt, who controlled the New York Central on the east margin of the river, wanted to own the Erie to ensure his monopoly of the service to Buffalo and potentially to Chicago. Vanderbilt's commitment was to robbing the public. The enduring contribution of his family to spoken literature was the expression, 'The public be damned'.[12]

The railroad business, however, was recognised as a key element in expanding the process of industrialisation outside Britain. In Britain the railway was also important to the changing nature of the economy. The City involvement in the railway boom was crucial but it was not always beneficial.

Then in 1835 came the City's first railway boom, as the number of officially listed companies (twenty-one in July 1835) almost trebled in the next twelve months. 'The whole active interest of the Stock Exchange has lately directed their almost exclusive attention to shares in Railways', noted the *Circular to Bankers* by February 1836.[13]

The production of industry required an efficient transport system to distribute raw materials and deliver finished goods. The first lines of organised passenger transport were encouraged through initiatives such as those demonstrated by Thomas Cook who used the railways to further the cause of temperance in 1841. Morals were being applied to the fallen. The passage below provides a point of reference to the birth of modern tourism.

The excursion took place on 5 July 1841; this was a Monday, perhaps a variety of 'St Monday', the unofficial holy day, or holiday, which workers often awarded themselves. Anyway, in the morning a large body of excursionists, variously numbered at 570 and 485, gathered at Leicester Station…Marshalled by Cook, they climbed on board one second class carriage and nine 'tubs', the open, seatless carriages in which third class passengers travelled during the early days of rail, and set off on the eleven mile journey.[14]

To a large extent, the travel rather than leisure activities of the Victorians were shaped and met by the railway. Whilst the railways had initially be the mode of transport for the rich, offers such as the 'shilling days', and initiatives by agents such as Cook, meant the system gradually began to be accessible to all levels of society.

> Between 1825 and 1935 no fewer than fifty-four Railway Acts were passed. In 1835-7, and again in 1844-6, the floating of companies and the dealing in railway shares, attended by vigorous speculative activity, reached such a state of frenzy as to merit the name of 'Railway Mania'. Capital was raised in hitherto unparalled quantities.[15]

The development of the railways should be viewed in the context of its influence in generating several mini-bubbles, amongst the line operators, suppliers of iron and locomotives and the necessary raw materials. The development of the railway is well served in Henry Grote Lewin's *The Railway Mania and Its Aftermath*, which provides the definitive text on the subject.

> In the 1830s, railway development was buoyed up by another speculative boom...There were few enough rules in the early days of joint-stock companies, and the reputation soared of those who succeeded in turning 'scrip into gold', such as George Hudson, 'the Railway King' who controlled a third of the system by 1845. Hudson made his attractive profits by paying the dividends of existing lines with capital raised for new branches; when the great mania of the 1840s, which he helped promote, faltered in 1848, he was exposed and fled the country – but not before mileage had risen to over 8,000 and the network had been extended from Aberdeen to Plymouth.[16]

The excitement for speculation was a factor in generating the extensions to the railways, but revenue and return on investment was lower than expected. The realisation that quick profits would not be attained produced fluctuation in shares; a series of boom and bust episodes made the investment rotate in cycles with varying degrees of bubble-like conditions being shaped by confidence and the fickle nature of it.

> The year 1850 provides the low-water mark of the reaction, after which by slow degrees confidence returned, and railway promotion resumed a normal course. With this year, therefore, our consideration or discussion of new railway proposals ceases, except in so far as it may be necessary to allude to them in explanation of point in connection with the lines of the 'mania' period proper. On the other hand, the construction and completion of the lines sanctioned in the years 1845-47 naturally extended over a further period, and overlapped into the next epoch, which may be designated as the 'middle ages' of railway history.[17]

The slump in financial activity in the 1840s began to thaw and interest was revived in a range of sectors, railway stock being considered a valuable investment.

The 1840s saw 'railway mania' sweep across the country. Thousands of ordinary people put their savings into dozens of railway companies. Some lost everything; others made fortunes. By 1851 7,000 miles of track were in use. That year over six million people travelled by train to the Great Exhibition in London. Canal operators went bankrupt or were bought by railway companies. Stagecoaches and turnpikes disappeared, and country roads remained deserted until the arrival of the motor car.[18]

The opportunities were widely recognised, but the risks which were exaggerated by the poor management in the railway companies (a feature that appears to be consistent) were numerous.

In 1844 the Stock Exchange for the first time found in the railways a medium for active speculation, and their possibilities attracted the imagination of the public. Thus the older companies were disagreeably roused from their position of security by finding themselves threatened on all hands by new schemes for railways in their neighbourhood. To protect their own interests, therefore, their only course lay in supporting such proposals as could be turned into feeders of their own established lines, and in promoting rival schemes in the case of those whose effect was bound to be inimical.[19]

The large sums that had been raised were widely publicised creating a rush to be part of the speculative adventure. The attraction of the investment coupled with the development in management of steam and the improvements in locomotive technology created the impression of radical transformation that would continue to expand indefinitely. It was this feature that triggered the frenzy, an event widely noted for its importance, which can be discerned in previous and subsequent bubbles.

In the early 1860s much British capital was sunk in railways and shipping at home, but above all this period is remembered by the excessive and unwise promotion of joint-stock companies which followed the recent Company Acts. A fever of speculation seemed to have seized the business community, and large commitments were recklessly undertaken in the hope of sharing in easy profits which the principle limited liability seemed to promise. The crash came in 1866, when the largest discount houses, Overend, Gurney and Co., formerly reputed to be as safe as the Bank of England, but lately imperilled by much speculative lending, collapsed with uncovered liabilities of £5 million, dragging many smaller firms down with it.[20]

The railways continued to expand, and with this expansion grew the concern that existing speculative shares were already in a mini-bubble with shares issued in the previous autumn gradually waning in demand.

The year 1846 may be said to mark the culminating point of the remarkable occurrence commonly known as the 'Railway Mania'. In it 270 Railway Bills received the Royal Assent, authorising the construction of 4,540 miles of new railway, and the raising of new capital to the amount of £95,625,943, with borrowing powers for an additional £36,087,272.[21]

The extensive social impact of the railways in Britain is captured in the famous book *Middlemarch*, by George Eliot which subtly reveals the impact of industrialisation on provincial towns and villages. Whilst the impact of the railways continued well into the twentieth century, the investment opportunities were limited to particular offerings that caught the imaginations of specialists. On 1 January 1948 the railways of Britain would be unified. Fifty years later, the mini-boom in privatisation would collapse in the form of Railtrack.

Foreign Loans Revisited: Expanding Bubbles

Continued recklessness in the investment market was perpetuated by the waves of opportunity resulting from the various developments of the period. To meet the demand in foreign loans, the new dealing room in the Stock Exchange reflected the interest in evolving markets and foreign securities, which appeared throughout the world, not without criticism, in 1823.

The interest in foreign loans had re-ignited at the beginning of the century. Accessing information, particularly from abroad, remained a laborious process. Names like Barings and Rothschild, however, would become synonymous with City institutions, wielding excessive financial and political power. Investors, entrepreneurs and innovators realised that the improvements in transport and communications would allow the exploration of commodities and trade to advance to a degree not possible during the Mississippi Bubble. Options, where a speculator would pay an agreed sum for the right to buy or to sell a stock at a certain price on a given date in the future, added to the excitement and controversy.

Barings led the way and raised its name to new heights in 1817 by successfully bringing out three issues for the indemnity-laden French Government that raised a total of 315m francs (over £12m)...In 1818 another French loan was less successful but Barings had made the point. That same year Nathan Rothschild began the fight back, issuing a £5m loan to the Prussian Government.[22]

The theory that investors were continuing to seek profit and interest is well typified by the move into foreign loans. In the nineteenth century, many objected to investment abroad, claiming it was unpatriotic.[23] The demand for foreign investments, however, led to arguments between agents and customers, haggling over high prices, and confusion in regards to applications.

In 1822 came the year of the foreign loan. Nathan Rothschild established his dominance in this market by floating sizable loans for Prussia, Russia (traditional Barings country) and the Neapolitan Government, and above all there was widespread enthusiasm for making loans to the newly liberated countries of Latin America. Emissaries from Colombia, Chile and Peru all came to London, all were greeted warmly by merchants-turned-contractors who knew a handsome margin when they saw one, and all were ruthlessly exploited.[24]

The activity in foreign loans continued apace, encouraging calls for reform in trading conditions. New dealings were opened, but the institutional structure continued to demonstrate weaknesses. The problems and high prices led to a lull in trading, but by 1824 the animation was re-started with South America being particularly notable. The fall came a year later when the speculation took on the guise of a mania.[25]

The collapse of the absurdly overblown boom in foreign loans and company promotions, speculative overtrading in imported commodities, rashness on the part of the country banks, Bank of England policy that veered between complacency and an over-sharp contraction of credit – all these things, in hotly debated proportions, played a part.[26]

The bubble in foreign loans that had been noted in the first half of the nineteenth century surfaced again at various intervals throughout the century. In the early 1870s new opportunities were again noted in international investments.

The period ended in the 'boom' of 1870-4, marked by much investment in heavy industry at home, railways in America and Government loans for various purposes in Europe and the Near East. Germany and the United States, the rising industrial giants, enjoying the heady wine of their post-war 'foundation years', experienced a crash in 1873; in England where expansion had been greatest in the heavy industry working to longer contracts, the decline set in only in 1874-5.[27]

The nineteenth century would not be the end of speculative adventures on a grand scale. New opportunities were opening up and investors again sought gain from speculation. Investment flowed into new opportunities. Fortunes were won and lost, and the speculative mania continued to engross investors, who quickly forgot losses and celebrated gains. With each speculative wave, new methods of trading were invented, institutions improved structures, and rules, with varying degrees of effectiveness, entered the fray to gradually attempt to introduce order to limit the chaos.

Twentieth-Century Bubbles

The waves of bubbles that expanded throughout the world were driven by the changing nature of physical transport and communications. World War I resulted in the wider accessibility of the motor car, a period recognised as industrial Fordism, which fundamentally altered the nature of communities. Whilst in 1919, Thomas Cook became the first travel agent to offer trips by air, it would not be until after the end of World War II that air travel would be accessible to mass tourism and business travel.[28]

The telegraph, radio, television, telecommunications and the Internet ushered in a social revolution that continues with on-going innovation in a range of related areas. Although not an exhaustive inclusion, the manias presented below are considered within this context.

Real Estate Bubble and the 1929 Crash

The great depression in America in the 1920s was the result of a double-bubble scenario. The first and minor bubble, which eventually led to the great crash of 1929, was the Florida Real Estate Bubble.

> One of the most remarkable features of the post-war economic expansion was the boom in real estate investment and building construction. The conditions in America were almost the exact opposite of those prevailing in Britain, for rents remained for some years at a high level, building costs were low, and credit was abundant...Development in some of the states, such as California and Florida, had all the characteristics of a mania. The population of Miami soared from 30,000 in 1920 to 75,000 in 1925. Swollen advertisement columns enabled the Miami Daily News one day in the summer of 1925 to print an issue of 504 pages, the largest newspaper in history. Older established cities like Chicago and New York acquired new skylines.[29]

The trigger for the burst of speculation was the purchase of land in Florida by farmers wanting to get away to a warmer climate during the winter months.[30] Soon New York bankers followed suit, also wanting land with a warmer climate. The situation was exaggerated by the option to purchase land with a mortgage, buyers only having to put down a 10% deposit. This financial mechanism added to the demand by increasing the circle of investors and their ability to purchase and speculate on land prices.

Interest in Florida real estate grew rapidly, and large areas of swampland were soon exchanging hands for $1000 per acre. The demand was so great that dirt was brought in to fill swamps, in order to sell more land.

The Florida boom contained all of the elements of the classic speculative bubble. There was the indispensable element of substance. Florida had a better winter climate than New York, Chicago, or Minneapolis. Higher incomes and better transportation were making it increasingly accessible to the frost-bound North. The time indeed was coming when the annual flight to the South would be as regular and impressive as the migrations of the Canada Goose.[31]

The peak of the bubble saw one-third of the population of Miami working in real estate, and competition amongst the rich to own the biggest estates. Status was an important consideration, particularly to the emerging 'middle class' who were happy to promote and realise the benefits of increasing affluence.

The bursting of the Florida Real Estate Bubble was an 'act of God' arriving in the form of a hurricane, which destroyed properties and added to the flight in the supply of new buyers. Throughout 1925 and 1926 prices began to fall, although unevenly at first, depending on the location. The link between the Florida Bubble and the subsequent stock market crash was the switch by middle class America from investment in property to the stock market, a move surprising in its optimism and volume.

It is widely understood that things had gone to pieces in Florida. While the number of speculators was certainly small compared with the subsequent participation in the stock market, nearly every community contained a man who was known to have taken 'quite a beating' in Florida. For a century after the collapse of the South Sea Bubble, Englishmen regarded the most reputable joint stock companies with some suspicion. Even as the Florida boom collapsed, the faith of Americans in quick, effortless enrichment in the stock market was becoming everyday more evident.[32]

The search for a get rich investment is recognised as an American trait, the so-called 'American Dream'. It must, however, be viewed in the context of wide opportunity and the advanced development of marketing, which accompanied numerous investments. This is particularly notable in the development of radio and television, and the related waves of consumer booms.

The Wireless Bubble

The Wireless Bubble comes before the dotcom bubble by almost 80 years, but it is similar to it. The role of new technologies, particularly stocks related to communications, attracted investors keen to realise the hype and substance associated with new developments in the area. Interestingly and anecdotally the term WWW was also used, by RCA (Radio Corporation of America), to describe the technology involved in this bubble of the 1920s. By March 1928,

> Radio, in many respects the speculative symbol of the time, gained 18 points. On the following day it opened 22 points above the previous close. Then it lost 20 points while the behaviour of the trading in the stock was being investigated by the Exchange, gained 15 points and fell off by 9. A few days later, on a strong market, it made another 18-point gain.[33]

In the 1920s, WWW was recognised as World Wide Wireless (very weird in a contemporary setting). Kirkland's impressive account of the visionary developments in American economic life includes the passage below, which is interesting beyond its historical record in the contemporary light of video-text mobiles (clearly, the innovation can be reapplied and interpreted in the twenty-first century).

> Meanwhile the electrical industry had returned to its first triumph, communication. Scientists in the late nineteenth century had decided that many forces moved in waves. If these could be actuated, amplified and controlled, telegraphing and telephoning could dispense with wires, and messages, perhaps even images, could be sent through the air...One of the first to apply these principles was Guglielmo Marconi, an Irish Italian who patented in Great Britain the wireless telegraph. By 1902 he was to send a full message across the Atlantic.[34]

The communications industry developed rapidly through the early part of the century. Early on its effects both in terms of speculation and social consequences were recognised.

Regular wireless telephone services between London and New York came somewhat later, for the application of myriad varieties of tubes and of their surrogate, the transistor, to radio broadcasting, television and computers was the accomplishment of the war and interwar periods. Forthwith electronics opened doors, detected submarines, and carried presidential fireside chats to the voters. Thus automation and the mass media jeopardized the values placed upon work and reading by centuries of civilisation.[35]

The full expansion of the bubble began after World War I (concomitantly to the Florida Bubble), when both the US and UK economies were again rebuilding. Wireless technology came out of military innovation and spread to the commercial sector. It was evident that the technology held possibilities, but these were originally seen as lying in point to point communications – the same market as wired telegraph messages. In the UK, the introduction of the telegraph service began with difficulties and losses:

> In 1899-1900 the expenditure on the telegraph service was £3,504,837; the receipts £3,350,000, – but the real annual loss on the service [The Post Office] is estimated at close on a million...In 1907-1908 eight stations for the transmission of messages by wireless telegraphy on Marconi's system were acquired by the post office. In that year 3266 radio-telegrams were sent out to ships, and 27,727 inward messages were received.[36]

It soon transpired that a better use for the technology was a few-to-many service – ideal for broadcasting. With this knowledge broadcasting companies attempted to transmit anything which they believed would interest the public enough for them to purchase the receivers that manufacturers were producing. The manufacturers were making money from the sale of receivers, but much like dotcoms, people could not think how to make profits from broadcasting itself. Numerous companies went under whilst trying to solve this problem, leaving investors cautious.

Eventually the answer was found. Exactly as dotcom entrepreneurs would discover, the way to make money was through national advertising (as done by independent radio stations) or by charging for the service (like the British Broadcasting Corporation).

Although there is no clear peak to the Wireless Bubble, which may be as a result of the emerging 1929 bubble that no doubt affected the rise and fall of share prices for broadcasting companies, it is clear that the bubble grew. Certain factors can be discerned, such as the trigger event (new technology), speculation, failure of major institutions (broadcasting companies), and base-building in recovery. In addition, two new factors emerge. Firstly, the fact that the companies had no clear method of making money is seen in this bubble as well as in the previous study of the South Sea Bubble and, in the next chapter, the Dotcom Bubble. Secondly, the recovery of the industry as a whole, which has not been seen in the other historical bubbles is studied (this may be a new phenomenon of increased bubble activity). This demonstrates that there is always the possibility of a new bubble emerging in the same field but in a different investment environment.[37]

There is always a trigger event in bubbles. At the time of writing in 2003/4, the reliance on the Internet as a key form of accessing information and exchanging communications through email is producing a range of opportunities. The developments in nanotechnology (micro technology), gains in efficiency and emerging and unforeseen developments relating to e-business and e-commerce could reinvigorate the dotcom mania albeit in a different form from its predecessor.

Wall Street Bubbles and International Political Economy

In the early part of the twentieth century the economic climate in America as a whole could not have been better. Business was booming, and as a result the same 10% down credit available for mortgages was also offered for the purchase of stocks.

From 1926 to 1929 prices rose, and speculative buying was prevalent. A variety of new financial innovations emerged with national banks setting up security affiliates to deal with large investments. For smaller investors the number of investment trusts grew from 40 to 770 in eight years.

> In Wall Street in the later 1920s, where speculation in stocks reached a degree of intensity and subtlety and an extent of public participation probably not matched anywhere before or since, it is doubtful that it occurred to any of the speculators that they were recapitulating the movement patterns of their subhuman ancestors swinging from tree to tree. Nor did this occur to the explainers and defenders of speculative activity, led by the authorities of the New York Stock Exchange, emphasized as lyrically as their gifts would allow the creative, human, even almost superhuman accomplishments of speculation and speculators...The critics of unrestrained speculation, whose voices were relatively few and muted in the age when the business of America was business, questioned the argument's factual basis, insisting that actually speculation had played only a minor role in the growth of American enterprise. But they went further and questioned its morality.[38]

A year before the crash the commodity price level had begun to fall. The sign that highlighted the risk was the collapse of a major financial empire, Clarence Hatry. When the Federal Reserve Board issued a warning about speculative credit on 7 February 1929, people began to listen and share prices started to fall. Whilst the financial institutions tried to limit a fall in the value of assets, it was an impossible investment atmosphere; people and the business community feared prices could only fall.

> The prevailing political economy allowed the world's central bankers to try to help by lowering interest rates quickly once the Wall Street bubble had burst, but this did little good when every other circumstance was persuading the world's capitalists to cut lending to countries whose prices and incomes had been geared to a continuing inflow of capital.[39]

The spiral of the mini-bubble bursts within the bubble as a whole can perpetuate a recession, but it is conditional on a range of factors and influences.

> The ending of that boom in the 'Wall Street crash' of October 1929 and the further reduction in American lending then instigated a chain reaction which appeared uncontrollable: the lack of ready credit reduced both investment and consumption; depressed demand among the industrialised countries hurt producers of foodstuffs and raw materials, who responded by desperately increasing supply and then witnessing the near total collapse of prices – making it impossible for them in turn to purchase manufacturing goods. Deflation, going off gold and devaluing the currency, restrictive measures on commerce and capital, and defaults on international debts were the various expedients of the day; each one dealt a further blow to the global system of trade and credit.[40]

The wider economy began to stagger from the uncertainty of the looming recession. Production faltered, although initially not alarmingly, and unemployment began to rise. The concern over the length and depth of the recession had an impact on Wall Street, which began to falter. There were still pockets of bullish behaviour determined to avoid or at least suspend the full descent of prices.

The atmosphere of concern hit confidence. Galbraith, in his classic study of the period, observed the downturn. The collapse of the enterprises of Clarence Hatry in England, the general fear regarding split stocks, and the recognised speculative fever peaking, created a rapid slide that involved large numbers of private investors.

Fraudulent activity had been embedded in the bubble (a recurrent theme notable in the South Sea Bubble and the Railway Mania). Bank officials had been stealing money from depositors to play the market.

By 24 October 1929, with the selling flood underway, one Michigan bank was down $2 million, which had risen to $3.6 million just one week later. It became clear that the money could not be repaid.

In the passage below, which can be noted in some of the similar responses to the problems at Enron, WorldCom, and the auditors Arthur Andersen (an almost timeless feature), the crash of the bubble in 1929 exposed the operation of malfeasance in investment bubbles.

> Just as the boom accelerated the rate of growth, so the crash enormously advanced the rate of discovery. Within a few days, something close to universal trust turned into something akin to universal suspicion. Audits were ordered. Strained or preoccupied behaviour was noticed. Most important the collapse in stock values made irredeemable the position of the employee who had embezzled to play the market. He now confessed [the numerous employees who had played the markets through diverting funds illegally].[41]

Although the banks and politicians intervened at this stage to try to stabilise prices, it was too late. In the liberal America, government intervention in the markets occurs through subtle means, but the effects are similar to other forms of government interference.

Everyone wanted to sell, and with no one willing to buy brokers found themselves with unsold orders at the close of trading.

The crash left America in a depression from which it did not directly recover for more than ten years, a factor that contributed to international political and economic instability (the psychological impact of the crash continues to haunt investors. The event is used as a measure against major falls that follow, but it does not prevent them).

The links between investment, politics and economics are explicit in the Wall Street Crash. Like previous bubbles, a series of interventions and events from a range agents and sites led to a precarious investment environment.

Panic, when it arrived, spread rapidly. The consequences of the falls in the markets produced an atmosphere of alarm, where ripples of discontent flowed within economies and between states.

> When in the 1930s the market economy failed to prevent the growth of mass unemployment in the industrial countries, and the ruin of peasant proprietors in the West's industrial hinterland, liberalism came under fire from Right and Left alike. By a curious coincidence the 1913-19 period was neatly bisected by the great Wall Street crash of October 1929 which ushered in a decade of economic depression and political crisis.[42]

The key stages of the demise of the American Bubble are listed below:

Phase	Description	Added feature	Description
1	Florida Real Estate	1	Wider stock market interest
2	10% down option	2	Investment trusts
3	Inflation in asset prices	3	Irrational investment
4	Overtrading and speculation	4	Inadequate regulation
5	Gullible public joins in	5	Leverage increases
6	Commodity price levels fall	6	Depositors' money used
7	The selling flood begins	7	Clarence Hatry collapses
8	Too many stocks to sell	8	Inconsistent patterns
9	The Great Depression	9	Massive losses
10	9 years on recovery begins	10	Base-building

Figure 6.1

The fundamental difference seen in this bubble, highlighted by Galbraith, was the extended inflation and burst of the bubble over time. In previous bubble scenarios the two factors occurred rapidly, but as the 1929 crash had been building for almost ten years, the repercussions also took longer to emerge and resolve.

The material in this chapter goes on to assess the influence of bubbles largely arising in the United States and the consequences of them on the international political economy.

Studying historical bubbles and applying Cohen's model to them has shown that some stages are more relevant than others. In addition common factors seemingly lacking in the literature include:

- A lack of investment vehicles offering returns equal to those promised/suggested by the bubble stocks leads to mass investment in the bubble
- Confidence of companies attracts investors
- Over valuations
- Unjustifiable stock prices
- The presence of 'virgin' investors as well as the 'gullible public'
- Build-up time is proportional to time of after effects

Highlighting these new factors demonstrates the benefits of using history as a basis for exploring theories of bubble activity. In order to assess the relevance of these new points, as well as the stages highlighted in the literature, the material will turn to contemporary bubbles, which occur in greater frequency and volume.

Boom and Bust: The Bubble Scenario

The material above has demonstrated how several bubbles can occur independently and overlap to produce a rapid rise and collapse in speculative activity. The explosion of mini-bubbles is continued in the next chapter, which identifies the stages in the TMT (technology, media and telecommunications) bubbles. This will be considered in the context that recurring waves of bubbles exist. The passages above have indicated that bubbles contain trends and countertrends, a condition related to the short-term reality of asymmetric information.

The boom and bust scenarios, which may contain bubble activity, may have detrimental effects on economic policy and growth. It is not a guaranteed relationship. The removal of fluctuations in a range of markets, could however curtail investment opportunities to the degree that international liquidity and economic growth is impaired.

Notes

[1] Morgan (1984) p.367.

[2] Watney (1998) p.24.

[3] See S. B. Saul's, *The Myth of the Great Depression 1873-1896* for a superb guide in problematising economic and financial history. The quote itself can be found on pp 53-54.

[4] Hobsbawn (1975) pp 62-63.

[5] Fischer (1996) p.158.

[6] Francis, J. (2001) p.73.

[7] Landes (1998) p.257.

[8] Francis, J. (2001) p.116.

[9] *Ibid*, 117.

[10] Poulson (1981) p. 280.

[11] Jay (2000) p.215.

[12] Galbraith (1977) p.49.

[13] Kynaston (1994) p.102.

[14] Brendon (1991) p. 6.

[15] Thomas (1957) p.293.

[16] Morgan (1984) pp 452-454.

[17] Lewin (1936) p. xvii.

[18] *Op cit*, Watney, p. 23.

[19] Lewin (1968) p. 4.

[20] Thomas (1957) p .438.

[21] Ibid, p.480.

[22] *Op cit* , Kynaston, p. 45.

[23] The *Commercial Chronicle* being a particularly vocal critic of the unpatriotic nature of foreign loans.

[24] *Op cit*, Kynaston, p. 50.

[25] Tulipomania returns in the cloak of foreign loans.

[26] *Op cit*, Kynaston, p. 65.

[27] *Op cit*, Thomas, p.440.

[28] See the excellent anthology of air journeys by Ludovic Kennedy, which captures the full excitement of the emergence of commercial air travel.

[29] Bagwell, P. and Mingay, G. (1970) *Britain and America 1850-1939*, p.258.

[30] The waves of property speculation continue with rich Jewish New Yorkers about to retire.

[31] Galbraith (1992 [1954]) p.32.

[32] *Ibid*, p.35.

[33] *Op cit* (1992 [1954]) p.40.

[34] Kirkland, E. (1969) *A History of American Economic Life*, p.307.

[35] *Ibid*, p.307.

[36] Porter, G. (1912) *Progress of a Nation*, p.564.

[37] For example in the wireless world of the early twentieth-first century technology, such as the WiFi or 802.11b represent an easy and relatively painless way to hook up to the web, download emails or access a corporate intranet. Taylor, P. (2002) 'Unplugged and fully connected', p.16.

[38] Brooks (1969) p.80.

[39] Sayers (1967) p.53.

[40] Kennedy (1989) p. 364.

[41] *Op cit*, Galbraith, p.153.

[42] Lichtheim (1972) p.145.

Chapter 7

Electronic Bubbles:
Dotcoms and Telecoms

Introduction

Having considered a number of historical bubbles in previous sections, this chapter turns to the waves of technology, telecommunications and media bubbles that appeared throughout the 1990s in the advanced post-industrialised countries of America, Europe and Japan, and to a lesser extent emerging economies. In the vanguard were companies such as Cisco, Qualcomm, Nokia and Yahoo which attracted, thrilled and frustrated numerous investors. Other mini-bubbles appeared and took flight. The chapter recognises the overlap of the bubbles featured below, but attempts to separate each e-boom, where opportunities exist. It is posited at the outset that the Dotcom Bubble and the fortunes of the telecommunications industry are indelibly linked; both were, in effect, riding off each other.

The boom in technology stocks has been mentioned earlier in the book, but the material set out below covers the investment bubbles that resulted in a return to the speculative adventures set out in the previous chapters. It is argued from the outset that the technology revolution had similarities to the South Sea Bubble, with initial substance being recognised before a chaotic rise in new companies produced an unsustainable market. In both cases the role played by government is important. It differed from the Railway Mania of the nineteenth century,[1] but shared similarities in the manner in which dotcoms appeared to spontaneously captivate investors.

It is has been noted that puzzles are commonly associated with steep asset rises, which can compound predicted outcomes. When considering tech stocks it should be kept in mind that equities were generally overvalued in the 1990s. The good times and the bad times tend to be exaggerated by 'the markets'. Whilst key factors can be discerned through observation of asset prices, the mechanism that initially alters the direction of an investment is less conducive to study. The trigger event that leads to a swelling or implosion of the bubble may not be a direct intervention, but a series of subtle actions and reactions that produces a timed change at a certain point, not necessarily immediately. It is at this point that reference to linear models becomes problematic; the higher movements are not underpinned by technical forecasts or asset management. On the contrary, swelling is fuelled by emotion, which is fickle and high risk. Whilst technical trading is an important activity, irrational price signals at the peak of the bubble make outcomes more a work of fiction than analysis.

On the one hand, the recognition of the impact of the decision-making process within institutional investment needs to be noted. On the other hand, an approach that is sensitive to the quirks and accidents that are imbedded in the markets (something can always go wrong or right and not in the way expected or predicted) reveals the limitations of manipulation whilst not lessening its presence.

Markets for e-Bubbles: The Twentieth-Century e-Revolution

The twentieth century had its share of fluctuations. Shares were hit during the 'Great War' only to recover in the early 1920s. The depression throughout industrialised economies led to shares in Britain in 1936 falling, only to pick up in the 1950s.

> The history of world capitalism has been one of dominant powers in relative economic decline being challenged by the growing economic – and, in the past, military – strength of newly emerging powers with growing market shares and ambitions.[2]

Vietnam and Korea disturbed investments, with investors consumed with uncertainty of recurring wars and the escalation of them. The consequences of the events in the Middle East, exaggerated by the counter hegemonic activities of OPEC, coupled with Lyndon Johnson's ambitious economic strategies during difficulties in Vietnam, produced an uncertain investment climate. The subsequent interventions and retreats by Richard Nixon contributed to stagflation and a lengthy bear market in the early 1970s, which damaged international growth. The collapse of Bretton Woods in 1973 marked the end of the postwar boom – the 'Golden Age of Capitalism' – and ushered in two decades of instability.

The problems associated with the oil supply paradoxically inspired a revolution in the management structure, a development that led to the reorganisation of the flow of the production, storage and distribution.

The import of petrodollars to the industrialised world and export of foreign loans to developing countries in the early 1980s produced an unrealistic investment environment. The subsequent rise in interest rates, restrictive monetary policies and a wide lack of caution in the context of lending produced serious structural difficulties, which continue to produce debt burdens to the developing countries in the long term. Western banks were generally able to restructure and reschedule loans without damaging future profits. This period is well documented in the book and TV documentary *A Face Worse than Debt* (1989) by Susan George.

The changes associated with the management and production structure in the 1980s were mirrored by deregulation in the international finance structure. Elsewhere, the introduction of just-in-time, downsizing and computer aided design and computer aided manufacturing (CAD-CAM) technology, altered the structure of labour and the related trade unions, and fundamentally altered the organisation and operation of business.

Within the changing nature of the international business environment the nexus of communication flows produced a rapid acceleration of the new ideas and innovation. The results of creativity and flexibility were prominent in new business models and operations, a shift underpinning the future success of large organisations.

The exponential change in technology and telecommunications that occurred in the industrialised world accelerated economic growth. Technology had been democratised. Knowledge as a commodity gained ascendancy, a development captured in the book *Funky Business*; albeit not as the main topic.

> Technology is not just a matter of nuts and bolts or bits and bytes. It is not a sideshow, but the ultimate in mass participation. It is curious – and a little daunting – to think back just a few decades. In the 1950s, 1960s and 1970s, technology was the domain of the military, rocket scientists, obscure academics and professors working in the R & D departments of pharmaceutical companies. Technology was Nobel laureates, Uri Gagarin, Apollo, missile systems and radar. Then it became commercialized, hijacked by entrepreneurial geeks. Creators of weapons of mass destruction dumbed down (or dumbed up, depending on your prejudices) to become instruments of mass entertainment.[3]

Whilst technological developments and the numerous firms associated with it captured the imagination of entrepreneurs and investors, the markets for its products and services were uneven, but overwhelmingly positive. Markets, however, needed time to mature. The full opportunities associated with the rapid transformation of communications, production and consumption were not immediately understood, producing excitement and ignorance.

The underlying problems associated with technological development were also ironically present during the revolution; innovation became exhausted by an uncertain market. In the article 'Informational overshooting, booms and crashes', in the Journal of Monetary Economics, the limitations of technology driven cycles were made explicit.

> To see the problem, remember the lesson of both history and economic theory – that rapid technological progress eventually leads to a slowdown in profit growth. This can be because the flow of new innovations eventually dries up, or because firms have inflated hopes of what the new technology can do, and therefore over invest in it, or because the new investment leads to a rising demand for labour, which eventually leads to rising wages.[4]

The series of technological developments can be mapped back to the success of satellite communications in 1957, the appearance of the mobile telephone in 1973, the Internet in 1983, innovation in genetic engineering, perhaps most notable with cloning in 1996 and the mapping of DNA.[5] *InternetWeek* in 1999 celebrated the birth of virtual commerce. It was expected that e-commerce and content sites would leverage multiple ASP services to improve the overall value proposition for their sites. Many of these services would be transparent to the user who would be unaware of the real-time virtual partnerships making their experience possible.[6] The appearance of nanotechnology in 2000, which continues to develop, provides a snapshot of an incredibly creative on-going period, which continues to have repercussions in a range of industries and sectors.[7]

> Corporate investors and venture capitalists have doubled their investments in nanotech over the past two years, with $1bn (£640m) flowing into nano projects, according to Josh Wolfe, partner with the Lux Capital Group. Mr Wolfe says that people are as excited about nanotechnology now as they were about the internet back in the early 1990s. And just as new companies slapped a dot.com on their name to take advantage of the internet investment frenzy, so they are starting to add nano to their names to ride this wave.[8]

The interest in new technologies and investment in them were typical of an emerging series of new markets that pulled attention away from traditional companies such as pharmaceuticals, tobacco and manufacturing. The models for presenting a solid business case were momentarily suspended, the bubble had become a frenzy where any idea was given financial support.

Many analysts tend to believe that the October 1987 stock exchange crisis as well as the Dotcom Bubble and its nirvana in 2000 were due to the irrationality of the agents involved. This is not necessarily the case, as explained by André Orlean, leading researcher and specialist of financial matters. In his view, the very nature of the speculative game leads investors to speculate with more concern for the majority's opinion than for objective values.[9] The idea that following the majority as an investment strategy has been considered in an earlier chapter, its importance here sheds light on the series of mini-bubbles. It is clear that waves, exaggerated by intricate patterns, attract private investor sentiment and media interest. The corresponding investment produces a series of small bubbles, which are not conducive to simplistic interpretation.

> Herd behaviour is not necessarily the blind following of others. Indeed, investors must take account of the opinions of others because no one person can research everything individually. A fundamental difficulty that all investors face, then, is how to judge the source of opinions that others have about the outlook for investments. We would like to pool the information that the others used to arrive at their opinions, but we cannot know where they received their information. In certain circumstances, we may assume that more information underlies their pronouncements than actually exists. This problem affects even our interpretation of stories presented in the media.[10]

The cycle and trends relating to the greater numbers of investors joining the investment in dotcoms and telecoms was imbued with the innovative energy, which contributed to the widening of the bubble. In an incisive article in the *Investor Chronicle*, the author considered the book, *The Gorilla Game*, in assessing the fortunes of internet shares. The piece explained how to look at technology stocks during the period, and made clear how technology may or may not change established markets – the outcome being dependent on a range of variables.

> Described how some new technologies – such as Apple Macintosh's graphic innovations – are simply absorbed by the established players. The technologies do not transform their markets. 'But at other times, the technology leaps out of its niche market and into the mainstream. It becomes a mass market phenomenon the PCs, local area networks, laser printers, relational databases, cell phone voice mail and electronic mail all have since 1985.'[11]

The mechanical and physical world caricatured in Charlie Chaplin's *The Modern Age* had been overtaken by virtual capital. Commodities in the form of intellectual capital and knowledge-related products and services continue to maintain importance and interest.[12] The icon and media driven world embraces the Electronic Bubble, which influences the flow of information at all levels.

The New Economy: Another Boom, Another Bust

The canvas on which the stock market boom of 1982-2000 occurred runs parallel with the emergence of the new economy, a selective belief in free markets shaped by the ideas emerging from the new right and Washington Consensus. The selective freeing of markets in the Western world through the dismantling of the trade barriers and commercial obstacles produced an animated business environment in search of new possibilities in a range of diverse markets. States, firms and markets shared similar objectives and policy in a market-driven landscape. The new realities of the markets and the changing relationship with holding debt widened speculative activity amongst private investors, a development that would produce a series of mini-bubbles.

The move towards the new economy can be tentatively mapped back to the emergence of the new right in the form of Reaganomics, a series of economic policies supportive of The Chicago School of Economics. On the other side of the Atlantic, the economic policies of Margaret Thatcher's government from October 1979 onwards removed the remaining controls on foreign exchange. The paradigmatic shift in economic policy ushered in the explicit end of the wavering interest in socialism and Keynesian influenced economic policy albeit explicitly. The change was dominant but not total of course; many countries in the 1980s had socialist governments, France for example.

In the world economy, foreign exchange rates created significant economic and political tensions within and between nations. Politics, economics and investment are related through a nexus of triggers, events and relationships. Whilst the overlaps can be unravelled, anomalies remain, which introduce the factor that curtails sustained manipulation. Interest rates are related to fluctuations in the economy, and trends in interest rates are related to trends in inflation rates. Unstable exchange rates forced governments, willingly and reluctantly, to produce economic policies that were sensitive to the links between the domestic and international economy. Throughout this period major events impacted on the markets, but the positive trend continued up to the very late 1990s.

The internationalisation and interdependence of financial markets accelerated the need to widen reform: restrictions increasingly appeared archaic. For example, the structure and ownership of firms did not reflect the demand for holdings, and new methods to regulate the emerging and vast range of financial products needed to be introduced. In Britain the changes were introduced in October 1986, under the banner of *Big Bang*, a move that coincided with the global market for finance.

Almost one year later in October 1987, the global financial crisis consumed the markets and temporarily downgraded the positive economic assessment. The fall was triggered across the Atlantic by the loss of confidence in the economic policies of the US Government, which had spread panic to the markets. Its inability to redress the significant problems associated with the Federal Budget Deficit damaged confidence. Whilst the concerns spread throughout the markets, a sustained crisis did not materialise, and markets resumed their upward trend.

The need to limit negative contagion and the potentially destructive speculation led to increasing co-operation and harmonisation in the financial strategies between states. The ERM provided, for example, a structure for the integration of economies.

Black Wednesday in 1992, however, illustrated to governments their limitations in manipulating the macroeconomic environment. In the wake of an international speculative avalanche, heavy selling of the British pound on the money markets prompted the raising of the base rate twice on 16 September to 15%. When this failed to preserve the value of sterling relative to the Deutschmark, the Chancellor of the Exchequer Norman Lamont withdrew Britain from the exchange rate mechanism and effectively devalued the pound.

In an interesting development across the Atlantic, the Federal Reserve was hard at work increasing the money supply; the excess money filtering through the banking system being redirected to stocks, pushing up share prices and increasing price earning ratios.

The flow of money to the markets through the central banks swelled the economy, producing an income surplus which was increasingly directed to the markets through private investment and indirectly through the various pensions, mortgage and investment funds operated by the financial sector.

From October 1998 to March 2000, NASDAQ was the proud beneficiary of two of history's biggest bubbles. First came the collapse of Long-Term Capital Management, a hedge fund backed by some of the biggest names around, including two Nobelists in economy, a failure that so terrified Greenspan that he went on a bubble binge. Then came the Y2K scare. There was only a brief gap between those sustained infusions of liquidity, so NASDAQ's P/E ratio rose, more or less continuously, from the 80 range to 351 in the course of the index's run from 1,425 to 5,000. Along the way, thousands of corporations came to believe that the NASDAQ-based creatures of the New Economy would put them out of business if they didn't buy gazillions of dollars' worth of tech gear. During this bubble, the U.S., and much of the industrial world had one of the biggest capital-spending booms of all time.[13]

The inflated asset prices listed on various stock exchanges continued to inflate in the first few months of the twenty-first century. The increasing concern over bloated equities, however, continued to raise the alarms throughout the markets. The telecom sector appeared exposed from the high debts incurred in the acquisition of the 3G licences.

The view that the surge in technology stocks was unsustainable produced a gradual shift in investor preferences. Markets and indexes began to rupture with investment seeking new opportunities in less swelled markets.

Globalisation: Electronics Empires and *Manufacturing Consent*

The contested term 'globalisation' has become a recognised factor in business literature and practice. The work by Kenichi Ohmae reflected the shift in models that reflected the global business environment and the end of the nation state (perhaps prematurely). Whilst few products actually adhere to a rigid global model, the shift to a global business platform was part of the strategic goals of some multinational companies, Motorola for example. Although concern is noted in weak markets where no presence may be more beneficial to the operations of the organisation, it was felt desirable to be in all markets to limit the learning curves of competitors. It is notable that the widening arena for business is evolving from the Western model to incorporate new experiences and perspectives, a condition accelerated by the recognition of global brands and the seemingly ceaseless development of new product and services.[14] The global nature of the military-industrial complex and the ability of firms to obtain lucrative contracts from international institutions to deliver a variety of projects throughout the world are producing a coherent international business and financial structure.

The ironic fortunes of Marconi during the bubble provide a business case study that will be studied in numerous management training programmes. Marconi disposed of its military contracts and GEC (white goods) to focus on the teleology telecoms markets. When the general stock market fell and the telecoms were straggled with huge debts from the licences, Marconi lost its tech related markets and its shares plummeted. The shift away from the military-industrial complex by Marconi is perhaps one of the biggest mistakes in business history. In the post-electronic boom environment:

> The centre of gravity of defence manufacturing has shifted decisively back into the civilian sector, as well. Large contractors still assemble the guidance system

and explosive in a smart bomb and the complex mix of steel and silicon that makes up a Nimitz-class aircraft carrier. But the components that account for much of the cost and all of the astounding precision and agility of the new weapons – powerful chips, together with countless layers of software that make them function – are manufactured by the same companies that build microprocessors for PCs and amplifiers for cell phones.[15]

The dominance of Silicon Valley, which introduced incredible change with it in actual markets, produced a 'mind set' that generated developments in the new economy. The numerous innovations and firms related to the 'silicon valley' idea, continues to impact on the possibilities for technology and investment (from Pixar to the numerous nano-inspired innovations). Whilst new innovation is hampered by a lack of investment, positive signs are beginning to emerge.

In the 1990s, the financial structure became operational on a global platform. Investors and firms had the ability to trade in various time frames and markets. Investment was the inspired medium of exchange, entering and leaving investments and markets in hyper time frames, producing an integrating exchange network operational on a global scale.

> For instance, most foreign exchange transactions today take place through a round-the-world, round-the-clock market that connects the dealing rooms of London, New York, Tokyo, Zürich, Frankfurt, Hong Kong, Singapore, Paris and Sydney…It is clear, even without delving into the often obscure technical details of financial markets, that much of today's foreign exchange, banking, securities, derivatives and insurance business occurs with considerable delinkage from territorial space.[16]

The revolution in information technology, integrated communications and the explosion of programmes and products, heralded the arrival of the electronic revolution and reinforced the global trends operational in a variety of domains. The developments should not be separated from the wider bubble, each stage is crucial to its nature and shape. The growth in opportunities arising from the Internet was carried by the large telecoms, searching in all markets for profits.

When reflecting on the nature of globalisation, it is useful to recognise that the process has been unfolding for centuries, each successive scientific leap making possible the e-boom of the late twentieth century. The process of globalisation occurs in various sites, but it is intrinsically linked to the various e-waves. The central force is related to the heightened awareness and accessibility of information, a flow democratised by relative access. The crowd, therefore, is not necessarily irrational, but buy into waves or bubbles in a considered manner, a development not widely present in historical bubbles active in previous centuries.

Japan: Bubble to Bust

The Japanese bubble economy was powered by the culminate wealth derived from decades of spectacular growth. Its success was driven by productivity, creativity and high performing Japanese technology stocks, a boom that faced numerous difficulties in the 1990s.

The Tokyo Stock Market had performed remarkably well between the years 1982-1989 (the success of the Japanese in innovation, production and labour relations being repeatedly cited in the discipline of international relations as an example of the loss of hegemony in the United States).[17]

In the early 1990s, fears that the miracle in Japan was in trouble led to a flight of investment capital. The bubble in Japan faltered with slips in share prices in 1989. The vast inflation in property, for example, was noted. It was claimed that the grounds of the Imperial Palace in central Tokyo were supposedly worth more than all the real estate in California. The property market collapsed with falls in real estate and commercial property investments, investments which were impaired by bad debts and widespread fraud.

Japan suffered a financial and real estate bust but has warded off an industrial one. The Japanese banks and insurance companies were riddled with bad debt. Tokyo City Bank, the fortieth largest in Japan, and Sanyo Securities, among others, filed for bankruptcy in late 1997. The Japanese Government, pressured by the crisis, had to open up its financial industry.[18]

In response, the Nikkei share index fell sharply and interest rates were raised. Cohen captures the selling flood that burst the spectacular economic miracle which had visited Japan since the early 1980s. Within two years a conspicuous collapse in share trading, ever soggier land and property prices, announcements of poor financial results by key companies, plus never ending tales of major business and political scandals had shaken national pride.[19] The boom in Japan had faltered, the economic miracle flawed by the unending creep of reality.

Japanese television broadcasts transmitted pictures of shocked employees and management, some in tears from the shame of the financial meltdown. The boom had produced bloated real estate expectations, a stock market that had lost sight of realistic company profits, and a banking system that demonstrated severe structural flaws; the bust left behind a weak investment environment and negative to slow growth.

Whilst Japan's economy has continued to struggle with serious structural difficulties, relatively weak growth and output, and zero inflation, the Japanese economy remains important to the global economy. If it had ruptured to the degree to which some reports have claimed, international financial turbulence would be more apparent. The signs of a reversal in the region's economic fortunes are also noticeable in relatively strong fund performance. Whilst structural difficulties remain, many of the problems have been resolved or are being addressed.

The Dotcoms Revolution: On-Line Manias and Discontents

Although widely used, the exact meaning of the term dotcom is unclear. One requirement however is that a dotcom company must have an Internet address (it is, however, debatable if having a www address is enough to be a dotcom, hence some confusion). The dotcom would not exist, were it not for the Internet. The Internet and Internet-related technology stocks appeared in the 1990s and tumbled in 2000 and early 2001. During the rush to capitalise on dotcoms, venture capitalists and entrepreneurs courted each other in frenzied business relationships to push forward new companies towards initial public offerings. In complement, financial institutions offered favourable terms for investment in dotcom start-ups. This led to overvaluations and an expectation that prices would continue to rise indefinitely. The development in dotcoms cannot be studied without recognising the role of the telecoms industry, which was caught out by the high stock market in general and the inflated cost of the 3G licences. In the frenzy of the dotcom market, few were interested in fundamentals and the importance of related industries. The passage below illustrates a familiar pattern:

> in the post-bubble history of the tulip business may lurk some clues on the fate of the dotcoms, many of which have been liquidated, while others have seen their values fall by as much as 90%. After the bubble burst, the trade in bulbs did not disappear. Eventually, bulb growers learnt how to turn a profit again. They converted their business from a seasonal one to one that could produce all year round, something that e-tailers have still to learn. The fact that the business graveyard is overflowing with dotcom corpses tells us less about the future role of the internet in our economic lives than it does about the propensity of some to irrational exuberance.[20]

The vehicle for the heightened profile of the new economy produced dramatic flotation and sharp rises in similar shares; dotcoms entered the mania phase. The relentless additions to the dotcom market attracted new investors keen to take advantage of the electronic gold rush. A flurry of flotation activity such as Lastminute.com generated vast media interest and propelled other initial public offerings into the forefront of speculative interest. The see-saw fortunes that are notable in the evolving business of Lastminute.com illustrate the high risk nature of the investment. On 1 March 2000:

> Online travel shop Lastminute.com has released quarterly results showing a turnover double that of its entire previous year. It has also announced the details of its share offering, valuing the company at up to £350m. However, turnover still only reached £409,000 for the three months to 31 December, with the firm recording an operating loss of £6m over the period. But it claims the numbers of subscribers are rising rapidly – from 25 February the company has 1.1 million subscribers to its service, almost double the amount it had achieved by the end of December. Lastminute.com intends to IPO on the 21 March and looks set to be the latest in the line of high profile UK Internet flotations following Freeserve and QXL.[21]

A few months later, the bullish atmosphere of the dotcom investment had withered; a reality check sent prices tumbling. Time magazine ran the story:

> In the three months since lastminute.com, a two-year-old London-based business-to-consumer website, became a publicly held company, Hoberman has watched his firm's share price soar on a thrust of hype, then take a harrowing plunge when investors around the world began unloading tech stocks. During one four-week stretch Hoberman lost $80 million. And though Hoberman, 31, and his co-founder, 27-year-old Martha Lane Fox, don't control the company's stock price, its freefall has, however unfairly, transformed the pair's public image from the sexy evangelists of Europe's dotcom revolution to fallen angels brought low by too much wealth and success too soon. Though Hoberman and Lane Fox remain irrepressible, the experience at times wears on them. 'It's a little like when you finish finals at university,' Hoberman says. 'People don't realize how much work and strain go into the IPO. You feel as if there can't be any euphoria.'[22]

Three years later, nearing the end of 2003, Lastminute.com are again in the news with strong signals for growth and optimism. The business has improved its operations in line with more traditional business models, improving operations and its customers' awareness of the firm's service and added value.

Lastminute.com, the online booking and travel website, said it will have a positive cash flow earlier than expected. Announcing an increased loss for its third financial quarter, Lastminute said its performance during the past 12 months and the acquisition of French travel website Degriftour in October strengthen the company's position. Lastminute announced a net loss of £9.47m during the three months to 30 September compared with £9.27m in the previous quarter. This brings the net loss to £35.7m for the past 12 months.[23]

The rapid boom in dotcoms highlighted in the above resembled the initial stages of an irrational bubble scenario. The combination of new technology, coupled with the atmosphere of generic change and the wide media interest, established the dotcom as an integral part of seismic change affecting the economic global environment. The numerous chat rooms, bulletin boards, and editors in the various media, added to the excitement, which pushed up prices and made investment a rational choice (it was a natural condition to copy and emulate the apparent success of similar investors).

Whilst Britain and the Scandinavian countries led the Mobile Phone Bubble, the United States was in the vanguard of the Dotcom Bubble. The new economy gathered momentum through the wider use of on-line trade. Features of the new economy and business communications revolution evolved through the mechanism of e-commerce (company to customer relationship networks) and e-business (business2business networks including supply chain management, logistics, collaborative advantage) which generated new opportunities. The passage below illustrates how some firms embraced the Internet from an early stage: an awareness of fundamentals not conclusively being abandoned in the e-explosion.

Although Amazon.com and bn.com captured the headlines (and investor interest), Borders, Inc. on the other hand quietly implemented a strategy to harness the benefits of integration. Compared with the abrupt about-face in the attitudes of many 'clicks and mortar' retailers who were forced to modify their virtual world strategies by the real world needs of their clients, Borders sought from the beginning to benefit from channel synchronization that the new technologies made possible.[24]

Whilst E-bay, Amazon and Lastminute.com have survived the extremely difficult period that followed the e-crash, numerous other operators were not as fortunate. The future outlook for tech stocks is relatively positive: the combination of innovation with sound business practice over the long term to gain substance and creativity being a good investment despite warnings to the contrary.

E-Nightmares: The Dotcom Adventure Collapses

In 2000, the Dotcom Bubble burst, an event captured on the e-screens of the NASDAQ, the stock market commonly associated with tech stocks. The result of wide ownership of shares in the United States damaged individual wealth and growth, producing a salutary view of the opportunities to be gleaned from the wide embracement of an investment and equity culture. Whilst the NASDAQ did include non-tech stocks, it was considered the window of the dotcom boom. *Investment Chronicle* and *Barron's*, the US investment magazine, had been cautiously warning investors of potential falls. Despite the wide recognition that the incessant flood of unique changes driven by ideas, technology and investment, which influenced the new economy paradigm and reinforced the impression that the boom would continue without obstacle, was important, the impression that difficulties lay ahead could not be concealed. Articles, like the passage below, increasingly appeared in the financial press around the winter and spring of 2000.

> So is the Internet leading to economic nirvana – and does the dotcom mania make sense? Not quite. The internet may be transforming business; but it is not rewriting economics to enable the American economy to expand at its current rate without dangerously overheating. Nor does the explosion of e-commerce justify the current high prices of many Internet related shares. On the contrary, all the signs are that the markets remain in the grip of a technology related bubble.[25]

Investors who had piled in money into particular dotcoms were obviously exposed, investors who held a basket of tech stocks had a limited ability to manoeuvre, and investors who held dotcom stock and other non-sector investments were able to readjust portfolios without being caught in the e-freefall. In Britain, tech stocks were hit by a media scandal. In the excitement, the presence of fraud and cheating developed. The well-known English newspaper, the *Daily Mirror* generated controversy in relation to its stock picking section in the financial pages. The column, 'City Slickers' hit the headlines when it appeared reporters were making money from the tips they were promoting. Reporters were accused of ramping stocks by offering tips on shares, which were often exaggerated, buying tips they promoted and cashing in before the prices fell.[26]

On the date of the bust, as with previous bubbles, the fall cloaked countertrends and investment moving against the trend, albeit temporarily. For example, in 2001 the FT UK markets could write:

The dotcom bubble may have burst but the smaller quoted company sector can still look back on a fairly satisfactory year. Both the FTSE SmallCap index and the Hoare Govett Smaller Companies Index outperformed the blue chips of the FTSE 100. Admittedly, it was not a bumper year in absolute return terms – just 5.5 per cent for the SmallCap – but the sector did hang on to the substantial gains achieved in 1999.[27]

Despite some minor evidence to the contrary, the collapse of the Dotcom Bubble left investors with heavy losses. The warnings of impending doom were widespread before the crash. It was clear that the telecoms market was haemorrhaging from huge debts.

Will Hutton, author of the valuable *The State We're In*, reported on the reckless atmosphere of the Dotcom Bubble:

'Legacy' companies that produce water, food, beer and electricity, making more than £3.5 billion between them and employing more than 250,000 people left the elite FT index of Britain's top 100 companies to make way for a clutch of companies, some of which have yet to make any money at all. But the newcomers represent the new economy, high technology and the Internet – and for that investors will pay almost anything.[28]

In Britain again, the collapse of Boo.Com sent serious warnings throughout the markets. In the United States, profit warnings issued by Microsoft and Intel added to the flight of investment from dotcoms. On the one hand, the flight from Internet companies led to a collapse in the rush of investment into initial public offerings. Existing enterprises suffered from the absence of cash flow substance and weakening optimism. The loss in favour of dotcoms to venture capitalists led to a flight of capital resulting in the haemorrhaging of the industry; investment moved into more secure stocks. In a flood of articles in the financial press, the obituaries of dotcoms were listed daily. A report from August 2000 in the weekly journal, *The Economist*, captured the implosion of the bubble.

America has, as ever blazed the trail; as its list of dead dotcoms lengthens, so do the shadows over the best-known of them all, Amazon.com. Over the next few months hundreds of European fledglings are likely to suffer the same fate as boo.com and clickmango.[29]

The fears in America of a substantial crash ushered investors elsewhere in foreign markets to dump tech stocks. In the UK, investors repositioned portfolios and directed investments to established companies that had relatively sound business plans and healthy cash flow records (blue chip companies that introduced technology to cut costs, improve efficiency and

develop new markets were identified and received investment interest –
although markets began their downturn).

> Examples of these 'clicks and mortar' companies (so called because they have
> a foot in both the real and the virtual companies) are the Pru, Pearson and The
> Gap in the UK; and Citigroup and Schwab in the US.[30]

In the United States, the action of the Federal Reserve in increasing
interest rates further damaged investment in Internet-related investments.
The flight from dotcoms became an avalanche with many investors and
dotcom entrepreneurs caught in the selling frenzy.

The subsequent anti-trust action taken against Microsoft signalled
further the problems associated with the loss of power in the industry. The
deflation in the bubble for dotcoms, however, has not resulted in the end of
the Internet and its opportunities. For example in e-retailing, on-line
markets are maturing and improvements are being made to purchasing and
distribution. New systems, intellectual capital and logistic management
need investment, which provides wider investment opportunities and
benefits the economy.

The industry has moved well beyond the requirement just to have a
website address. Business fundamentals and strong on-line management are
improving services and delivery, a development that is returning credibility
to dotcoms and their longevity.

Telecommunications: Who Needs Friends?

The deregulation, liberalisation, mergers, acquisition and foreign direct
investment prevalent throughout the telecommunications industry
generated a rapid boom. In recognition of the developments within the
industry that increased pressure on finite bandwidth, governments in
Western Europe milked the companies of their investment money during
the Dutch auctions for 3G licences. The telecoms industry was caught in
the related frenzy: NTL, Vodaphone and Orange spending billions to obtain
licences, a move that would subsequently stop investment in new
development. The problem also of associated debt (driven in part by the
high costs associated with laying fibre optic cables), in the late 1980s,
resulted in on-going financial difficulties, high mobile penetration rates in
Europe and ushered rapid change throughout the telecom sector and
inflated costs. The relationship between telecoms, dotcoms and government
is made explicit below.

1. Governments demanded extortionate fees for the 3G licences
2. The stock market slump hit the telecoms industry at the worst possible time (debts were exposed through the investment in 3G licences)
3. The dotcom industry was reliant on the telecoms industry
4. Nepotism operated throughout the bubble

The changing nature of the customer's expectations and the incessant flow of new products and services from the telecommunications networks and related industries generated a boom in the sector (the telecom boom produced the rapid transformation of the number system, a development accelerated by intense use of mobile phones and the Internet). Modifications to the telecommunications infrastructure, the appearance of tele-clusters in the telecoms markets (driven by liberalisation), and the need to provide quick and reliable communications networks to transport new modes of information-related products, produced active interest throughout the industry. The problem with the new innovation was the lack of incoming cash streams. Customers had become accustomed to free internet services. Companies such as NTL used the Internet network as a loss leader. The difficulties in not finding sustainable profit streams for new innovation and technology proved damaging.

> Telecom and internet companies offer free internet service off the peg so anybody with a strong brand or a clever marketing idea can now enter the market and that is just what they are doing. Now there are alternatives to companies with strong brands like Tesco and British Telecom. There are others where access has been rolled into some value added service like banking (Barclays, egg) or business information (hemscott.net).[31]

Nonetheless, the wider enthusiasm for IPOs, rapid technological changes (developments such as WAP [wireless applications protocol] and the mobile Internet, were not, however, exempt from criticism, particularly with relatively slow connection speeds). The plethora of new products fuelled both by consumer demand and intense competition propelled the telecommunications industry into the media spotlight.

Despite rapid innovation, the telecoms industry struggled to take advantage of the synergistic opportunities produced by telecommunications and the media. Rupert Murdoch's Sky TV Corporation prevented further development in the area with numerous legal clauses related to cable TV. Telecoms are dependent on new opportunities for Broadband and Voice Call, with new innovation locked in the rigorous process of the variable business case (not necessarily a negative condition, although lack of available investment clearly is). The new reality is the need to make sustainable and profitable sales to customers.

Whilst European governments damaged the future of telecoms, the European Union ushered in standardisation and co-ordination of the telecoms industry, a condition underpinned by the single standard GSM introduced by European governments,[32] a development that briefly gave European-based companies an edge over their American rivals. The accumulated debts, however, associated with the wireless gamble have not been lessened by the realisation of shortcomings in expected profits, which failed to meet the initial optimistic forecasts.

In Britain, the boom in mobile phones continued. Vodaphone obtained the UMTS (Universal Mobile Telecommunications System) licence. The costs associated with the acquisition of the new licences had produced a radical restructuring of the industry.

The astonishing growth in the UK mobile phone market is reflected in new figures released by two of the four main networks. Orange said 430,000 new customers had signed up to its service in the second quarter of the year, outstripping market forecasts by 45,000. And One 2 One has taken on 400,000 new subscribers during the quarter, an increase of 150% on the figure for the same period last year. The statistics mean a mobile phone is sold in the UK every four seconds. Nearly 17m people now own them – more than a quarter of the population. And some analysts expect that figure to double over the next year or so. 'It's fair to say mobile has gone mass market in Britain,' one analyst said. Shares in Orange jumped on news of its figures. Although it made its first profit only last year, Orange has grown rapidly and in February announced plans to create 2,000 jobs over two years as the market grows. It is Britain's third biggest mobile telephone company and now has 2.9m customers. Bosses have promised it will be the first British cellphone group to develop integrated data, Internet and electronic commerce capability.[33]

Nokia and Ericsson, both registered in Scandinavia, have used the single European wireless network infrastructure, GSM, and co-operation amongst European telecommunication carriers, to gain international strategic advantage.

The European spectrum auctions have resulted in a massive transfer from shareholders to governments. As a consequence, some of Europe's more financially stretched telecoms elite may have to break themselves up to pay 3G bills.[34]

The boom in mobile phones has not been without its critics. The rapid expansion of mobile phone masts and the health-related issues associated with direct mobile phone use has disturbed investors, concerned that new regulations may be introduced to limit the concern.

It is difficult to see where the telecoms industry will go forward; many continue to be crippled by high debts and costs servicing existing debts.[35] Where will the industry go? How will it make money? The new infrastructure that will carry the new generation of voice IP and related products is not without risk. New transmitters and mobile phone masts are straggled with high landlord costs. Customers may also find the prospect of viewing an image held on the mobile phone for more than a few minutes an unsatisfying prospect. The industry will thrive or fail on how willing its customers are prepared to pay for the new services, many of which are introduced back to back in a confusing non-customer friendly series of promotions.

Communicating Mini-Bubbles: Losing Value and Raising Costs

Like the South Sea Bubble and the railway manias before, numerous fraudulent practices were introduced to take advantage of the rabid speculation. In a repeat of the Dotcom Bubble, which was not entirely separate, companies did not have realistic business plans, secure fundamentals and healthy cash flow predictions. Revenues were calculated without any underlying substance, and valued through crude multiples. Examples of stocks from the Tech Bubble, which are less well-known, were Intelligent Environments, Sci Entertainment Group, Geo Interactive Media. Another fact about these is that some of them changed their names after the losses to try to relaunch and do the same all over again.

The demand and supply of stocks were complicated further through the merger and acquisitions of telecoms operators and manufacturers, partly motivated by opportunities provided by third generation licences and a highly competitive market fuelled by new products, deregulation, strong consumer demand and expanding credit facilities.

Major companies took dramatic losses. Marconi for example, which had been at the forefront of the initial wireless revolution, ironically became a major casualty. Despite difficulties throughout the industry, the opportunities to manipulate and cut mobile phone prices through new contract packages and international mobile roaming to cut cost generated an industry seeking to exploit new openings producing new optimism: the broadband boom being one example of renewed interest in the industry. Porn and sport may offer some sound business opportunities, but the risks are numerous.

Media Bubbles

The ability of the various media to exploit the developments in digital, satellite and cable television propelled a multi-channel industry keen to deliver bespoke programming as a pay-to-view service. Major companies for example Kirch Gruppe's media monolith, developing the Premiere Pay-TV Service, held contracts on events such as Formula One. In Britain, the spectacular problems at ITV digital made clear the importance of content to paying customers.

The media wave is also related to the Internet boom and the possibilities realised by digital transmission. A passage commenting on the cultural industries, sheds light on the greater exposure of the cultural experience, and its manipulation by the various media, and vice versa.

First, we observe an increasing interweaving between the media and/or the cultural industry, and other branches of what I characterize as an industry of experience. 'The former media' have become part of a widely expanded and at the same time internally more integrated, leisure industry. Take the Disney concern – it represents the start of a complete industry of experience with strong links between the virtual media (written, visual, sound) and the material world of clothing and toys, theatres, restaurants, theme parks, shopping malls and sports stadiums. Furthermore, digitalization of aspects of the cultural environment has initiated a greater mobility and manipulability of images and experiences. As a result there is an increase in the experiences open to people, more demand for people's attention, more skilful and efficient ways of attracting people, and highly demanding, spoilt consumers.[36]

The expectation that the synergy between sport and the media would produce a phenomenal entertainment product produced a mini-bubble, which was unsustainable due to poor audience engagement. The opportunities associated with sports publicity, advertising and merchandising seemed to guarantee success. The various media, particularly television, expected sport to attract high viewing figures and the take up of specialised channels to guarantee income flows. The expectation was flawed through undue attention to consumer wants.

The Sports Bubble, although not defunct in all media, disappointed predictions of Pay TV. The poor revenue streams associated with the Media Bubble rapidly disappointed investors, who departed from further exposure.

The ever decreasing circles that bind sport and the media continue to rupture the bubble, a factor that is sending alarm through a network of related industries and organisations. The sport and media nexus could benefit from the new opportunities provided in next generation mobiles, with improved image quality, power source and faster downloads.

Emerging businesses such as iTunes (Apple Music Store), which allows customers to legally download songs, are notable for their initial success: making money and producing healthy cash flows is fundamental to sustaining the e-business model. The initial success of the iPod mini, a credit card sized digital music player from Apple, illustrates the recurring bubble-type cycles.[37]

Conclusion: Onwards Electronic Bubbles

The electronic bubbles arising from the successive waves of e-booms were embedded with the riddles of speculation. The frenzy was propelled by the recognition of an e-adventure. On the one hand, fundamentals were ignored by entrepreneurs and investors in the stampede to obtain spectacular gains. On the other hand, the implosion of the e-adventure has resulted in both established companies building in the e-factor and new companies incorporating the lessons of the period; the latter appearing with new confidence and expectations.

The overlapping relationship between telecoms and dotcoms will continue, however, to complicate the future performance of each sector. It is expected in future that a boom in mergers, collaborative strategies and partnerships will emerge, providing the investment environment for a bubble.

Notes

---

[1] Michael Miller illustrates in an informative piece that 'the mainstream press is declaring that the technology boom is over for good. Business spending on information technology is flat. The market for technology stocks is down. Despite the recession, the pace of innovation in technology continues to advance. Intel predicts that by the end of the decade there will be 1.5 billion computers with broadband connections and 2.5 billion phones with more processing power than today's PCs. It predicts that by the end of the decade there will be 1.5 billion computers with broadband connections.' If this is viewed in the context of action of Alan Greenspan and central banks outside the United States where massive amounts of cash are being released into the system at ever lower interest, a revived boom in tech related stocks looks a strong possibility.

[2] Kitson and Michie (1995) p.3.

[3] Ridderstråle and Nordström (2002) p.57.

[4] Zeira (1999) p.239.

[5] A special feature in the journal *Geographical* captures the flows embedded in globalisation: 'Like so many world-changing processes, globalisation began with a technological breakthrough. In 1971, an engineer at Intel in California's Silicon Valley, as it became known, produced the world's first Microprocessor. These modern marvels are now so commonplace that we have dozens in our homes and don't even think about it. The microprocessor enabled the computer, faster communication networks and, eventually, the Internet. These in turn made possible the instantaneous transfer of money and information, which became the driver for the process we now know as globalisation', p.44.
[6] Evans (1999) p.18.
[7] See http://www.nanalyze.com/forums/topic.asp?TOPIC_ID=268 for investment developments and discussion in Nanotechnology.
[8] Anon (2002) 'Investors bet on hi-tech breakthrough', BBC Front Page, 5 September 2002: http://news.bbc.co.uk/1/hi/business/2234333.stm.
[9] See Orléan, 'Les marchés financiers sont-ils rationnels? (Are Financial Markets Rational?)' (2003) pp 58-62.
[10] Shiller (2002) p.18.
[11] Carr (1999) p.12-15.
[12] Check on-going investment in techs and other related stocks on Raging Bull, an important and useful message board. http://ragingbull.lycos.com/cgi-bin/static.cgi/a=index.txt&d=mainpages.
[13] Coxe (2003) p.34.
[14] The Disney Corporation launches a new product every few minutes.
[15] Huber (2003) p.19.
[16] Scholte (2000) p.52.
[17] See Michael Crichton's business thriller *Rising Sun* to reconsider the atmosphere in the US, which felt Japan was taking over the American economy. Japan's then alleged motto, 'Business is War', is interesting on consideration of financial, economic and political events.
[18] Rugman and Hodgetts (2003) p.507.
[19] Cohen (1997) p.330.
[20] Stelzer (2000) p.4.
[21] Cardiner (2000) 'Lastminute.Com posts strong results ahead of its IPO', 1 March, http://www.silicon.com/news/500020/1/1016092.html.
[22] Ratnesor (2000) 'The New Moguls': http://www.time.com/time/europe/specials/eeurope/process/lastminute.html
[23] Lynch (2003) 'Lastminute shares fly on positive news.' 10 October 2003. http://www.computing.co.uk/News/1114824.
[24] Nevaer (2002) p.14-15.
[25] Anon (2000) p.21.
[26] BBC Panorama 'Dot.Com Fever', broadcast 3 April 2000.
[27] http://surveys.ft.com/ukmarkets2001/.
[28] Hutton (2000) p.3.
[29] Anon (2000) p.20.
[30] Anon (1999) p.30.
[31] Evans (1999) p13.
[32] See 'America rides the wireless wave' for a cautious note on Europe's lead in Telecommunications. The article suggests that the US has two long-term advantages: the nexus of innovative enterprises and the wide access to capital. Anon (2000) pp 77-78.
[33] Anon (1999) 'Business: The Company File – Britain Mad about Mobiles': http://news.bbc.co.uk/1/hi/business/the_company_file/383818.stm.
[34] Anon (2000) pp.19-20.

[35] NTL filed for Chapter 11. The company has struggled with a £500m loan paying 19% interest, the high interest figure being a reflection of the company's specific difficulties and the perceived generic risk associated with telecoms.

[36] Mommass (2000) p.26.

[37] BBC News (18 February 2004) 'Thousands rush to order iPod mini': http://news.bbc.co.uk/1/hi/technology/3498839.stm.

Chapter 8

The Role of Institutions and the Response to Malfeasance

Introduction

The debate between the benefits of unfettered capitalism and the need to limit its worst excesses has historically motivated a range of ideologies: forces that operate throughout the world to shape political and social life (Al-Qaeda's plot to overthrow capitalism *à outrance*). The collapse of the institutions related to Soviet communism in the latter part of the twentieth century led to a euphoric claim of the end of history: capitalism won and communism lost. It was held that the progression of capitalism and the omnipotence of market democracy would continue without hindrance.

Whilst the story of the demise of a superpower can be debated, it is clear that an explicit alternative view to capitalism was suspended in the debris of the socialist experiment. The stampede that gathered during the 1980s to de-regulate free markets and limit the influence of labour representation altered the possibilities within and between markets; the republican revolution had begun.

With the ascendancy of new right thinking, the deepening of an individual's responsibility to 'make it happen', and the prevalence of a commercial solution to all problems, the markets boomed in anticipation of a sustained *golden age*. On the one hand, the consequence of the spread of capitalism and managerialism was the Corporate Bubble of the 1990s. On the other hand, the protests that have erupted in Seattle, Prague, London and Washington, whenever world leaders and their aides meet to discuss economic policy, demonstrate the failure of a final consensus.

With the disruption of corporate America following the decline in equities, woeful management in managing financial transparency and accountability, and the disturbing turn in world affairs, the twenty-first century opened in similar character to what John Maynard Keynes would recognise as a bad attack of economic pessimism.

This chapter considers the international institutional architecture charged with maintaining stability and limiting uncertainty. Financial markets are imbued with asymmetric information. The complexity continues to deepen with the on-going developments in the sector. Richard Dale argues that the world economy has been transformed by three key developments: globalisation of the financial services industry; functional integration of the banking and securities business; and financial innovation, particularly in the derivatives products area.

The key strand in the material below is therefore reflected in the need to assess the desirability for internationally applied standards of good practice in domestic policy making in relation to investment and the economy in general. Trends and countertrends will be considered to pinpoint the fault lines in economies and markets, where bubbles occur and spread opportunity and misery. In the development of the institutional and management theme, the strength and weaknesses of international co-operation in maintaining stability in the international financial and economic architecture is analysed to make clear the demands prevalent throughout the international system.

Politics and Commerce: Interests and Bubbles

Wealth and power cannot be separated from the nexus of social relations operational throughout society. Modern economies expand through innovation and investment, recognisable stages that evolve producing cycles for products and services. The nature of economic development during periods of rapid growth presents difficulties to policy makers charged with managing the economy within the state. On the one hand, the policy of central banks to allow cheap money into the system may lead to sudden bursts of growth and the appearance of mini-bubbles, which may have to be initiated to avoid an economic slowdown.[1] On the other hand, too tight a monetary policy may result in a slump in innovation, capital investment and entrepreneurial activity.

Interestingly, the courses that inform policy makers in this area rarely appear to include in-depth studies of financial bubbles and their consequences. An historical study that includes content and substance in relation to trade, commerce and market cycles would uncover bubble activity and forces which emerge from rapid asset inflation. Peter Jay, in the book *The Road to Riches*, includes a passage that illustrates the full implications of an emerging political economy:

> The whole business of human relationships in terms of command over people (politics) and things (economics) changes radically once (a) the number of people involved in a typical living and working location rise from tens to

hundreds and then to thousands and tens of thousands, and (b) the production system is generating a substantial surplus of output above what is necessary simply to keep the food producers and their families going. Suddenly, also (we are still speaking of millennia) there is real surplus wealth to argue about; and argument leads to conflict. There begin to be people who specialise in the whole embryonic business of politics, government and war, in short proto rulers, politicians and generals.[2]

The rapid, and also paradoxically staggered, development of capitalism unfolded throughout the world spreading influence and change (it clearly ignores some regions, sub-Saharan Africa for example). Whilst capitalism is the key organising force in production, capital and labour in most parts of the world, it is not universal. Despite this, its impulse to expand is undeniable.

The on-going debate associated with the principles of capitalism, which should includes its failures, creates problems through the acknowledgement of unequal distribution of power and benefits. Whilst some positions do not directly accord with the prevailing force that underpins most economies and markets (for example, the work of Friedrich List who argued for the temporary implementation of protectionism to help infant industries) alternative approaches are not widely recognised.

> What was and is still needed in America is not the silencing of dissent, but a vibrant counterpoint to the chorus of promoters who virtually monopolised economic discussion in the 1990s. What will prevent bubbles and manias and mass delusions and maybe even bad government is a new set of public thinkers willing at least to entertain the notion that capitalism might not always allocate goods fairly or efficiently; that markets may not always be synonymous with democracy; that voting and collective bargaining are expressions of the popular will every bit as legitimate as are shopping and day trading.[3]

The patterns that can be gleaned from a long-term study of financial history, however, can be deceptive. The data implies that bull markets, for example between 1982 and 2000, are not common. Robert Shiller, author of the well-known book *Irrational Exuberance*, suggests that:

> There's been only two of them – the Twenties and the Nineties. If you take the US stock market from 1871 to 1991 and compute what the average annual growth rate of stock prices corrected for inflation has been, it's been two per cent a year. Of course, then it'll pay higher dividends so over that whole period you've got a return of something like seven per cent, but it has not been anything like the 1990s. But people still have this view of the world because they've seen it do this through their entire life – that the market has just gone

up and up. They want to know when is that starting again and that's the wrong question to ask.[4]

Whilst major bubbles that damage the economy as a whole are relatively rare, the presence of mini-bubbles is common in a range of markets. This point will be picked up later in the book. Despite the relative absence of severe problems undermining the international financial architecture, problems persist, which could lead to difficulties in future. The focus here turns to the need to enhance stability and limit uncertainty in the markets.

The Development of Regulatory Structures: Limiting Uncertainty; Sustaining Stability

The twentieth century is notable for the developments in the international regulatory structure. Keynes' classic work, *The Economic Consequences of Peace*, presents an incisive study of the failure of policy to provide equity and fairness. Nonetheless, the introduction and enforcement of regulations have continued to be applied in response to the increasing complexity of international political and economic affairs.

> Regulatory initiatives did not stop at national borders. As early as the mid-nineteenth century, European governments saw the need to establish rules at an 'international' (that is, largely Western European) level. Intergovernmental conferences in the second half of the century considered many such issues. Some were primarily of concern to investors, such as standardisation and interconnection of railways and telegraph systems, stronger maritime and fisheries laws and broadened patent and copyright principles. Telegraph and postal co-operation also developed in this way. Even the question of duelling came up for international consideration. But there also arose issues of direct concern to the new mass electorates and trade union movements – like sanitation, slavery and labour conditions. Public international bodies were founded in those years to codify and strengthen these rules, including the International Telegraph Union, the International Maritime Bureau, the Metric Union, the Patent Union and the Universal Postal Union. The International Association of Labour Legislation, predecessor of the ILO, was founded in 1901 to improve and standardise working conditions. These new organizations were the forerunners of the League of Nations and of the United Nations itself.[5]

The stock market boom of the 1920s perpetuated the wider interest in investment in stocks and shares. With stability underpinned by the Federal

Reserve,[6] positive trends were expected to continue without interruption. The world did not share equally in the boom.

> The twenties were a decade of high prosperity for the rich, and an Indian summer for the old regime. They were also a time of desperate poverty in Scotland, Appalachia, rural Europe, and urban slums throughout the world. Inequality put narrow limits on consumption. In the United States during the late 1920s, major industries began to suffer from excess capacity and insufficient demand. Industrial production began to fall. In October 1929, the American stock market crashed, and the world slipped into the Great Depression.[7]

The realisation of evaporating demand led to falling prices and a downward spiral in productivity resulting in unemployment and industry closures. The series of panics in the banking industry, which were related to the local conditions of falling real estate prices and agriculture, added to the depression.[8] Withdrawals and the decline of deposits accelerated bank failures. The frictions in the national financial architecture of the United States reduced bank reserves, money supply and bank credit, a knock-on effect removing swathes of purchasing power from markets culminating in chaos and contagious deflation.[9] The need to re-inject confidence in the markets led to the creating in 1934 of the Securities and Equities Commission, a body set up to regulate investments.

The Great Depression was fundamental to the growing popularity of fascism and was partly responsible for World War II. Ironically, the preparation for war generated a mini-boom on Wall Street with enthusiasm for the war dividend underpinned by the increasingly full order books of American manufacturers. Fragmented economic development is also related to cycles, which produces changes within and between socio-economic and political entities. The rally was short and the market did not recover its momentum until the end of the hostilities.

The agreement reached at the Bretton Woods United Nations Monetary and Financial Conference, held in 1944 in New Hampshire, introduced the foundations of an international financial order. The new structure was intended to limit the havoc accorded to turbulent laissez-faire markets. The new institutions would introduce capital controls and initially provide stability. The Bretton Woods institutions, the International Monetary Fund (set up originally to manage the exchange rate system) and International Bank for Reconstruction and Development, and the World Bank, would aid development and reconstruction.

The Fund is [was] required by its charter, the Fund Agreement, to appear in two roles, corresponding very roughly to those of a banker and of an umpire. In its former role the Fund engages in transactions with its members for the purpose of supplying them with additional means of international settlement, in broadly the same way that a bank grants advances to its customers, though we must beware of pressing this analogy too far. In its latter role, the Fund is required by its charter to administer and enforce certain 'rules of the game' laid down in the charter itself for the regulation of international monetary affairs.[10]

The Bretton Woods institutions evolved and overlapped in responsibilities and aims. The activities of the IMF and World Bank are imbued in controversy, which is, depending on the issue, both exaggerated and justified. The trail of businesses tracking to Washington to win lucrative contracts is one example of the influence of business on the decision-making process, an aspect that is perhaps unavoidable.

State co-operation continued in 1947 with the establishment of the General Agreement on Tariffs and Trade, which sought to dismantle trade policies that limited economic growth and encouraged trade between states.

GATT is a voluntary commercial treaty that came to represent the third pillar of US – British hegemony after World War II – the other two being the IMF and the World Bank (or IBRD). This multinational organisation monitors 90 per cent of world merchandise trade and has stimulated industrial countries to reduce their tariffs more than 40 percent to an average of less than 5 percent since its founding.[11]

In attempting to stabilise the economic fluctuations, Governments tried to limit and control, where possible, the persistent supply side shocks to the economy. The uncertainty associated with raw materials, energy prices, natural disasters, and a range of variables, whose changes over time were unpredictable, led to government regulation at the local, national, regional and international level.

Between 1950 and 1973, the real per capita GDP of Western Europe grew more than twice as fast as the secular trend and faster than any other comparably large group of countries. At the same time, cyclical fluctuations were mild and inflation rates socially acceptable.[12]

Throughout the 1950s and into the 1960s, the rebuilding of Europe and the management of the Cold War led to the increasing exit of dollars from the United States. The European and Japanese economies grew positively and the stability encouraged growth throughout the world.

The steady ten-year bull market floundered on the political issues: the deepening of the Cuban Missile Crisis. Nikita Khrushchev's decision to counter the position of American missiles in Turkey led to a superpower posturing that nearly resulted in far more than a temporary fall in the markets.

There was stagflation throughout the early 1970s, which contributed to the great bear market of 1975. As noted in the previous chapter, the manufacturing sector had responded to the difficulties with a revolution in management tools and practices. In particular, the changes to the production and management structure were initiated by the resource-dependent Japanese, recognising a new range of techniques were needed to boost efficiency and reduce dependence.

> The evolution of the biggest 50 firms reflects the changes in the post-war industrial structure. Since 1975 companies in information technology and telecommunications have risen to challenge the energy complex and the automanufacturers within the rankings. Moreover since the 1950s American dominance in the sphere of transnationalisation has been undermined by the rise of Western European and Japanese companies, although the latter have moved much more slowly into international production, preferring to focus their efforts on exporting Japanese manufactures.[13]

The revolutionary business models were adapted and modified in the United States and the industry of management books took off enormously. In response to the structural changes, authors such as Tom Peters would become business evangelists selling millions of copies, a market that is dominated by its own mini-bubble in guru management and business gobbledegook.

The increasing demand from multinationals to support their cross border activities with relatively easy access to foreign exchange markets encouraged the waves of deregulation. The intention of the Thatcher Government to reposition London as an attractive international financial centre underpinned the desire and acceptability of this trend to interests supportive of business.

> In London the rules of the Stock Exchange were amended in 1986 to allow acquisition of member firms by outsiders, including banks. In a one-step change, the banking and securities business was combined, thereby ending the separation of these activities, which had been a feature of the UK financial services industry for 300 years.[14]

The see-saw mentality associated with the introduction and repeal of regulatory actions is related to various trends operational throughout society, which become important at particular junctures. The shift in support for regulation and against it is noted in the extract below.

> Over the past twenty years, as investors have sought global open markets, they have become increasingly critical of national investment rules and regulations, giving rise to a dominant economic ideology of neoliberalism that has enshrined deregulation as a universal principle of rationality and prosperity. Some conservative economists and commentators even refer to regulation as 'repression,' comparing it by allusion to the arbitrary rule of dictators. Not surprisingly, mega-corporations prefer to carry on their business without any regulatory oversight. In these circumstances, the political potential for new global regulatory initiatives might seem bleak. But a global political movement is emerging and demanding more citizen control over transnational capital. Mass demonstrations in Seattle, Washington, Prague and other cities express public outrage and press for urgent solutions. Even the World Bank now refers to the 'inadequacy of regulatory and supervisory frameworks both at the global and country levels.'[15]

Despite the super-high interest rates of the 1980s and the shocks of 1987 (where during a selling frenzy, brokers stopped answering the phones to curb the demand to fill in sell orders – a condition that accelerated the fall and led SEC to allow individual investors to deal directly in future with market makers obliged to handle these transactions) the bull market of 1982-2000 was not stopped.

The previous chapter has considered the collapse of confidence in technology-related stocks and the general fall in equities. It is clear that the 1982-2000 bubble was in serious trouble before the assault on the World Trade Centre and the successive and damaging cases of corporate malfeasance. In a variety of sectors, stock market activity faltered and slumped. Market sentiment had changed, the media rapidly communicated the concern; anxiety was the notable presence in the markets. The corporate storm added to the malaise.

> But the most precipitous corporate collapse in American history is much more than a financial scandal. It is also a political scandal of historic proportion, with potentially huge public policy ramifications. There is no better example in modern times of the symbiosis between commerce and politics, between wealth and power, between access and influence. That this morality tale ultimately ends with truth and consequences might be heartening on one level, of course. But let us not forget that before the awful, inevitable, financial day of reckoning that has befallen Enron, its employees and its investors, the field of schemes for this calamity necessarily extended well beyond Houston. Enron's influence, and the taint of its collapse, touches Washington, D.C., and every state capital in America. The supposed elixir of government deregulation, limited liability,

and minimal reporting requirements for the energy futures, securities and accounting industries enabled the financial chicanery and excesses.[16]

The response of the Republican administration to the scandal initially appeared more rhetorical than substantive. The Sarbanes-Oxley Act passed by the US Congress however, introduced a range of measures that will impact on the operation of corporate America and the financial markets.[17] The Securities and Equities Commission has continued to add amendments, increasing the burden on senior management to provide rigorous internal control.[18]

The concerns related to conflicts that arise from the analysts within investment institutions and banks have been reviewed. For example, the analyst may praise a client company in a research paper to an investor client, but then rubbish the company in internal emails and conversations.[19] Congress has given new powers to the SEC in regard to analyst conflict of interest rules, an area of concern listed in the Sarbanes-Oxley Act.

The changes introduced to improve financial reporting and probity perhaps do not go as far as the populist days of trust busting,[20] a period during which Teddy Roosevelt used the Sherman Anti-trust Act to reduce the power of the industrial monopolies. The Sarbanes-Oxley Act of 2002 will however have numerous implications for finance professionals, many of which cannot at this stage be fully foreseen.

Corporate America had been severely shaken, but it has not been irreparably damaged; investors have notoriously short memories. Profits will continue to be made, but a return to the heights recorded during the Great Bull Bubble will take some time to recover, although it may be sooner than is currently touted.

The attack on the World Trade Centre publicised the extent of the problem relating to illegal money in the system or legal money with an illegal history and led to a response from the United States administration to limit the free flow of terrorist finance and fraud. Accounts around the world were frozen and organisations had their activities blacklisted. The policy highlighted the tension between the need to maintain a client's confidentiality and the desired transparency inherent in a financial record.

Whilst probity is crucial to a mature economy, it is extremely difficult for the private sector, including insurers, banks, bureaux de change and other financial institutions, to thoroughly identify suspicious transactions. This does not mean that procedures are not being implemented to limit the depth and spread of illegal money, which is substantial in all markets.

In the wider context of financial fraud, The Financial Action Task Force on Money Laundering (FATF) is an inter-governmental body whose purpose is the development and promotion of policies, both at national and international levels, to combat money laundering. The Task Force is therefore a 'policy-making body' which works to generate the necessary political will to bring about national legislative and regulatory reforms to combat money laundering. The emphasis lies in the co-ordination of supervision.

Investment Turbulence: Institutional Challenges in *Free* Markets

The heightened awareness of financial scandals has concerned investors in America and outside (although financial irregularities are anything but new). It has been suggested throughout the book that fraud is a common feature that occurs in investment bubbles, the earlier South Sea Bubble demonstrating similar features of wrongdoing.

The issues Susan Strange raised in the classic book *States and Markets* made explicit the poverty of ideas associated with the management of the international financial architecture. Although systemic risk has been greatly reduced since the 1990s, the book continues to stimulate wide discussion. Strange highlighted four key areas that presented on-going problems to the world market economy. The areas can be summarised:

- the management of sovereign debt
- the supervision and prudential control of banks
- the restoration of stability and credibility to exchange rates between the major currencies
- the bankruptcy of economic thought in a global financial structure.[21]

The revolutionary developments within the international financial system since the publication of *States and Markets* have been extraordinary. The introduction of integrated communications has resulted in an ever increasing mobility of finance. Governments recognise that economic autonomy is largely absent in an integrated and sophisticated economy. Major policy initiatives are cautiously put forward; the content needing guarding from the media.

Orthodox monetary theory sees monetary policy as a simple combination of day-to-day interventions within financial markets. The influence of the central banks in managing and co-ordinating policy is increasingly autonomous from direct political interference, unless the situation calls for interventions to be made in the national interest, an interesting and debatable arrangement.

As banking systems develop, monetary policies rely much more on indirect mechanisms than on direct ones; central banks themselves are perfectly aware of their own limitations in effecting liquidity without risking financial instability. In other words, at higher stages of banking development, central banks are generally perfectly aware of the limits of the traditional textbook monetary policy rules, so that in practice they choose to affect liquidity through a variety of means, including influencing mood of the bank supervision.[22]

Leertouwer and Maier illustrate in an incisive article on political business cycles that governments are limited in their influence over central banks. For example, the authors found in their study that 'no evidence was [forthcoming] that central banks activity engaged in short-sighted behaviour before elections'.[23] It is argued in this book that governments have a messy, subtle relationship with central banks and other key institutions operational in the economy.

Despite trends of co-operation, the problem of uneven regulation between states continues to cause problems.[24] The Basle Committee on Banking Supervision, the OECD and the International Securities Commissions (IOSCO) have initiated various programmes to encourage prudential regulation through a process of regulatory harmonisation.

By the mid-1980s a shift in the policy of prudential regulation became evident, away from rules pre-set within a strictly national framework, and towards a broader international collaboration at least between the G-10 central bankers. Apart from the timid start to globalisation of supervision, the 1990s resulted in: a more flexible regulatory framework which starts working transborder; greater weight on case-by-case evaluations of institutions; mathematical models using volatilities, simulation, non-linearities and other tools; and a major weight given to the reliability of financial reports by banks and other institutions... [25]

Whilst the procedures and the operations of banks have improved since the years of reckless lending and loose management, banks continue to be at risk from corporate malfeasance, a result of the embedded fusion between securities and banking.

The corporate scandals have unsettled investor confidence in the United States and re-focused the debate between the promotion of the American economic model of unhindered free-market capitalism and the need for regulation in the markets. At one extreme, which is not exclusive to speculation, orthodox economists argue that intervention results in less efficient markets:

Speculative capital abhors regulation. Regulations interfere with the cross-market arbitrage that is its lifeline. If speculative capital cannot freely operate, it cannot generate profits and must cease to exist. The opposition of speculative capital to regulation is thus not a matter of some technical or tactical disagreement but a question of life and death.[26]

The financial canvas encapsulates a web of public and private institutions intervening in the market to promote, protect and propagate a diverse range of interests. The need for regulation is related to the asymmetrical and sheer complexity of the nexus of markets, which deliver varying degrees of transparency in a range of financial products and services. For example, on the one hand there is a clear desire to counter anti-competitive behaviour. The move also acknowledges the embedded nature of imperfect information. Consensus is one of the main drivers of financial regulation. Ideological and political interference are no substitute for prudential regulation.

> ...the existence of a regulatory burden on banks' capital level, banks' portfolio, shares and so on, may give confidence to the consumers of financial services as they perceive that such a system is backed by monetary authorities...In other words, prudential regulation has made a positive contribution to the growth of banking, without which it would not be clear that banks could now run effectively.[27]

A case can be suggested that the poverty of ethics in business practices generally has undermined the quality of self and prudential regulation. Business schools and management training institutes have historically not directed time to this important area.

Despite improvements in some areas of banking, the problems of Enron and the auditors Arthur Andersen, WorldCom, Xerox and others highlight the potential for activities that disrupt investments and markets.[28] The method may be crude – spreading costs to a future time when the anticipated revenue might arrive and recording costs as assets – but it inflated the price of the stock well beyond its actual value, misleading investors and creditors.

This raises the issue of the real value of a company. The stock market 'value' of a company is the number of shares in issue multiplied by the share price. This is, however, the perceived value.

> The real value is the economic value, which is the net present value of the future cash flows discounted at the weighted average cost of capital. Growing the economic value involves enhancing future cash flows either by reinvesting cash flows into new projects where the return is in excess of the weighted average cost of capital or by continuing to improve the flows of the existing business.[29]

The additional influx of money is contributing to an excessive investment risk environment. Gilts, bonds, corporate IOUs are not risk adverse as Enron, Barings and British and Commonwealth demonstrate. If the measures that assess the strength of the corporate books are not to be trusted, even after the gloss has been removed, the absence of confidence will hit investment and banking, and economies in general.

It would appear that European insurers have limited direct exposure to the Worldcom crisis – although most institutions in the sector are not immune from the general fall-out. Nevertheless, weak institutions that have links will see their credit rating downgraded.

In Europe, one vehicle for developing legislation in this area is the European Union. 'An EU Directive on corporate responsibility is currently being debated which could have far reaching effects on levels of reporting' illustrates the desire to improve leadership.[30]

The recent companies that have allegedly succumbed to corporate malfeasance include:

Table 8.1

Corporation	Sector	% Share Price fall since 1st Jan 2002	Misdemeanour
Enron	Energy Trader	99.9	Accounting irregularities
Global Crossing	Telecoms	99.7	Chapter 11 following accounting irregularities[31]
Adelphia Communications	Cable TV	99.1	Filed for bankruptcy after director loans discovered
Peregrine Systems	Computer Software	95.8	Under SEC probe following accounting irregularities
Qwest Communications	Telecoms	95.6	CEO Joseph Nacchio fired
WorldCom	Telecoms	93.8	Enquiry into $3.8 billion accounting fraud
Dynergy	Energy Trader	88.9	Under SEC investigation over accounting irregularities
Imclone	Biotechnology	80	Former CEO Samuel Waksal charged with insider dealing
Tyco International	Industrial Conglomerate	79	CEO Dennis Kozlowski charged with tax evasion
Xerox	Office Equipment	33	$6bn mis-statement of earnings

Source: adapted from The Business 30 June/2 July 2002

Within the bull market of 1982-2000, the culture that underpinned the celebration of greed may be traced back to the beginning of the bubble, which reflected wider changes in politics and society. The period is brilliantly captured in fiction through the character John Self, consumer extraordinaire, in the book *Money* by Martin Amis.

The change in atmosphere is best identified in the words of the investment trader Ivan Boesky. In the commencement address, 18 May 1986, School of Business Administration, University of California, Berkeley, Boesky conveyed a view, 'greed is all right, by the way... I think greed is healthy. You can be greedy and still feel good about yourself'[32] that empowered a generation to seek material and financial gain.

This was picked up in the Oliver Stone film, *Wall Street* (1987), spoken by the Faustian character Gordon Gecko. In keeping with the sensationalism of the film, Boesky himself was later convicted of conspiring to file false documents with the federal government, involving insider trading violations, and agreed to pay $100 million in fines and illicit profits. Boesky cheated by using illegally obtained secrets about impending mergers to buy and sell stock before the mergers became public knowledge.

James Stewart's book, *Den of Thieves*, used the vehicle of wilful violations of securities law and ethical standards that undermined Wall Street's reputation during the take-over frenzy of the 1980s. Focusing on four major culprits Ivan Boesky, Dennis Levine, Michael Milken, and Martin Siegel – Stewart illustrates how the Securities and Equities Commission and US Justice Department were unable to enforce the regulations until serious damage had been conducted.

In co-operating with the SEC, Boesky brokered a deal and the problem of insider trading was highlighted. The investigation ruined Michael Milken and his firm, Drexel Burnham Lambert Inc., then one of the most powerful investment banks in the country.

It is clear that poor practices tend to go unnoticed or are ignored in a bull market. The flaws are flagrantly exposed in a bear market; the need to blame is paramount. It must however be noted that many apparently fraudulent activities go unnoticed or are not reported. The regulators in the United States claim to have the best standards. The use of prescriptive rules are however, seen as a weakness following the Enron scandal.

Whilst the culture celebrating gain by any means has not been totally defeated, the unhindered dominance of the masters of the universe is tempered by the introduction of regulations and self-control, which reflects the need for professionalism throughout the industry.

Contagion and Co-operation between States

States co-operate to limit the conflict that arises between them. History is littered with examples of relationships between states harmonised in the form of treaties to avoid a variety of risks that may lead to aggression. The potential dangers posed by the integration of markets produces a similar will to co-operate through the mechanism of the G10: the economic order of the financial systems being a key motivator.[33]

The serious financial and business developments in the United States are presenting problems for the rest of the world (the value of the dollar and corporate transparency). The value of the dollar being a key instrument in the success of the world economy, unless performance in growth improves outside the United States the economies of the world may have to rely on American leadership.[34]

The overlapping arguments about international financial contagion have been well considered by Vincent Cable in the book, *Globalization and Global Governance.*

> One relates to whether crises are in fact 'contagious' between countries. Another issue is whether they behave in a 'herd-like' way, aggravating the magnitude of financial crises. A third is whether the behaviour of investors is 'rational' ('herd-like' behaviour and contagion may be rational but still economically undesirable).[35]

Despite various challenges, states co-operate on a regional basis to limit the problems that may destabilise the economic security of a region. For example, the European Union will require all EU companies to comply with ISAB standards by 2005. Financial problems overlap different national sovereignties and laws, which requires a co-ordinated response. In September 2002, The Financial Stability Forum (FSF), chaired by Andrew Crockett, General Manager of the Bank for International Settlements, met in Toronto to review the potential vulnerabilities in the international financial system. Emphasis was also given to:

- addressing weaknesses in market foundations;

- improving transparency in the reinsurance industry; and

- reviewing progress in offshore financial centres to comply with international standards.[36]

In other areas, the G7 and its commission, the Financial Stability Forum, are encouraging the improvement of standards and co-operation between states. In seeking respective good housekeeping, the aim is to limit international financial turbulence.

Tax havens have worried the Organisation of Economic Co-operation and Development (OECD), the rich-country club, for some years. In 2000 it published a blacklist of 35 territories, many of them small island nations that were alleged tax havens. These include: Andorra, Anguilla, Antigua and Barbuda, Aruba, Bahamas, Bahrain, Barbados, Belize, British Virgin Islands, Cook Islands, Dominica, Gibraltar, Grenada, Guernsey, Isle of Man, Jersey, Liberia, Liechtenstein, Maldives, Marshall Islands, Monaco, Montserrat, Nauru, Dutch Antilles, Niue, Panama, Samoa, Seychelles, St Lucia, St Kitts and Nevis, St Vincent and the Grenadines, Tonga, Turks and Caicos and the US Virgin Islands.[37]

Tax havens continue to cause problems. For example, Irish tax authorities have reported collecting more than 111 million euros (£77 million pounds) in unpaid tax from offshore Jersey accounts.[38] It would appear substantial unpaid taxes lay dormant in other accounts, a total figure that can only be estimated.

Debate continues as to whether the havens could be subject to economic sanctions. Given the atmosphere of financial probity it is interesting to note that the Bush administration has not given complete support to the OECD initiative, concerned that it might in fact damage the financial industry in the US.

The robustness of the international financial systems has been tested in recent years. For example, the decline in the economic fortunes of Argentina provides an inside and outside reflection on how an economic system can potentially implode. In the mid-1990s, Argentina was recovering from years of economic turbulence and hyperinflation. The objective in restoring confidence in the economy by pegging the peso to the dollar initially stabilised the economy. The resulting loss of monetary control coupled with weak domestic growth and falling prices for agricultural products led to a decline in productivity and a rise in unemployment.

The introduction of currency devaluation may improve the position with regard to exporting in competitive international sectors and foreign currency earnings, which could be directed to debt repayment, but this is not without problems. The strategy will, however, cut the profits and investment assets of existing businesses. The public has clearly suffered in the decline and has lost confidence in the financial system and institutions. Through limiting access to savings, the Argentine public has reacted with understandable anger. Individuals do not have enough information to know which banks are safe (or all financial information is considered sceptically).[39] Therefore, in fright of a financial crisis, investors with savings in the banks behave rationally by attempting to withdraw deposits. The action leads to an irrational collective reaction, further accelerating the crisis.

Systemic Turbulence and Stability: The Fright from Flows

Despite a largely informal architecture of financial governance, the latter part of the 1990s and the opening part of the twenty-first century demonstrated the relative strength of the international financial system to withstand shocks: Mexico, the Far East, Russia, Brazil, Japan and China being the most notable. The waves of financial gloom emanating from the Asian crisis, the debris left by the implosion of the Long Term Capital Management, the technology boom and bust, the chaos of Argentina and the terrorist attack on the World Trade Centre have been met largely without serious structural and financial damage. This is, in part, related to the modifications made following the disruption caused by the Mexican peso devaluation of 1994/1995. The stability of the financial structure depends generally on the understanding of risk from all its participants. It is clear however that the system can be put under pressure from defeats within it. The defeats are often largely unrealised until a bust. For example:

> In 1997 the 'tiger economies' of South East Asia, which had symbolised economic success and efficient production methods during the 1980s and 1990s, were afflicted by economic crisis. Suddenly, issues which had been overlooked, or accepted as part of the way 'they did things over there' revealed a crisis of bad debt with collapsing currency values, recklessly extravagant lending causing bank failures, sharply weakened consumer confidence and substantially weakened stock markets, corruption, undue favouring of family and bad management, often concealed by the network of inter-company alliances and partnership.[40]

In the sector of banking generally, bank failures and financial disruption may generate systemic turbulence that damages growth and limits opportunities. In particular:

> Bank (depository institutions) failures are widely perceived to have greater adverse effects on the economy and thus are considered more important than the failure of other types of business firms. In part, bank failures are viewed to be more damaging than other failures because of a fear that they may spread in

domino fashion throughout the banking system, felling solvent as well as insolvent banks. Thus, the failure of an individual bank introduces the possibility of system wide failures or systemic risk. This perception is widespread. It appears to exist in almost every country at almost every point in time regardless of the existing economic or political structure. As a result, bank failures have been and continue to be a major public policy concern in all countries and a major reason that banks are regulated more rigorously than other firms.[41]

George Kaufman, in an excellent article, *Bank Failures, Systemic Risk, and Bank Regulation*, argues that the motivation for regulation needs to be monitored closely to determine the degree of inherent politics operational in the decision-making process. Where government has a specific financial involvement, it may be easier for it:

> to justify imposing other regulations that have primarily social and political objectives and are often in conflict with the objectives of the prudential regulations, e.g., credit allocation schemes. However, the bulk of the evidence suggests that the greatest danger of systemic risk comes not from the damage that may be imposed on the economy from a series of bank failures, but from the damage that is imposed on the economy from the adverse effects of poor public policies adopted to prevent systemic risk.[42]

Whilst the Asian crisis in the 1990s did not lead to a meltdown in the world financial system, on the contrary an argument for its successful containment could be easily made, there is evidence that infers the system could break down.

> The combination of various factors suggests that international capital markets may be very unstable. By their own behaviour they can trigger a collapse of currencies or (if exchange rates are floating) large exchange-movements. This can in turn contribute to financial instability in affected countries, to a greater extent than is justified by policy failures in those countries, suggesting that there is a deficiency in arrangements for stopping a market panic impacting on large numbers of countries. This in turn raises the issue as to whether there is need for an international lender in the last resort.[43]

The debate on the lender of the last resort continues to be split between the need to maintain confidence in the banking system and limit the decline in the money supply with the prudent management of the banks. In the globalised economy, the demand on such a lender requires access to phenomenal reserve funds, funds that may not be forthcoming in the existing financial and institutional architecture.

Despite the potential drawbacks to the lender in the last resort, the creating of Contingent Credit Lines (CCL), an IMF facility that enables the Fund to intervene and potentially reduce the risk of a system financial fracture, is a tool that may limit, if it were to materialise, a wide ranging meltdown.

The IMF cites five key areas in reforming institutional financial institutions active in a global economy.[44] These are:

- Transparency
- Developing and assessing internationally accepted standards
- Financial sector strengthening
- Involving the private sector
- Modifying IMF financial facilities and other systemic issues

To take one example from the above, the reliability of economic data in regards to transparency is constantly debated, reviewed, amended and modified with each successive revelation of additional information. Whilst the intention should be to produce reliable data, problems and anomalies will not be eradicated easily.

The complex issues that impact, shape and react to the international regulatory structures continue to produce challenges to the management of the international financial structure. It is clear that the central banks have increased powers, which are co-ordinated with other international institutions that *manage* the international financial system and investment flows between states. The G7 governments and G10 regulators hold the key to a workable financial architecture. It is recognised, however, that many problems are of a global nature and the financial architecture is largely constructed on national or regional lines.

The monetary policy of nations cannot ignore the need for bank regulation and supervision. The demand for harmonisation, co-operation and co-ordination between institutions raises the prospect for both solutions and potential conflict. Further regulation throughout the international financial architecture may limit financial crisis, but the result may expunge risk of its creative element and limit opportunity. One thing worse than investment bubbles may be no bubbles at all. The emphasis therefore should be on managing investment bubbles case by case, rather than eradicating them.

Notes

[1] Bernhard *et al* suggest 'the institutional structure of central banks – that is, their degree of independence from direct government control – varies across systems and over time. When a central bank is completely 'dependent,' its institutional structure permits the government to determine monetary policy directly. With a fully independent bank, by contrast, the government delegate monetary policy to an agent – typically the bank's governing board – and is restricted by statute from interfering with the agent's freedom of action in the monetary domain'. p. 695.

[2] Jay, P. (2000) *The Road to Riches*, pp. 40-41.

[3] Thomas Frank, (2002) 'Talking Bull', p.27.

[4] Robert Shiller (2002), Radio Debate, Analysis: Follow the Leader, BBC Radio 4, Broadcast 15 August 2002.

[5] http://www.globalpolicy.org/socecon/ffd/2000papr.htm.

[6] The Federal Reserve was charged with acting as the lender of last resort to the macroeconomy by, among other things, offsetting the impact of losses of reserves from the banking system for reasons such as a run to currency by depositors or gold outflows that threatened to reduce the money supply below appropriate levels. But the Federal Reserve was given discretion with respect to when and to what extent to do so. Unfortunately, as Milton Friedman and Anna Schwartz (1963) document, when the banking system experienced a run into currency during the Great Depression from 1929 to 1933, which dramatically reduced aggregate bank reserves, money supply, and bank credit, the Federal Reserve failed to inject sufficient offsetting reserves. As a result, the simultaneous attempt by nearly all banks to contract by selling assets led to large fire-sale losses and the largest number of bank failures in US history. www.cato.org/pubs/journals/cj16n1-2.html.

[7] David Hackett Fischer, *The Great Wave*, p.193.

[8] For a detailed study of the series of banking crisis during the depression, see Elmus Wicker, *The Banking Panics of the Great Depression*.

[9] For a critical analysis of the failure of the Federal Reserve to inject sufficient off-setting reserves see Milton Friedman and Anna Schwartz, *Monetary History of the United States* (1963).

[10] Brian Tew, *International Monetary Co-operation 1945-65*, p. 72.

[11] Robert A. Isaak, *Managing World Economic Change*, p.121.

[12] Toniolo (1998) p.252.

[13] Stephen Gill and David Law (1988) *The Global Political Economy*, p.194.

[14] Richard Dale, *Risk and Regulation in Global Securities Markets*, p.3.

[15] Quality of Growth 2000, http://www.globalpolicy.org/socecon/ffd/2000papr.htm

[16] 'The Enron Collapse: A Financial Scandal Rooted in Politics', The Centre For Public Integrity, 10 July 2002,
http://www.publicintegrity.org/dtaweb/report.asp?ReportID=10&L1=10&L2=10&L3=0&L4=0&L5=0.

[17] A summary of the Sarbone-Oxley Act of 2002 can be viewed at:
www.cpeonline.com/cpenew/sarox.asp.

[18] To review the stream of press releases issued by the US Securities and Equities Commission on the Sarbanes-Oxley Act, see: www.sec.gov/news/press2003-66.htm.

[19] see www.oag.state.ny.us/press/2002/apr/apr08b_02.html.

[20] Teddy Roosevelt used the Sherman Antitrust Act to break the power of the corporate players in the railroads, the first legislation enacted by the United States Congress (1890) to curb concentrations of power that interfere with trade and reduce economic competition. It

was named for US senator John Sherman, who was an expert on the regulation of commerce. One of the act's main provisions outlaws all combinations that restrain trade between states or with foreign nations. This prohibition applies not only to formal cartels but also to any agreement to fix prices, limit industrial output, share markets, or exclude competition. A second key provision makes illegal all attempts to monopolise any part of trade or commerce in the United States. These two provisions, which comprise the heart of the Sherman Act, are enforceable by the Department of Justice through litigation in the federal courts. Firms found in violation of the act can be ordered dissolved by the courts, and injunctions to prohibit illegal practices can be issued. Violations are punishable by fines and imprisonment. Moreover, private parties injured by violations are permitted to sue for triple the amount of damages done them.

[21] Susan Strange (1988) p.111.

[22] Philip Arestis and Malcom C. Sawyer, *The Political Economy of Central Banking*, p.2.

[23] Leertouwer and Maier (2002) p.220.

[24] Regulation is by nature ambiguous, particularly so when it comes to enforcement in the international context.

[25] Chorafas (2000) p. 5.

[26] Nasser Saber, *Speculative Capital*, p.167.

[27] *op cit* Chorafas, p.3.

[28] The need to improve management accountability and responsibility is crucial if financial irregularities are to be limited.

[29] Lever (2002) p.26.

[30] Law (2002) *Getting the Measure of Leadership*, p. 27. See the websites below for an overview of the financial regulation in Europe.
International Accounting Standards – European Commission submits views to IASC on its proposed new structure:
http://europa.eu.int/comm/internal_market/en/company/account/news/186.htm
Financial reporting: Commission welcomes creation of European Technical Expert Group:
http://europa.eu.int/comm/internal_market/en/company/account/news/creationeteg.htm
Views on a single standard by CPS:
http://www.cpshome.com/articles/adjustments_in_practice.html
Deloitte, Touche and Tohmatsu references:
http://www.iasplus.com/restruct/resteuro.htm
Very interesting document on how the single standards could appear:
http://www.iasplus.com/resource/feestudy.pdf
The European Federation of Accountants website:
http://www.fee.be/european/directives.htm
Modernisation of the accounting system: europa website:
http://www.europa.eu.int/rapid/start/cgi/guesten.ksh?p_action.gettxt=gt&doc=IP/02/1136|0|RAPID&lg=EN

[31] Chapter 11 may be commenced by the filing of a voluntary petition by the debtor, or the filing of an involuntary petition by creditors that meets certain statutory requirements. As with cases under other chapters, a stay of creditor actions against the debtor automatically goes into effect when the bankruptcy petition (whether voluntary or involuntary) is filed. The automatic stay provides a breathing spell for the debtor during which negotiations can take place to try to resolve the difficulties in the debtor's financial situation and propose a reorganisation plan. A corporation exists separately and apart from its owners, the stockholders.

Upon filing of a voluntary petition for relief under Chapter 11 (or, in an involuntary case under this chapter, the entry of an order for such relief) the debtor automatically assumes a new identity as the "debtor-in-possession."
http://www.abiworld.org/media/chapter11.html

[32] The Columbia World of Quotations. (1996).

[33] The G10 group of central bankers: USA, UK, Japan, Germany, France, Italy, Canada, Holland, Belgium, Sweden, Switzerland (and Luxembourg as Observer).

[34] See 'Flying on One Engine: A Survey of the World Economy', *The Economist* 2003.

[35] Cable, Globalization and Global Governance, p.74.

[36] The Financial Stability Forum, www.fsforum.org

[37] see http://www.escapeartist.com/taxhavens/taxhavens.htm

[38] see BBC Front Page '£77m Swoop on Jersey Accounts', 18 October 2003.
http://news.bbc.co.uk/1/hi/world/europe/3201230.stm

[39] In considering bank runs, systemic risk and deposit insurance, Spencer makes the point that 'the snag is that if for some reason people panic and demand their money without having a genuine cash requirement, a bank will not be able to repay everyone', p.193.

[40] Neil Harris, *The European Business Environment*, p.38.

[41] www.cato.org/pubs/journals/cj16n1-2.html.

[42] *Ibid*, cato journals.

[43] Cable (1999) p.74.

[44] The main sections include: *Transparency*, the intention is to make the relevant financial and economic information available to financial markets and the public. The IMF state that 47 countries now subscribe to the IMF's Special Data Dissemination Standard (SDDS), which encourages member countries to provide detailed and reliable national economic and financial data. In its surveillance of members' economies, the Fund continues to actively encourage members to release Public Information Notices (PINs), which describe the IMF Executive Board's assessment of a country's economy and policies:

Developing and assessing Internationally Accepted Standards, In encouraging compliance to rules and regulations the IMF has prepared experimental country case studies known as ROSCs (Reports on the Observance of Standards and Codes) that assess a country's progress in observing internationally recognised standard and codes.

Financial Sector Strengthening, the IMF and the World Bank have intensified and enhanced their assessment of countries' financial systems through joint Financial Sector Assessment Programs (FSAPs), which serve to identify potential vulnerabilities in countries' financial systems. With IMF input, the Basle Committee on Banking Supervision is addressing gaps in regulatory standards.

Involving the Private Sector, the IMF claim better involvement of the private sector in crisis prevention and resolution can limit moral hazard, strengthen market discipline by fostering better risk assessment, and improve the prospects for both debtors and creditors.

Modifying IMF Financial Facilities and Other Systemic Issues, as referred to above, the IMF created a new instrument of crisis prevention in 1999, Contingent Credit Lines (CCL). The CCL is a precautionary line of defence readily available to member countries with strong economic policies designed to prevent future balance of payments problems http://www.imf.org/external/np/exr/arcguide.htm.

Chapter 9

Rhythms and Interventions: Studying the Ebbs and Flows of Bubbles

Introduction

The previous chapters have considered bubbles from Tulipomania to the dotcom and telecom implosion. The material below returns to analyse the various theories that sought to make clear the inner workings of bubble activity. With reference to the literature pertaining to bubbles, various approaches will be considered to identify the specific features of speculative activity, which propel prices higher or deflate positions in sudden falls.

The nature of bubbles (long-term and spectacular asset rises), waves (successive but staggered positive increases, medium to long term) and maxi- and mini-bubbles (short-term up and downs occurring in rapid bursts, usually related to sparse trading) will be separated to determine the nature of the price increase and parameters of each category.

One point needs to be held throughout the discussion: bubbles do not have a clear beginning or end (the origin is commonly fuzzy, the initial trigger multifaceted). It is apparent that bubbles begin relatively innocuously, gradually gaining momentum before rising spectacularly to an unsustainable peak and dropping ungraciously.

There are similarities in the study of bubbles to the work undertaken in the analysis of hurricanes and storms (natural and social catastrophes share devastating impacts). Research directed to the appraisal and interpretation of hurricanes, which includes analysis of variables that contribute to the disturbance arising in the natural world, helps to shed light on the progression of bubbles in the social arena.[1]

The comparison between speculative activity and natural phenomena is considered with the objective of improving the predictive capabilities as a priority. In linking the assessment model in hurricanes and storms to bubble activity the similarities become explicit:

- Stage 1   Investigate the causes and magnitude of the bubbles.

- Stage 2   Monitor the growth (history) of the bubbles and previous occurrences of bubbles to highlight similarities and differences.

- Stage 3   Produce an assessment of the key features of the bubble including an analysis of the factors and actors involved.

- Stage 4   Consider the consequences of bubbles and the wider economic environment and assess policy and regulation to contain or limit disturbance.[2]

- Stage 5   Implement actions to limit the destructive traits associated with investment bubbles.

It should be clear that the points raised above are similar to the approach taken in this book, which highlights the stages in the analysis of the bubbles, not in the bubbles themselves. Further research could be initiated to discern the depth of the relationship between investment bubbles and hurricane studies.

It was made clear in the introduction that aim of the book was to understand the development and collapse of bubbles within the context of international political economy.[3] To reiterate, the knowledge related to recognising why bubbles intensify nearing the peak (why do they pick up force and collapse suddenly?) is important to financial, economic and political policy through the nature of the damage it causes. The need to have forecasts to assess the potential instability of a bubble is therefore relevant to politicians, economists, investors and regulators.

The study undertaken has been sensitive to the details of prior manias, making explicit the role and importance of time (speed, speculation and crash); an analysis of symptoms (or variables) operating in the market, which appear to contribute or frustrate bubble activity (including the psychology of collective irrationality, mass madness, collective panic); and the important role of government in investment bubbles (politics and the government) shaping, influencing or ignoring speculative frenzies and market volatility.

The ever-present theme through the book has been the importance of timing in investment speculation. The issues emerging from the point of execution of a buy or sell order (an action largely dictated by where the investor is in the investment chain) are related to the processors of asymmetric information.[4] It is argued that the decision-making process that informs this action is related to the intervention of power, or insight gleaned from a specific position in the speculative environment – access to information which others do not have – that facilitate speculative advantage (this is notable both in the rise of the bubble and in its subsequent fall, recognising that investors join in and leave at unco-ordinated stages).

Emerging Trends: The Challenge of Change

In response to the turbulent global economic conditions, investors have moved into cash or have directed funds to the property market, which has resulted in property price bubbles in a number of countries. Australia, New Zealand, Britain, The Netherlands and China to name a few have seen a rapid rise in property prices. The increase in property prices has been driven in part by the redirection of funds from markets such as Asia, dotcoms, telecoms, and equities in general. Coupled with low interest rates and relative easy access to funds, the Property Bubble has been developing throughout the world. In the context of investment strategies, the boom in residential and commercial property prices, albeit uneven, provides insight into generic speculative activity.

> Housing decisions are more often than not crucially dependent on the availability of mortgage financing and in times of stability and optimism mortgage lenders will lend on favourable terms because of their positive expectations about the future prospects of the economy...The boom phase will, initially at least, magnify itself. However, as mortgage rates start to rise, instability will creep in. When mortgage borrowers start to default on their mortgages, mortgage lenders will become more wary and the whole process will start to falter...so the housing market will be prone to the same speculative forces and frenzy effect that characterize other asset markets.[5]

Investment environments are conditional on the degree of competition and static status of the asset in question. Michael Porter in the book *The Competitive Advantage of Nations* (1990) makes it clear that companies that fail to adapt to the competitive realities in the business environment decline and fail.

> The reason so few firms sustain their position is that change is extraordinarily painful and difficult for any successful organisation. Complacency is much more natural. The past strategy becomes ingrained in organisational routines. Information that would modify or challenge it is not sought or filtered

out...smaller firms or those new to the industry, not bound by history and past investments, become innovators and the new leaders.[6]

Similarly, assets of all kinds pass through cycles, the progression of which is determined by a range of variables active in an on-going fluid process. Likewise, the product life cycle is a guide model. At some point, its direction is altered to reflect the changed nature of its position, a snapshot derived from the numerous decisions in the market, which is conducive to generalisations, but is not fully satisfactory in terms of presenting a full explanation.

It has been noted that a range of indicators have pointed to a change in the fortunes of Japanese funds and dotcoms although both need room to find sustainable positions. Investors may, however, be attracted by low prices. This adheres to the base rebuilding scenario where, following spectacular falls bargains become available and a steady return to market ensues, usually in gradual tentative stages. The rise is difficult to sustain if no other positive element is present other than cheapness. The advantageous trend may continue with new investors recognising the rise and returning to the market. The trend however is conditional on: 1, the nature of the recovery (is there substance to it?); 2, the extent of previous losses and the context in which the recovery emerges (are related and non-related products and services rising in value?); 3, is there a notable feature that makes it different from the previous asset rise? (Is the infrastructure different? Is the problem that influenced the previous fall resolved? Is there a new factor underpinning the revival?)

The ebbs and flows in investment can be recognised in the swings in tastes for different kinds of investments (each shares uncertain prediction). For example, the development in broadband may lead to a crash in the office property market. The improvements in video conference and web cams may also be a sign that this change may be on the horizon, coupled with the demands placed on the infrastructures of cities, particularly transport. The wider acceptance and benefits of working from home may become increasingly acceptable to employees and employers, resulting in a fall in demand for office space (correspondingly, rental values may fall).

Whilst the signposts to future economic activity are rarely clear, the investment culture in large organisations is cautious. The corporate world is learning to 'live within its means'. This does not mean that innovation will cease, although projects that can realise return on investment and profit in six to twelve months will be preferred to projects that present a high long term risk. Despite the environment of considered investment, markets remain poised to erupt in activity.

The Internet is producing a changing world. What is coming next? How will work be organised in the next twenty years? What will be the changes in the things we buy? What will be the way we buy things and what will be the logistics involved in supplying and receiving them? One thing is certain:

> Thanks in part to money, the population of the world has doubled since the war, and these additional people on the Chinese mainland, in India and elsewhere in Asia are baying for money. A single prototype CD and its player halved the value of all the world's stock of vinyl discs in an instant; and somewhere in the world are warehouses of flared trousers, superannuated toys, seaplanes and armoured trains, mainframe computing power and so on that cost labour, ingenuity and seas of money to make and are now worthless in money. For the world, as we have said, is a battleground of wishes, which are limitless and cannot be satisfied except for a moment.[7]

The passage above refers to an obvious human trait: the on-going desire to satisfy wants and needs. It also explains a lot in relation to bubbles. Wants are obviously limitless, occasionally satisfaction is perceived to be attainable through the bubble, which inflates and offers a psychological ride to the realisation of untrammelled wealth. Although disappointment tends to be a generic reward, each seemingly believes that the opportunity exists to beat the market or in the very least obtain rewards from it.

The ability to access key information from a variety of sources is a fundamental part of successful speculative activity. There is, of course, no simple method to achieve perfect information. Professionals studying the stock market still get it wrong, especially in bubbles.[8] Even when investors act on good information and take a considered approach to the investment, it is almost impossible to beat the markets. Despite limitations, the use of indicators, such as a bubble model sketched out below can be useful in improving the chances of reducing the exposure to risk and maximising the benefits of speculation.

The ability to recognise major changes in the markets at an early stage is determined by the recognition or the notice of triggers that will change the direction and nature of the market. The early exit of key investors during a bubble, which may or may not be initially recognised by the wider investment community, gradually filters through a nexus of information networks that triggers further buying and selling strategies.

The trading patterns that are reflected in crowd trading occur in the markets with reference to a) peer pressure; b) psychological neurosis; c) rational and irrational investment speculation recognised in frenzied investment. Speculation that is related to the frenzied investment bubble is conditional on:

- An asset that is underpinned initially by a degree of substance
- Wide availability of credit or an increase in the wider generic prosperity
- A vehicle, for example, facilitated by the various media, that further popularises the asset through direct or related news
- A generic belief that the price will continue to rise
- The operation of social networks conducive to the communication of signals including related positive 'triggers', gossip or rumour of increasing returns from the engagement with the bubble

The presence of variables in the markets makes an exact science problematic. Politics, economics, society, technology, environmental, legal and cultural influences, as well as an emotional impact and accidental interventions from numerous sources shape (along with the supply and demand of the share itself) its performance and volatility. Nothing can be guaranteed.

The investment that seems to grow in a relatively consistent and persistent manner disguises an accompanied range of possibilities, some being conducive to manipulation, which may or may not alter its general direction at any point.

Theoretical Positions in Understanding and Mapping Bubbles

It has been mentioned in the introduction that the model by Cohen is underpinned by a lot of anecdotal, although historical, evidence. This does not undermine its value, which is noted in introducing some coherence in the studies of bubble activity. The model draws on the work collected by Kindleberger, who is indebted to Minsky. Cohen is firm in her view that the vehicle propelling bubbles is chaos.

Markets contain a degree of chaos, accidents and anomalies – erratic patterns are part of the rise and fall in assets prices. The strength of the model by Cohen is that it recognises the successive and unregulated interventions in bubbles. The weakness of the theory lies in its limited recognition of specific and direct interventions made to the market.

The model is useful, but does it help us to understand bubbles? In part, the answer must be yes. The work on chaos theory in relation to bubble activity should be further explored to simulate chaotic patterns in the markets. Markets, in this context, can be viewed as a series of puzzles; each bubble presents differing and unique patterns.

The reality that a series of largely subtle interventions produce and deflate bubbles should not however be ignored. Markets are manipulated but not by sinister forces (although on occasion that goal may be the prime motivation). The natural propulsion of markets oscillated by supply and demand produces opportunities. The potential to shape the market lies in the ability to recognise and act on the information, which may be reliable or be a rumour. Markets move because full information is impossible.

The model below integrates previous stages and illustrates the various theoretical positions that have contributed to understanding the progression of bubbles. The model omits stages that are perceived to be of less relevance and adds new stages that have been revealed throughout the investigation.

Table 9.1

Theorist	Description of Stage	Further comments
Schabacker	Economy recovers from previous bear market	Anticipation
Cohen	Trigger event	A new industry/idea that has not been seen before
Bagehot	Few investment vehicles	Other investment vehicles do not offer equally high 'promised' returns
Cohen	Easy credit/financial innovations	Bubble companies are highly geared and personal credit is available to investors
Minsky	Euphoric Economy	'it is different this time' view
Minsky/ Cohen	Ridiculous ventures/fraud	Detectable if applying rational investment criteria such as company profits, order book analysis
Cohen/ Bagehot	The selling flood/panic sell off	Caused by hysteria. Good stocks are affected by involvement of frauds and ridiculous ventures
Cohen	Debt deflation	Lasts similar length of time as build-up to bubble

Sheeran and Spain (2004)

The model above demonstrates that the series of stages is identifiable in bubbles. Schabacker is noted initially and shapes his deliberations in terms of fundamental analysis:

> Fundamental factors therefore include balance-sheet items, corporation management, prospects for the business, price earning ratios and basically – all things that normally and logically have a bearing upon the future state of the company's position and profit.[9]

Schabacker argues that:

> All that the average operator needs to do, therefore, in order to turn fundamental considerations from a stumbling block to a definite profit aid, is to place himself in such a position that he can also anticipate the future development or publication of such fundamental factors.[10]

Schabacker recognises the limits of the theory, but suggests that common sense approaches track carefully the range of the factors both within the company and its external business environment. These include an analysis of the structure of the industry, the place within it and related industries. Further considerations include an assessment of customer service, supply chain, procurement and the health of the order book. Each presents insight to produce a platform from which to base a realistic assumption on the future asset movement of a specific company.

The model built by Cohen recognises the stages within a bubble through the recourse to the alphabet alert, which recognises a series of phases in the rise and fall of bubbles.[11] This view is conditional on the perspective of the investor: each sees and recognises the steps or stages through experience.

It can be easily inferred that not all experiences are the same in the context of investment speculation. Therefore, to state the obvious, not all investment strategies or bubbles are the same. They may exhibit particular features, but they do not follow a predetermined pattern, otherwise the element of gambling, which underpins all investments to a degree, is removed to the point that the investment culture is stifled or removed. Nonetheless, regularities occur, but exceptions are ever present, waiting to break out, defeating easily firmly held perspectives and realities. This feature does not abandon rigour; on the contrary when considering financial forecasts and analysis all anomalies must be considered to reduce risk and error.

Despite the notable challenges in models created to make clear the progression of speculative activity, Cohen identifies eight key phases in bubbles with two further phases that recognise debt deflation and base-rebuilding (the point of recuperation where some investors regain confidence and return to the market). Cohen cites the eight key phases:

1.   Asset interest (Phase one: onset of bubble, trigger event)
2.   Cheap credit (Phase two: growth in credit and money supply)
3.   Inflation in asset prices (Phase three: rising prices)
4.   Overtrading and speculation (Phase four: pure speculation and exaggerated expectations)
5.   Gullible public joins in (Phase five: mass participation at the peak)
6.   Nagging doubts form (Phase six: concern that assets may not sustain positive trend)
7.   The selling flood (Phase seven: the serious selling begins)
8.   The panic sell off (Phase eight: the crash, panic and stampede into cash)

   Within each of the categories listed above, investors may act rationally or irrationally. The key to understanding the behaviour is derived from decoding the availability of information at each point, a factor that rests with each investor's actual relationship with it (triggers may be recognised, missed, acted upon or ignored). This is particularly evident during phase six (fraudulent practices in particular are disguised in a range of legal relationships).

   Each decision is informed by experience and intuition, the outcome of which is dependent on the value of the flow of information (power arises through the ability to judge and react), which ultimately determines the success or failure of the investment.

   Bagehot suggests that assets rise suddenly due to the absence of alternative investment opportunities returning acceptable gains. In this context, the absence of strong investment vehicles (a level conditional on the general investment mood and the range of alternatives available) exaggerates an existing bubble producing disturbance; money flows towards its greatest advancement. Writing on the manias that followed the South Sea Bubble, Bagehot captures the frenzy of moving into investments that promise high returns.

> In 1825 there were speculations in companies nearly as wild, and just before 1866 there were some of like nature, though not equally extravagant. The fact is, that the owners of savings not finding, in adequate quantities, their usual kind of investments, rush into anything that promises speciously, and when they find that these specious investments can be disposed of at a high profit, they rush into more and more. The first taste is for high interest, but that taste soon becomes secondary. There is a second appetite for large gains to be made

by selling the principal which is to yield the interest. So long as such sales can be effected the mania continues; when it ceases to be possible to effect them, ruin begins.[12]

The mood of the market in Bagehot's analysis is crucial to understanding why bubbles suddenly pick up force. The excitement generated by actual high returns is communicated through the investment chain, which attracts a fresh burst of investment with investors seeking similar gains. New investment money arrives in the form of virgin investors, also seeking to take advantage of the gains – this it is not irrational, but it is unsustainable and the final climb to the peak is followed by a fall, which invariably damages the investors least able to abscond from the investment, a flight which for numerous reasons is shaped by the distance between the investor and the market (spatiality determines also the ability to increase wealth and limit its losses).

The influx of new investment to the rising stock is fuelled also by availability of credit to the small investor. The recognition that high returns can be achieved by entering a particular rising investment attracts money from investors who have other assets but, noticing the unequal returns, either transfer assets to cash for the investment or seek additional gearing to take part.

Cohen makes this the second step in her model, presenting the early access to credit as being an important factor in the later rise. With an increasing money supply:

> Everyone becomes a buyer in the hope of making quick gains and selling is delayed in the expectation that prices will rise even further. Reassured by the almost effortless accumulation of easy profits, the concept of 'fair value' is heedlessly jettisoned. Conversion from caution to high-risk taking can affect the most cautious sophisticates and stolid professionals at the very moment when it lures all the novices and outright speculators, just when the peak looms into view.[13]

The abandonment of 'fair value' is an important point: the asymmetric moves are related to an underlying reality and a perception of it introduces disparities. In an earlier chapter the difference between the price of a stock and the real value of the company was noted. In rapid rises and falls, the underlying value of the company remains the same, although it obviously has an impact, certainly over time. The issue however is the rise and fall of prices, which are conditioned by supply and demand and the generic mood in the market.

In the book, *The Trouble with Capitalism* (1998), Shutt warns of the long-term damage caused by a feverish investment climate to a range of markets, industries, products and services:

> This is because the over enthusiasm of investors – born of sheer desperation to find profitable outlets for their surplus funds – may induce either excessive expansion of capacity in relation to demand growth potential or else overvaluation of the companies involved. In either case the effect may be to destabilise the latter financially – through undue pressure to maximise short-term profits and associated speculative takeover interest – with the end result that the businesses concerned may be distorted and the successful development of promising new product markets thereby prevented or delayed.[14]

In the case of the bubbles scenarios, the gradual and on-going rise in the asset price deludes investors through a transfer of confidence (the steady rise implicating that previous and unrelated bubbles were a separate phenomena, details which will not occur in the existing bubble).

Minsky recognises the influence of euphoric money on the bubble scenario and goes against the theory of efficient markets hypothesis.[15] Volatility is considered in reference to Keynes, where expectations are shaped by uncertainty but are led by mass sentiment. Confident that the bubble is a different investment environment from previous bubbles the on-going rising investment stages are perceived to be a guide to future expectations, a position that largely ignores the need for caution. It should be kept in mind that the damaging variables that impact on the sustainability of bubbles continue to be present in all bubbles, although they may take different forms; this is also relevant to the appearance of hurricanes and storms, which are composed of similar natural variables acting in some way – although in different combinations on each occasion.

The role of the banking system is central to Minsky's views on speculative investment: the flow of money within the system propelling the bubble rise. Minsky further illustrates the flows of money to a variety of investments through a reference to the 'financial fragility hypothesis'.

> In the theory, Minsky reiterates that finance and investment are interdependent and exert crucial influences on the development of the business cycle. Minsky's theory is based upon the insight that there are three basic types of 'financial posture' that together make up the debt structure underlying the financing of investment decisions: hedge finance, speculative finance and Ponzi finance. These different forms of financing involve different levels of risk for both the borrowers and lenders because they are funding investment projects with differing spreads of expected returns.[16]

The vortex of endogenous and exogenous investment flows produces an atmosphere of expectation both in the nature of the bubble and investment in it. The associated dynamics that attract interest produce opportunities for the manipulation of the situation through recourse to dubious practices.[17] The appearance of ridiculous ventures discussed in an earlier chapter, most explicitly in relation to the South Sea Bubble, and the generic identification of widespread fraud produces further factors that are relevant to bubbles activity. The Internet boom too had its share of scams.

> Some scamsters have used the Internet in the same way that con artists have used newspaper ads, the telephone, and other communications media to pitch their schemes. The old cold calling method done from the boiler rooms has given way to e-mail messages and Web sites that can reach millions of potential investors cheaply and instantly. The business of fraud has simply become more efficient. On the Internet it is much easier to get the word out about bogus get-rich-quick opportunities, hot stocks 'tips', and investments too good to be true.[18]

The increasing realisation that fraud and ludicrous business cases are embedded in the bubble produces a reaction in the stage listed by Cohen as *early nagging doubts.*

> It seems odd that the peak in each case is followed by a halting pause of early nagging doubts, marked by a gentle downward drift in prices from the all-time highs. This is a breathing space as people await events. However, if almost everyone has been a buyer, resulting in an enormous imbalance of buys over sells, it seems reasonable to wonder where the next buying surge can come from.[19]

The nagging doubts can however be disguised by the uncertainty surrounding the final stages of the bubble. There are investment flows to and from the bubble, which differ in volumes, presenting clues to the possibilities of future outcomes. This is not direct manipulation, but a considered appraisal of the information available, which may only be, at this stage, available to the few.

In addition to the stages presented in the model outlined by Sheeran and Spain, six modified influences are recognised:

1. A generic *atmosphere of public interest* attracts irrational investors (as seen in South Sea Bubble and Dotcom Bubble). The irrational nature of investor behaviour is irrational only in the context of hindsight. An asset that has recognisable and transparent substance will attract

investment. The point to examine is the psychology of the investor as the asset price becomes caught up in a bubble scenario.

2. Bubble stocks are over-valued from the outset. Methods of avoiding the use of conservative valuation techniques include the assertion that the market will act differently 'this time'. This was the case with dotcoms – enthusiasts believed that the revolution was permanent.

3. Increase in 'virgin' investment, i.e. those who have never invested before are drawn to invest because of the level of hype about the bubble stocks and the degree of available financial resources.

4. The Impact of government regulation or government action, as exemplified in the South Sea Bubble (the Bubble Act) and the Telecoms sector (Western European governments milking the industry in relation to 3G licences).[20]

5. The role of central banks (the impact of low interest rates) on the gradual rise in asset prices and bubble development. In the low interest rate environment, money flows back to the market (albeit in a slow uptake).

6. The unfolding of unanticipated and highly animated actions, which arise in various coded and explicit forms. High volume trading ahead of wider market moves.[21]

The need to expand on point four lies in the acceleration of global flows. International political economy recognises the nexus of relations betweens states and markets: the domains are not separate. This arena becomes heightened in terms of fault lines emerging from bubbles, which necessitate management and regulation.

Boom, distress and panic are transmitted between national economies through a variety of connections: arbitrage in commodities or securities (and marking up or down prices in one market when they change in another, without actually buying and selling), movements of money in various forms – specie, bank deposits, bills of exchange, interest rates changed through uncovered arbitrage, cooperation among monetary authorities, and readily neglected, pure psychology. These connections, moreover, can take various forms and may be interrelated in various ways.[22]

It is this dynamic that places the study of bubble activity within its lens of political economy. Government needs to be sensitive to the overlaps and links that couple states and markets in assessments and the application of policy to promote or limit bubble activity.

> ...As noted earlier, markets have an inherent tendency to expand and bring everything into their orbit. New demands are constantly stimulated and new sources of supply sought. Further, markets are subject to cyclical fluctuations and disturbances over which the society may have little control; specialization and its resulting dependencies increase vulnerabilities to untoward events. In short, markets constitute a powerful source of socio-political change and produce equally powerful responses as societies attempt to protect themselves against market forces.[23]

The need to monitor the development, spread and implosion of bubbles is shaped by the interconnectedness of politics and economics within and between states. It is posited that in future bubble phenomena will cause serious systemic disruption. Investors will increasingly become comfortable investing in shares outside familiar exchanges, the separate exchanges may themselves merge although, an integrated stock market looks unlikely in the short term.

Whilst constraints on investments are facilitated through regulation and money supply, the psychological expectations in relation to financial returns on investments are unrealistically high (through which criteria is poor performance measured?). The condition is noted by Bagehot that disappointment in alternative investments generates investment bubbles through money seeking the best return; limited choice directs flows towards specific investment vehicles.

Money initially flows from within the system. The investment environment is short-term and erratic. Debt deflection is notable in the markets; low interest rates are producing mini-bubbles in property and some investment funds. The next speculative adventure may be driven by short memories and the need to prop up disappointing pensions.

Notes

---

[1] Walter Bagehot in Physics and Politics (1875) presented an analysis of the relationship between the natural and social sciences, a connection that could be applied to economic and financial analysis and the movement of markets propelled and restrained by various investment strategies.

[2] *Lombard Street* (1917) by Walter Bagehot continues to be a classic text that demonstrates how a central bank, as lender in the last resort, should behave in response to a banking crisis.

[3] The nature of bubbles incorporates finance into economies via investment. Ulrich Beck in the book *The Reinvention of Politics* (1997) p.130 recognises the need to reconceptualises the relationship between politics and business, 'the age-of-And experiment of joining business and politics is therefore taking place simultaneously on several levels and is running in different directions. First, management must be conceived of as a kind of electoral district in which consent must be continually obtained over again, even if it is not organised in the form of a mandate (management training so forth). Second, it is necessary to open management strategies and methods, including personnel technology, organizational and labour market policies, to the dependence on publicity and consensus and to criticize and reorganise them on the basis of appropriate alternatives'.

[4] Uneven information in the markets is a natural condition. The link between prices on the stock market and the real economy are perhaps too tenuous to be used in practice by policy markers outside the context of a guide. Bain and Howells in *Monetary Economics: Policy and Its Theoretical Basis* (2003) p 367, suggest 'given that the flow of benefits from virtually all financial assets lies in the future and thus the current price must incorporate something of the agent's view of the future, scarcely any class of assets is immune from the search for potentially useful information. So far, we have considered the possibility of uncovering market's expectations of future interest rates (of different kinds) and possibly of inflation. Most ambitiously, it has been suggested in recent years that financial markets might be made to yield information about future developments in the real economy.'

[5] Baddeley (2003) p.196-197.

[6] Porter (1990) p.52.

[7] Buchan (1997) p. 277.

[8] Investment clubs may outperform professional traders on occasion, however over the long term the ability to assess and respond to the wealth of information that emerges continually, a situation that favours the institutional investor.

[9] Schabacker (1999[1934] p.85.

[10] Ibid (1999[1934]) p.94.

[11] Found in Cohen (1997).

[12] Bagehot (1917) pp 131-132.

[13] Cohen (1997) p.338.

[14] Shutt (1998) p.193.

[15] The efficient markets hypothesis is based on the notion that share prices accurately reflect all available information about both the economy and all individual companies. If the market is efficient, the aggregate market view of a company, as reflected in the share price, is the best possible guide to the true underlying value of the company (extract from Keasey *et al* p. 147).

[16] Baddeley (2003) p. 131.

[17] The scandal of Enron in American corporate life highlighted other problems inherent in financial and business circles. Arthur Andersen, once proud bearers of probity, had successive problems before the exposure of Enron in Britain. A feature by Robert Lea in

Management Today (2002) reported: 'Blacklisted from Government work for 15 years following the DeLorean scandal, Andersen was put back on the roster when New Labour swept to power. Indeed Andersen people worked closely with Gordon Brown's Shadow Treasury team on New Labour's economic agenda. It quickly won official contracts, including the audit on the Millennium Dome and work on the planned sell-offs of the NATS air traffic control business, the London Underground and British Nuclear Fuels.'

[18] Perkins and Perkins (1999) p. 201.

[19] Cohen (1997) pp 11-12.

[20] Cohen on the last page of her book (p.378) states 'perhaps we should stress the key role played by muddle-headed people in authority'. The starting point in the *International Political Economy of Investment Bubbles* is indeed we should.

[21] James Rosenau illustrates this point in the book, *Turbulence in World Politics* (1990: p.304) 'This is what happened when the world's stock markets crashed on October 19, 1987: "program trading" based on the information processing capacities of high speed computers swept the markets into outcomes that none of the existing macro regulations had anticipated.'

[22] Kindleberger (2000) p.119.

[23] Gilpin (1987) p.20.

Chapter 10

Reflections and Recriminations: The End of All Bubbles?

Reflections

The beginning of the twenty-first century has been marked by falling markets on a global scale, a slump in productivity and historically low interest rates. Despite examples of selective countervailing trends, the generic investment picture is depressed. Is this the end of investment bubbles?

New markets and opportunities are emerging. For example China appears well positioned to reap the potential opportunities arising from rapid growth, its release from the shackles of humiliation, and associated great power status; nanotechnology looks set to encourage a revived technology wave, the consumer keen on all things small; and efficiency gains derived from collaborative strategies and integrated networks, including supply chain and logistics, will improve productivity, albeit unevenly within sectors and industries.

The demand for cheap capital from anywhere in the world continues to intensify. The material presented in the book suggests that bubbles, waves, and mini and maxi short-term asset rises, continue to impact on economies throughout the world. Where they occur, how they progress and in what form they collapse is conditional on the operation of a range of factors and countervailing variables, which produce the bubble phenomenon (these influences were highlighted in the previous chapter).

It has been noted that bubbles in future are likely to be global in scope. Risk deepens and widens with integration. The debate pertaining to the management of the international financial architecture is shaped around the ability of existing international institutions to *adequately control* the flows of capital between states and the bubbles that arise within economies. Are new institutions required to respond to the problems relating to the wired global nexus of markets or are the existing controls satisfactory?

The trend for investors to adopt investment strategies that lie outside their immediate knowledge of markets is gradually increasing. There is a shift in investor culture that may encourage greater activity in unfamiliar exchanges, a change motivated by the realisation that is necessary to assess and act on opportunities wherever they occur.

Cultural obstacles remain, however, as most investors are reluctant to move outside their immediate investment boundaries. For small enterprises and individuals, the perceived difficulties relating to research (which may be in a different language), fear of high commission, red tape and other financial liabilities such as taxes, limit speculation. This is changing through increased transparency and the need to seek advantages wherever they can be found. It should be kept in mind that it is the small investor who brings liquidity to the markets. Decisions may, however, be handled by an institution which has the strategic resources and scope to take advantage of global investments and the resources available to undertake cross-border research assessments.

The increased competition occurring on a global scale is pressuring business, labour and markets to adopt flexible operations. Traditional industries such as manufacturing are finding that rising costs in some areas are encouraging firms to restructure or to relocate.

In the service sector, businesses that have markets in the rich industrialised world are re-routing services to consumers through call centres. For example, a customer's query to a company in Manchester may be routed to and addressed by a call centre in India. Flows of information, knowledge, commodities and capital of all kinds are generating new investment environments which present investment opportunities in mature and emerging markets. In both manufacturing and the service sector, competitive advantage and business development depend on networking. Information is a commodity with the ability to inform, increase and destroy investment bubbles.

Established markets are also reaping the benefits from the range of efficiency gains generated by the rapid technology changes that have been introduced since the 1980s. The infrastructure that transports information and knowledge through the various communication tools available is expanding geographically and advantages are increasingly being gained (existing systems and networks being run nearer to intended capacity, waste being generally addressed and noted). How companies respond to emerging opportunities produced by developments such as broadband will influence the shape of profits and the nature of survival.

The need to be aware of the operation of bubbles is crucial in the deceptive investment environment. Assets have been known to vanish into thin air (Enron), certainties have become failures (Marconi) and no dot hopers have become e-monoliths (Amazon). The history of investment bubbles suggests that intense speculative activity is not consigned to it. New speculative perils are poised to repeat similar investment adventures, which may place serious pressures on the interconnected system.

Recriminations

How the political and regulatory architecture responds to the series of structural changes occurring throughout the world will determine the shape and positive and negative consequences of investment bubbles. It is the flow of money to the markets and the condition of the investment environment that facilitates or limits the potential for bubbles (an uneven world in terms of production and consumption is a natural condition).

Governments mess with the markets. Through the implementation of a range of policies in relation to economic growth, regulation and stability, interventions influence the markets on an everyday basis, producing gains and losses in various measures.

Whilst international institutions manage elements of the system, domestic government provides the platform for firms to flourish or stagnate in the competitive environment. It is clear that the investment environment is partly shaped by the political structure and its numerous relationships with the economy. The state is influential in the rise and demise of investment bubbles. The state has not disappeared; it continues to operate in the new world realities.

Following a dramatic investment decline, strategies are initiated to take advantage of the weakness in the markets to stock pick and identify investment bargains. The potential to take advantage of speculative depression leads to a recovery in kind: the literature relating to the historical readings of investment bubbles demonstrates how fears of crashes relax with the passing of time. The realisation that Keynes's famous quote 'one certainty is that we are all dead one day' increases the desire to take risks to improve individual or collective wealth. It does not, however, fully explain the appearance, development and demise of bubbles.

Psychological factors are extraordinarily important in the rise and acceleration of bubbles, certainly when the crowd of investors recognise the possibilities and join in the investment. The earlier stages are dominated by other factors such as the generic investment environment. Other conditions prompt a series of questions. Are there alternatives providing similar returns? Is the money supply increasing the level of wealth throughout the economy? Is the asset part of a technological breakthrough? Is the asset desirable in some way other than its material gain? Is the political structure enhancing or limiting the conditions for investment? Do investment strategies have to be implemented to become bubbles?

The initial beginnings of a bubble are introduced by the realisation of ideas (the previous chapters have demonstrated that the ideas that lead to bubbles can be simple or spectacular): ideas in the presentation of an asset associated with speculation, be it a tulip bulb, a railway, or a dotcom (the recent IPO of the French Internet Company Iliad on 8 January 2004, which resulted in a 26% appreciation of its share price in its first month, highlights the fashion of speculation, other IPOs in the sector are expected to follow). Ideas in the method through which investment is attracted, triggered and promoted facilitate the opening run, which attracts other investors keen to emulate the first round of success.

It was posited, at the outset, that fear and greed shape the rise and fall of investment bubbles. This work illustrates that the presence of features beyond a strict reading of psychological factors, including emotional triggers, are responsible for the bubble phenomenon.

The International Political Economy of Investment Bubbles demonstrates that various forces are juxtaposed in a struggle to shape the eventual and eventful outcome of speculative advantage. The role played by the state in the process should not be underestimated.

Bibliography

Abreu, D. and Brunermeier, M. (2003) 'Bubbles and Crashes', *Econometrica*, Vol. 71, No. 278, pp. 377-378.

Aldcroft, D.H. (1977) *From Versailles to Wall Street 1919-1929*, London: Allen Lane.

Alexander, J. (1963) *Economic Geography*, New Jersey: Prentice Hall, Inc.

Allen, F. and Gale, D. (1999) 'Bubbles, crises, and policy', *Oxford Review of Economic Policy*, Vol.15, No.3, pp 9-18.

Amis, M. (2000 [1984]) *Money*, London: Penguin Classic.

Anon (1994) 'Merger Mania II', *Fortune*, Vol 130, Issue 7 p.20.

Anon (1999) 'The workshop of a new society', *The Economist*, 31 December 1999, pp 19-20.

Anon (1999) 'How to invest in the technology revolution', *Investors Chronicle*, 1 October, pp 30-31.

Anon (2000) 'Milking the dotcom mania', *Business Times*, p.16.

Anon (2000) 'Dotty about dot.commerce?' *The Economist*, 26 February , pp 21-22.

Arestis, P. and Sawyer, M.C. (2000) *The Political Economy of Central Banking*, Cheltenham, UK and Northampton, MA, USA: Edward Elgar.

Arrighi, G. (1994) *The Long Twentieth Century*, London and New York: Verso.

Ashley, M. (1952) *England in the Seventeenth Century (1603-1714)*, London: Pelican.

Backhouse, R.E. (2002) *The Penguin History of Economics*, London: Penguin Books.

Baddeley, M.C. (2003) *Investment: Theories and Analysis*: Basingstoke: Palgrave.

Bagehot, W. (1875) *Physics and Politics: or Thoughts on the Application of the Principles of 'Natural Selection' and 'Inheritance' to Political Society*, London: King.

Bagehot, W. (1917) *Lombard Street: A Description of the Money Market*, London: John Murray.

Bagwell, P.S. and Mingay, G.E. (1970) *Britain and America 1850-1939: A Study of Economic Change*, London: Routledge and Kegan Paul.

Bain, K. and Howells, P. (2003) *Monetary Economics Policy and its Theoretical Basis*, Basingstoke: Palgrave.

Baker, M. (2003) 'Law's Paper Revolution End Up as Pulp Fiction', *The Daily Telegraph: Your Money Supplement*, 10 May 2003, p. B2.

Baldwin, J. (1957) *The Flush Times of Alabama and Mississippi*, New York: Sagamere Press.

Balen, M. (2003) *A Very English Deceit*, London and New York: Fourth Estate.

Balls, E. and O'Donnell, G. (2002) *Reforming Britain's Economic and Financial Policy*, Basingstoke: Palgrave.

Basile, A. and Joyce, J.P. (2001) 'Asset Bubbles, Monetary Policy and Bank Lending in Japan', *Applied Economics*, Vol. 33, No.13, pp.1737-1744.

Beck, U. (1997) *The Reinvention of Politics*, Cambridge: Polity Press.

Beck, U. (1992) *The Risk Society: Towards a New Modernity*, London: Sage Publications.

Bernhard, W., Broz, J.L. and Clark, W.R. (2002) 'The Political Economy of Monetary Institutions', *International Organization*, 56, 4, Autumn pp.693-723.

Boesky, I. (1985) *Merger Mania*, New York: Holt.

Boyer, C.B. (1989) *A History of Mathematics*, New York and Chichester: John Wiley and Sons.

Boyle, R. and Haynes, R. (2000) *Power Play: Sport, the Media and Popular Culture*, Harrow: Pearson Education.Winston.

Braudel, F. (1981) *The Structures of Everyday Life: The Limits of the Possible*, Volume 1, London: Collins.

Braudel, F. (1982) *The Wheels of Commerce*, Volume II, London: Collins.

Brendon, P. (1991) *Thomas Cook – 150 Years of Public Tourism*, London: Secker and Warburg.

Brenner, R. (2000) 'The World Economy at the Turn of the Millennium', *Review of International Political Economy*, Vol. 8, No.1, Spring, 6-44.

Brooks, J. (1972 [1969]) *Once in Golconda: A True Drama of Wall Street 1920-38*, London: Pelican Library of Business and Management.

Brooks, J. (1975) *The Go-Go Years*, Dublin: Gill and Macmillan.

Brown, R. (1988) *Group Processes*, Oxford: Blackwell.

Buchan, J. (1997) *Frozen Desire: An Inquiry into the Meaning of Money*, London: Picador.

Burton, J. (1972) *World Society*, London: Cambridge University Press.

Burton, J. ed., (1986) *Keynes' General Theory: Fifty Years On – Its Relevance and Irrelevance to Modern Times*, London: The Institute of Economic Affairs.

Cable, V. (1999) *Globalization and Global Governance*, Royal Institute of International Affairs, London: Pinter.

Camilleri, J.A. and Falk, J. (1992) *The End of Sovereignty?: The Politics of a Shrinking and Fragmenting World*, Aldershot: Edward Elgar Publishing Limited.

Campbell, J. and Bonner, W. (1994) *Media, Mania and the Markets*, London: Fleet Street Publications.

Caporaso, J.A. and Levine, D.P. (1992) *Theories of Political Economy*, Cambridge: Cambridge University Press.

Carr, R. (1999) 'The Gorilla Game', book review, *Investor Chronicle*, pp 12-15.

Carruthers, B.G. and Babb, S.L. (2000) *Economy/Society*, London: Pine Forge Press.

Carswell, J. (1960) *South Sea Bubble*, London: Cresset Press.

Chorafas, D.N. (2000) *New Regulation of the Financial Industry*, Great Britain: Macmillan.

Christy, J.H. (2002) 'Rough Waters', *Forbes Global*, June 10 2002, 58-59.

Cipolla, C.M. (1970) *The Economic Decline of Empires*, London: Methuen and Co Ltd.

Cochrane, J.H. (2001) 'Book review – Famous First Bubbles', *Journal of Political Economy*, Vol.109, No.5, pp 1150-1154.

Cohen, B. (1997) *The Edge of Chaos: Financial Booms, Bubbles, Crashes and Chaos*, Chichester: John Wiley and Sons.

Cort, R. (1834) *Railroad Impositions Detected Bubble Speculations*, London: W.Lake.

Coward, N. (1956) *South Sea Bubble: Comedy in Three Acts*, London: Heinemann.

Cowles, V. (1960) *The Great Swindle: The Story of the South Sea Bubble*. London: Collins.

Coye, D. (2001) *Paradoxes of Prosperity: Why the New Capitalism Benefits All*, New York and London: Texere.

Coxe, D. (2003) 'The Bubble Master', *Maclean's*, Vol.116, Issue 29, p.34.

Crichton, M. (1993) *Rising Sun*, USA: Ballantine Books.

Dale, R. (1996) *Risk and Regulation in Global Security Markets*, Chichester and New York: John Wiley and Sons.

Dalton, J. (1993) *How the Stock Market Works*, New York: New York Institute of Finance.

Dash, M. (2000) *Tulipomania: The Story of the World's Most Coveted Flower and the Extraordinary Passions It Aroused*, London: Gollancz.

De La Vega, J. (1996[1688]) *Confusión de Confusiones*, New York and Chichester: John Wiley and Sons.

De Wit, B. and Meyer, R. (1997), *Strategy – Process, Content, Context: An International Perspective*, United States: West Publishing Company.

Delmer, A. (1864) *The Great Paper Bubble, or The Coming Financial Explosion*, New York: Metropolitan Record.

Dimson, E., Marsh, P. and Staunton, M. (2002) *Triumph of Optimism: 101 Years of Global Investment Returns*, Princeton: Princeton University Press.

Dubois, A (1938) *The English Business Company after the Bubble Act 1720-1800*, New York: Metropolitan.

Dicken, P. (2003) Fourth Edition, *Global Shift: Reshaping the Global Economic Map in the 21st Century*, London: Sage Publications.

Dostoyevsky, F. (1996 Edition) *The Gambler*, New York: Dover.

Driesum, R.V. and Hall, N. (2000) *Amsterdam*, London: Lonely Planet.

Drucker, P. (1993 [1950]) *The New Society: The Anatomy of Industrial Order*, New Brunswick (U.S.A) and London (U.K.): Transaction Publishers.

Ekelund, R.B. and Hébert, R.F. (1990) Third Edition, *A History of Economic Theory and Method*, New York: McGraw-Hill Publishing.

Eliot, G (1965 [1871-2] *Middlemarch*, London: Penguin Classics.

Erleigh, V. (1933) *The South Sea Bubble*, London: Peter Davis Limited.

Essinger, J. (1999) *Global Custody*, London: Financial Times Prentice Hall.

Evans, J (1999) 'Latest despatches from the wild frontier', *Investment Chronicle*, 22 July, pp 12-13.

Evans, C. (2002) 'Napoleon's corporate heirs', *Accountancy*, September, 68-69.

Feiling, K. (1975[1950]) *A History of England*, London: Book Club Associates.

Feis, H. (1974) *Europe: The World's Banker 1870-1914*, Clifton: Augustus M. Kelly.

Ferguson, B. (1978) *Hubble-Bubble*, London: Collins.

Ferguson, K. (2002) *Essential Economics*, Britain: Basingstoke.

Ferguson, N. (2001) *The Cash Nexus*, London: Allen Lane The Penguin Press.

Ferguson, P., Ferguson, G. and Rothschild, R. (1993) *Business Economics*, Basingstoke: The Macmillan Press.

Fischer, D.H. (1997[1996]) *The Great Wave: Price Revolutions and the Rhythm of History*, New York: The Softback Preview.

Flynn, J.T. and Pavlik, G.P. (1995) *Forgotten Essays: Selected Essays*, US: Foundation for Economic Education.

Francis, J. (2001[1850]) *Chronicles and Characters of the Stock Exchange*, London: Hindsight Books.

Frank, A.G. (1980) *Crisis: In the World Economy*, London: Heinemann.

Frank, T. (2002) 'Talking Bull', Weekend, *The Guardian*, 17 September.

Friedman, M. and Schwartz, A. (1963) *A Monetary History of the United States*, Princeton: Princeton University Press.

Fritschy, W. (2003) 'A 'Financial Revolution' Reconsidered: Public Finance in Holland during the Dutch Revolt, 1568-1648', *Economic History Review*, LVI, 1 pp. 57-89.

Fukuta, Y. (2002) 'A test for rational bubbles in stock prices', *Empirical Economics*, Vol. 27, No. 4, pp 587-600.

Fukuyama, F. (1995) *Trust: The Social Virtues and the Creation of Prosperity*, London: Hamish Hamilton.

Galbraith, J.K. (1974) *Economics and the Public Purpose*, Great Britain: Andre Deutsch.

Galbraith, J.K. (1977) *The Age of Uncertainty*, London: BBC and Andre Deutsch.

Galbraith, J.K. (1987) *A History of Economics: the past and the present*, London: Penguin Books.

Galbraith, J.K. (1991[1958]) *The Affluent Society*, London: Penguin Books.

Galbraith, J.K, (1992 [1954]) *The Great Crash 1929*, London: Penguin Books.

Garber, P. (2000) *Famous First Bubbles*, Cambridge Mass.: MIT Press.

Garrett, G. (1932) *A Bubble that Broke the World*, Boston: Little, Brown and Co.

Geisst, C. (2002) *Wheels of Fortune*, Hoboken: N.J.Wiley.

Giles, C. and LeRoy, S. (1998) 'Arbitrage, martingales and bubbles', *Economics Letters*, Vol.60, No. 3, pp.357-362.

Gill, S. and Law, D. (1988) *The Global Political Economy: Perspectives, Problems and Policies*, New York and London: Harvester Wheatsheaf.

Gilpin, R. (1987) 'The Nature of Political Economy', in Goddard, C.R., Cronin, P. and Kishore, D.C. (2003) *International Political Economy: State-Market Relations in a Changing Global Order*, Basingstoke: Palgrave.

Gladwell, M (2000) *The Tipping Point: How Little Things Can Make A Big Difference*, London: Abacus.

Glautier, M.W.E. and Underdown, B. (1991) *Accountancy Theory and Practice*, Belmont: Pitman publishers.

Gleich, J. (1987) *Chaos*, Great Britain: A Cardinal Book.

Gould, J.D. (1972) *Economic Growth in History: Survey and Analysis*, London: Methuen and Co Ltd.

Groom, A.J.R. and Taylor, P. (1990) *Frameworks for International Cooperation*, London: Pinter Publishers.

Hailey, A. (1975) *The Money Changes*, London: Pan Books.

Hale, J. (1994) *The Civilization of Europe in the Renaissance*, London: Fontana Press.

Hamilton, A., Madison, J. and Jay, J. (1996[1911]) *The Federalist*, London and Vermont: Everyman.

Harris, N. (1999) *The European Business Environment*, Basingstoke: Palgrave.

Harrison, J. M. and Kreps, D.M. (1978) 'Speculative Investor Behaviour in a Stock Market with Heterogeneous Expectations,' *Quarterly Journal of Economics.*

Harte, N.B. ed., (1971) *The Study of Economic History*, London: Frank Cass and Company.

Hawkings, D.T (1995) *A Guide to Staff Records of the Railway Companies of England and Wales 1822-1947*, Public Record Office: Alan Sutton Publishing Ltd.

Hayek, F.A. (1971 [1944}) *The Road to Serfdom*, London: Routledge.

Helmore, E. (2001) 'Inside the $100m Club: The Dotcom Entrepreneurs Who Have Lost A Fortune, *The Guardian*, Online, pp 2-3.

Hellenier, E. (1994) 'From Bretton Woods to Global Finance', in Stubbs, R. and Underhill, G. ed., *Political Economy and the Changing Global Order*, Basingstoke and London: Macmillan.

Helweg-Larsen, M. and Sheppard, J.A. (2001) 'Do Moderators of the Optimistic Bias Affect Personal or Target Risk Estimates? A Review of the Literature', *Personality and Social Psychology Review*, Vol. 5, No.1, pp 74-95.

Henderson, A.J. (1975) *London and the National Government, 1721-1742: A Study of City Politics and the Walpole Administration*, Philadelphia: Porcupine Press.

Hibbert, C. (1986) *Cities and Civilization*, Britain: Weidenfeld and Nicolson.

Higgott, R. (1994), 'International Political Economy', in Groom, A.J.R. and Light, M. ed., *Contemporary International Relations: A Guide to Theory*, London and New York: Pinter Publishers.

Hobsbawn, E. (1977[1962]) *The Age of Revolution 1789-1848*, London: Abacus.

Hobsbawn, E. (1993[1975]) *The Age of Capital 1848-1875*, London: Abacus.

Hobsbawn, E. (1990 [1989]) *The Age of Empire 1875-1914*, London: Abacus.

Hobsbawn, E. (1995[1994] *Age of Extremes: The Short Twentieth Century*, 1914-1991, London: Abacus.

Hoekman, B. and Kostecki, M. (1997) *The Political Economy of the World Trading System: From GATT to WTO*, Oxford: Oxford University Press.

Hofstede, G. (1997), *Software of the Mind*, New York: McGraw-Hill.

Holton, R.H. (1992) *Economy and Society*, London: Routledge.

Honderich, T.H. ed., (1995) *The Oxford Companion to Philosophy*, Oxford: Oxford University Press.

Hoppit, J. (1986) 'Financial Crises in Eighteenth-Century England', *Economic History Review*, pp.39-58.

Howkins, J. (2001) *The Creative Economy*, London: Penguin Books.

Huber, P. (2003) 'Military-Industry Complex, 2003', *Forbes Global*, 12 May, p.19.

Hurd S. and Mangan, J. (2001) Essential Data Skills for Business and Management, *Office of National Statistics*, Bishops Stortford: Statistics for Education.

Hutchenson, T.W. (1981) *The Politics and Philosophy of Economics*, Oxford: Basil Blackwell.

Hutton, W. (1996[1995]) *The State We're In*, London: Vintage.

Hutton, W. (2000) 'From .com to .bomb', *The Observer*, 12 March, p.16.

Isaak, R.A. (1995) *Managing World Economic Change: International Political Economy*, New Jersey: Prentice Hall International.

Israel, J.I. (1995) *The Dutch Republic: Its Rise, Greatness, and Fall 1477-1806*, Oxford: Clarendon Press.

Jackson, R. and Sørensen, G. ed., (1999) *Introduction to International Relations*, Oxford: Oxford University Press.

Jay, P. (2000) *The Road to Riches*, London: Phoenix.

Johnston, R.J., Taylor, P. and Watts, M. ed., (2002) *Geographies of Global Change: Re-mapping the World*, Oxford: Blackwell Publishers.

Kahneman, D., Tversky, A. and Slovic, P. (1982) *Judgement Under Uncertainty*, Cambridge: Cambridge University Press.

Kahneman, D. and Tversky, A. (1979) 'Prospect Theory: Analysis of decision under risk', *Econometrica*, Vol.47, pp. 263-91.

Kaldor, N. ((1980[1964]) *Essays on Economic Policy II – IV. Policies for International Stability; V. Country Studies*, London: Duckworth.

Kaufman, G. (1996) 'Bank failures, Systemic Risk and Bank Regulation', *Cato Journal*, Vol. 16, No.1, pp 17-45.

Kaufman, G. (1998) *Bank Crises, Cause and Analysis*, Greenwich: JAI.

Kaufman, G. (2000) *Bank Fragility and Regulation*, Amsterdam: JAI.

Keasey, K., Hundson, R. and Littler, K. (1998) *The Intelligent Guide To Stock Market Investment*, Chichester: John Wiley and Sons.

Kennedy, P. (1989) *The Rise and Fall of Great Powers*, London: Fontana Press.

Keynes, J. (1919) *The Economic Consequences of Peace*, London: Macmillan and Co.

Kindleberger, P.C. (1978) *Manias, Panics and Crashes*, New York and Chichester: John Wiley and Sons, Inc.

Kindleberger, P.C. (2000c) Comparative Political Economy: A Retrospective, Cambridge Mass. and London: MIT Press.

Kirkland, E.C. (1969) *A History Of American Economic Life*, Fourth Edition, New York: Appleton-Century-Crofts.

Kitson, M. and Michie, J. (1995) 'Trade and Growth: A Historical Perspective', in Michie. J. and Smith, J.G. (1995) *Managing the Global Economy*, Oxford: Oxford University Press.

Klein, N. (2002) *Fences and Windows: Dispatches from the Front Lines of the Globalization Debate*, London: Flamingo Original.

Knight, F. (2002[1964]) *Risk, Uncertainty, and Profit*, Chicago: Augustus M.Kelley.

Knox, P. and Agnew, J. (1989) *The Geography of the World Economy*, Great Britain: Hodder Headline PLC.

Kolb, R.W. and Rodriguex, R.J. (1996) *Financial Markets*, Oxford: Blackwell Publishers.

Kynaston, D. (1994) *The City of London: A World of Its Own 1815-1890*, Vol.1, London: Chatto and Windus.

Landes, D. (1999) *The Wealth and Poverty of Nations*, London: Abacus.

Langford, P. (1992) *A Polite and Commercial People – England 1727-1783*, Oxford: Oxford University Press.

Lash, S. and Urry, J. (1994) *Economies of Signs and Space*, London: Sage Publications.

Law, J. (1705) 'Money and Trade Considered, with a Proposal for Supplying the Nation with Money', pamphlet held at the British Library Kings Cross.

Law, S. (2002) 'Getting the Measure of Leadership', *ProfessionalManager*, pp. 26-28.

Lea, R. (2002) 'Shredded Lives: The Agony of Arthur Andersen', *Management Today*, October, pp. 46-53.

Lee, C.H. (1977) *The Quantitative Approach to Economic History*, London: Martin Robertson.

Lefèvre, E. (1994) *Reminiscences of a Stock Operator*, New York: Wiley.

Lewin, H.G. (1968) *The Railway Mania and its Aftermath 1845-1852*, New York: Augustus M. Kelley.

Lewis, M. (1989) *Liar's Poker*, London: Hodder and Stoughton.

Lewis, M. (1999), *The New New Thing*, London: Hodder and Stoughton.

Lewis, M. (2001) *The Future Just Happened*, London: Hodder and Stoughton.

Leertouwer, E. and Maier, P. (2002), 'International and Domestic Constraints on Political Business Cycles in OECD Economies: A Comment,' *International Organisation*, Vol.56, No.1, Winter, pp. 209-221.

Lever, K. (2002) 'Stock markets and business reality: a finance director's view', *Accountancy*, September.

Leys, C. (1989) *Politics in Britain: From Labourism to Thatcherism*, London: Verso.

Lichtheim, G. (1972) *Europe in the Twentieth Century*, London: Weidenfeld and Nicolson.

Littlewood, J. (1998) *The Stock Market: 50 Years of Capitalism at Work*, London: Financial Times Pitman Publishing.

Lukes, S. ed., (1986) *Power*, Oxford UK and Cambridge USA: Blackwell.

Lunt, W.E. (1962) *Financial Relations of the Papacy with England 1327-1534*, Massachusetts: The Mediaeval Academy of America Cambridge.

Lux, T. and Sornette, D. (2002) 'On rational bubbles and fat tails', *Journal of Money, Credit and Banking*, Vol. 34, No. 3(1), pp. 589-610.

Mackay, C. (1996 [1841]) *Extraordinary Popular Delusions and the Madness of Crowds*, New York: Wiley Investment Classics, John Wiley & Sons.

McRae, H. and Cairncross, F. (1973) *Capital City: London as a Financial Centre*, London: Eyre Methuen.

Mandel, E. (1978) *The Second Slump, A Marxist Analysis of Recession in the Seventies*, London: NLB.

Manstead, A.S.R. and Hewstone, M. eds., (1996), *The Blackwell Encyclopaedia of Social Psychology*, Oxford: Blackwell.

Marrewijk, C.V. (2002) *International Trade and the World Economy*, Oxford: Oxford University Press.

Matlin, M. W. and Stang, D. J. (1978) *The Polyanna Principle. Selectivity in Language, Memory, and Thought*, Cambridge, MA: Schenkman.

Mayer, H.E. (1972) *The Crusades*, Oxford: Oxford University Press.

Meltzer, A. (2002) 'Rational and Irrational Bubbles', *Central Banking*, Vol.XlIl, No.1, pp 36-45.

Melville, L. (1921) *The South Sea Bubble*, London: Daniel O'Conner.

Mennis, E.A. (1999) *How the Economy Works: An Investors Guide to Tracking the Economy*, Second Edition, New York: New York Institute of Finance.

Miche, J. and Smith, J.G. eds., (1995) *Managing The Global Economy*, Oxford: Oxford University Press.

Mill, J.S. (1848) *Principles of Political Economy*, London: Penguin Classics.

Miller, J. (1720) *An Interesting Account of the South Sea Scheme*, London: S. Gilbert.

Miller, M.J. (2003) 'Rejecting the Doomsayers', *PC Magazine*, Vol. 22, Issue 12, p.7.

Minsky, M. (1982) *Can 'It' Happen Again? Essays on Instability and Finance*, Boston: M. E. Sharpe.

Minsky, H. (1986) *Stabilizing an Unstable Economy* (20th Century Fund Report), Yale: Yale University Press.

Mommass, H. (2000) 'De culturele industrie in het tijdperk van de netwerkeconomie (The cultural industry in the age of the networked economy)', *Boekmancahier*, Vol. 12, No. 43, pp 26-46.

Morgan, K. (1984) *Oxford Illustrated History of England*, Oxford: Oxford University Press.

Morrison, J. (2002) *The International Business Environment: Diversity and the Global Economy*, Basingstoke: Palgrave.

Morton, J. (1997) *Investing with the Grand Masters*, London: Financial Times Pitman Publishing.

Moschandreas, M. (2000) *Business Economics*, Second Edition, United Kingdom: Thomson.

Murphy, C.N. and Tooze, R. eds., (1991) *The New International Political Economy*, Hampshire: Macmillan.

Nevaer, L.E.V. (2002) *The Dot-Com Debacle and the Return to Reason*, Westport, Connecticut: Quorum Books.

Newhausrer, R. (2000) *The Early History of Greed: The Sin of Avarice in Early Medieval Thought and Literature*, Cambridge: Cambridge University Press.

Nyhus, E.K. (2001) 'Life-cycle and dispositional routes into problem debt', *The British Journal of Psychology*, Vol. 92, pp. 423-446.

Ohmae, K. (1995) *The End of the Nation State*, London: Harper Collins.

Oliver, J. (2000) 'Growth enhancing bubbles', *International Economic Review*, Vol. 41, No.1, pp.133-151.

Olson, W.C. and Groom, A.J.R. (1991) *International Relations Then and Now: Origins and Trends in Interpretation*, London and New York: Routledge.

Orléan, A. (2003) 'Les marches financiers sont-ils rationnels? (Are financial markets rational?) *La Recherche*, May 2003, No. 364, pp 58-62.

Oudard, G. (1928) *John Law: a Fantastic Financier 1671-1729*, London: Jonathan Cape.

Parker, G. (1979) *Spain and the Netherlands 1559-1659*, London: Fontana Press.

Pen, J. (1958) *Modern Economics*, London: Pelican.

Pennington, D.H. (1970) *Europe in the Seventeenth Century*, London and New York: Longman.

Perez, C. and Puffert, D. Rev. (2003) 'Technological revolutions and financial capital: the dynamics of bubbles and the golden ages', *Journal of Economic History*, Vol. 63, No.2, pp. 615-616.

Perkins, A.B. and Perkins, M.C. (1999) *The Internet Bubble: Inside the Overvalued World of High Tech-Stocks – and What You Need to Know to Avoid the Coming Shakeout*, New York: Harper Collins.

Petal, A.B. (1997) *The Mind of a Trader*, London: Financial Times Prentice Hall.

Peters, E.E. (1994) *Fractal Market Analysis: Applying Chaos Theory To Investment and Economics*, New York and Chichester: John Wiley and Sons.

Pettinger, R. (2000) *Investment Appraisal: A Managerial Approach*, Basingstoke: Macmillan Business.

Pevitt, C. (1997) *The Man Who Would Be King: The Life of Philippe D'Orleans, Regent of France*, Britain: Weidenfeld and Nicolson.

Phillips, B. (2000) 'The Stock Market – Friend or Foe?', *Company Accountant*, August, pp. 19-29.

Piquard, P. (2003) 'La fabuleuse histoire de l'économie', *Capital*, No. 143, August, pp. 36-90.

Plumb, J.H. (1957) *England in the Eighteenth Century (1714-1815)*, London: Pelican .

Porter, G.R. (1912) *The Progress of the Nation*, New York: Augustus M. Kelley.

Porter, M. (1998[1990]) *The Competitive Advantage of Nations*, Basingstoke: Macmillan Press.

Post, B. (2002) 'Big Ideas: From Frozen Peas to Penicillin to Spreadsheets. 85 Ideas that Have Changed the World,' *Forbes Global*, Vol. 5, No. 24, pp. 33-55.

Poulson, B. (1981) *Economic History of the United States*, New York: Macmillan.

Redhead, K. (2001) 'The Psychology of Personal Finance', *Company Accountant*, Issue No. 164, pp. 26-29.

Redhead, K. (2000) 'The Story of Gilts', *Company Accountant*, June, pp.11-15.

Rhinehart, L. (1998) *The Dice Man*, US: Overlook Press.

Ridderstråle, J. and Nordström, K. (2002) *Funky Business: Talent Makes Capital Dance*, Second Edition, London New York: Prentice Hall Financial Times.

Robbins, L. (1976) *Political Economy: Past and Present A Review of Leading Theories of Economic Policy*, London and Basingstoke: Macmillan.

Robinson, J. (1975) *Collected Economic Papers Vol III*, Oxford: Basil Blackwell.

Rosenau, J. (1990) *Turbulence in World Politics: A Theory of Change and Continuity*, New York and London: Harvester Wheatsheaf.

Rosenberg, J. (1994) *The Empire of Civil Society: A Critique of the Realist Theory of International Relations*, London and New York: Verso.

Ross, D. (2003) 'The Rise and Rise of Globalisation', *Geographical*, October.

Rowe, D. (1999) *Sport, Culture and the Media*, Buckingham: Open University Press.

Rozin, P. and Royzman, E. (2001) 'Negativity Bias, Negativity Dominance, and Contagion', *Personality and Social Psychology Review*, Vol. 5, No. 4, pp. 296-320.

Rowling, N. (1987) *Commodities: How the World was Taken to Market*, London: A Channel Four Book.

Rugman, A.M. and Hodgetts, R.M (2003) *International Business*, Third Edition, England: Pearson Education Limited.

Ruskin, J. (1970) *Unto This Last: Four Essays on the First Principles of Political Economy*, London and Glasgow: Collins Publishers.

Saber, N. (1999) *Speculative Capital*, Vol.6, London: Financial Times Prentice Hall.

Sakolski, A.M. (1932*) The Great American Land Bubble: The amazing story of land grabbing, speculations, and booms form colonial days to the present time*, New York and London: Harper and Bros.

Samuels, W.J. ed., (1979) *The Economy as a System of Power*, New Jersey: Transaction Books.

Saul, S.B. (1969) *The Myth of the Great Depression 1873-1896*, London: Macmillan and Co.

Sayers, R.S. (1967) *A History of Economic Change in England 1880-1939*, Oxford: Oxford University Press.

Schabacker, R. (1999 [1934]) *Stock Market Profits*, London: Financial Times Prentice Hall.

Schama, S. (1997) *The Embarrassment of Riches: An Interpretation of Dutch Culture in the Golden Age*, London: Fontana Press.

Scholte, J.A. (2000) *Globalization: A Critical Introduction*, London: Macmillan.

Schumpeter, J.A.(1986 [1954]) *History of Economic Analysis*, London: Allen and Unwin.

Sedden, E. (1966) *Modern Economic History*, London: Macdonald and Evens Ltd.

Sedgwick, R. (1970) *The House of Commons 1715-1754*, History of Parliament Series, London: History of Parliament Trust.

Sefton, C. (1999) 'Net one of us – if you can', *Investors Chronicle*, pp 12-15.

Seitz, J.L (2002) *Global Issues*, Second Edition, Oxford: Blackwell Publishers.

Shiller, R. (2000) *Irrational Exuberance*, Princeton: Princeton University Press.

Shiller, R. (2002) 'Bubbles, Human Judgement and Expert Opinion', *Financial Analysis Journal,* Vol. 58, No. 3, pp.589-610.

Shutt, H. (1998) *The Trouble with Capitalism: an Enquiry into the Causes of Global Economic Failure*, London and New York: Zed Books.

Singleton-Green, B. (2001), 'Reasons and Rollercoasters', News Editorial, *Accountancy*, April Issue.

Smith, A. (1974) *The Money Game*, London: Joseph.

Smith, A. (1974 [1776]) *The Wealth of Nations*, London: Penguin.

Sobel, R. (1965) *The Big Board: A History of the New York Stock Market*, New York: Collier-Macmillan.

Spencer, P.D. (2000) *The Structure and Regulation of Financial Markets*, Oxford: Oxford University Press.

Spero, J.E. (1977) *The Politics of International Economic Relations*, Fourth Edition, London and New York: Routledge.

Sprott, W.J.H. (1958) *Human Groups*, London: A Pelican Book.

Stark, W. (1954) *Jeremy Bentham's Economic Writings: Critical Edition Based on his Printed Works and Unprinted Manuscripts*, London: The Royal Economic Society, George Allen & Unwin Ltd.

Stelzer, I. (2000) 'Tulip mania holds lessons for dotcoms', *The Sunday Times*, Business Section, p.4.

Stewart, J.B. (1991) *Den of Thieves*, New York: Simon and Schuster.

Stiglitz, J. (2002) *Globalization and its Discontents*, London: Penguin.

Strange, S. (1986) *Casino Capitalism*, Oxford: Basil Blackwell.

Strange, S. (1988) *States and Markets: An Introduction to International Political Economy*, London: Pinter Publishers.

Strange, S. (1991) 'An Eclectic Approach', in Murphy, C.N and Tooze, R. (1991) *The New International Political Economy*, Boulder: Lynne Rienner Publishers.

Strange. S., Stopford, J. and Henley, J.(1991) *Rival States, Rival Firms: Competition for World Market Shares*, Cambridge: Cambridge University Press.

Suls, J., Martin, R. and Wheeler, L. (2000) '*Three Kinds of Opinion Comparison: The Triadic Model*', Personality and Social Psychological Review, Vol. 4, No.3, pp. 219-237.

Sutton, J. (2000) *Lords of the East: The East India Company and Its Ships 1600-1874*, Great Britain: Chrysalis Books Limited.

Tanous, P.J. (1997) *Investment Gurus*, New York: New York Institute of Finance.

Tayeb, M. (2000) *International Business: Theories, Policies and Practices*, London: Financial Times Prentice Hall.

Taylor, P. (1993) *Political Geography: World Economy, Nation-State and Locality*, New York: Longman Scientific and Technical.

Taylor, P. (2002) 'Unplugged and fully connected', *Financial Times*, October 1, p.16.

Tew, B. (1965) *International Monetary Co-operation 1945-65*, London: Hutchinson and Co.

Thomas, G. (1980) *Day the Bubble Burst: A Social History of the Wall Street Crash*, London: Arrow Books.

Thompson, E.P. (1990[1975]) *Whigs and Hunters: The Origin of the Black Act*, London: Penguin Books.

Toniolo, G. (1998) 'Europe's golden age, 1950-1973: speculations from a long-run perspective', *Economic History Review*, 2, p.252-267.

Trow, G.W.S. (1996) *Within the Context of No Context*, New York: Atlantic Monthly Press.

Tversky, A. and Kahneman, D. (1974), 'Judgement under Uncertainty: Heuristic and Biases', *Science*, Vol. 185, pp.1124-31.

Tversky, A. and Kahneman, D. (1986) 'Rational Choices and the Framing of Decisions', *Journal of Business*, Vo.l59, pp. 251-78.

Tversky, A. and Kahneman, D. (1992) 'Advances in Prospect Theory: Cumulative representation of Uncertainty', *Journal of Risk and Uncertainty*, Vol. 5, pp. 297-323.

Valdez, S. (2003) *An Introduction to Global Financial Markets*, Fourth Edition, Basingstoke: Palgrave.

Van Thienen, F. (1951) [Het Noord-Nederlandse Costuum van de gouded eeuw] *The Great Age of Holland 1600-60*, London: George G. Harrap and Company Ltd.

Verdier, D. (2001) 'Capital Mobility and the Origins of Stock Markets, *International Organization*, Vol. 55, No. 2, Spring, pp 327-356.

Waine, P. and Walker, M. (2000) *Takeover*, Chichester: John Wiley and Sons Ltd.

Watney, J. (1998) *The Industrial Revolution*, Andover: Pitkin.

Weber, M. (1927) *General Economic History 1864-1920*, London: Transaction Publishers.

Weber, M. (2001[1930]) *The Protestant Ethic and the Spirit of Capitalism*, London: Routledge.

Weinberg, N. (2003) 'Criminalizing Capitalism', *Forbes Global*, 12 May, pp.50-52.

Wenner, L.A. ed., (1998) *MediaSport*, London: Routledge.

Wicker, E. (1997), *The Banking Panics of the Great Depression*, New York: Oxford University Press.

Willman. P (2000) 'Risk, Greed, Sound and Fury', *Business Strategy Review*, Vol 11, Issue 2, pp 72-74.

Wolf, M. ed., (2002) 'The bubble will keep deflating', *The Financial Times*, 14 May, p. 23.

Wolfe, T. (1988) *The Bonfire of The Vanities*, London: Picador.

Wood, C. (1992) *The Bubble Economy: The Japanese Economic Collapse*, London: Sedgwick and Jackson.

Zakay, D.,Zur, N., and Tsal, Y. (1986) 'The Relativity of Unrealistic Optimism, *Acta Psychologica*, Vol. 93, pp. 121-134.

Zeira, J. (1999) 'Informational Overshooting, Booms and Crashes', *Journal of Monetary Economics*, Vol 43, No.1, pp 237-257.

Index

References from Notes indicated by 'n' after page reference